BRISTOL'S PAUPER CHILDREN

Victorian education and emigration to Canada

Shirley Hodgson

Bristol Books CIC, 1 Lyons Court, Long Ashton Business Park,
Yanley Lane, Long Ashton, Bristol BS41 9LB

Bristol's Pauper Children
written and researched by Shirley Hodgson

Edited by Clive Burlton

Published by Bristol Books 2017

ISBN: 9781909446113

Copyright: Shirley Hodgson (shirleyhod2@aol.com)

Design: Joe Burt

Printed by: TJ International, Padstow, Cornwall

Author photograph courtesy of David Emeney/Bristol Museums, Galleries and Archives

BRISTOL BOOKS

Bristol Books CIC is a not-for-profit Community Interest Company that publishes important and untold stories about lives, communities, places and events that have significance and interest in Bristol and the surrounding area.

ABOUT THE AUTHOR

SHIRLEY HODGSON was born in 1935 and her working life was devoted to the care and education of children across Bristol. She first trained as a nursery nurse and then as a primary school teacher. She worked in several Bristol schools including Victoria Park Junior School in Bedminster, where she was head teacher for ten years before retiring in 1992.

She was introduced to the story of the British Home Children who were sent to Canada from the 1860s during a lecture by Dr. Moira Martin from the University of the West of England. Little was known about Bristol's Pauper Children who were part of this exodus, so Shirley set about investigating what had happened to them and the role Bristol institutions and individuals played in the street children's education and emigration. This book is the result of her painstaking research, which has taken her across the UK and Canada as well as closer to home in Bristol, where Shirley volunteers with a group of family historians at Bristol Archives, transcribing and indexing records.

Shirley is a strong advocate for the institutions that care for the city's civic and community records. She's also a member of the Friends of Bristol Museums, Galleries and Archives, where she sits on the Executive Committee and helps to raise funds for Bristol Museums Service.

ACKNOWLEDGEMENTS

I ATTENDED A FAMILY HISTORY conference a number of years ago in Exeter, and listened to Dr Moira Martin of the University of the West of England talk about the emigration of children from Bristol to Canada. She engaged my interest, recommended reading material and shared some of her research with me; I wish to acknowledge the part she played.

I also wish to acknowledge the foresight of Richard Burley, formerly Senior Archivist at Bristol Archives, who unknowingly opened my mind to the idea of writing a book. When I was initially researching through the records he suggested that I might write an account of my research. This didn't seem practical at the time, but when it became possible to work with Bristol Books, I could still hear his words; thank you Richard.

I am very grateful to all the Canadians I have met who have helped me to understand the position of the British Home Children, including: Marion Crawford, former president of the Middlemore Atlantic Society who welcomed descendants of the Bristol children to their meetings; Mary-Ellen Badeau, who guided me around the records of the home children in New Brunswick Archives; Dr Patricia Roberts-Pichette whom I met at Ottawa Archives; and Chris Sanham, who sent me information about the children from Bristol.

A big thankyou for the input and advice received from Clive Burlton and Joe Burt because you have turned this piece of writing into a professional piece of work and I have appreciated being able to learn from you both.

I also wish to acknowledge all the help and support I have received from the staff at Bristol Archives, Bristol Museums Service and Bristol Library; without their services this project would have been so much harder to achieve.

My grateful thanks to my husband Peter, who supplied me with endless cups of coffee and even the odd glass of wine, as I took over the dining room table. He has struggled through piles of ironing, answered the telephone and ignored my monosyllabic answers when he needed to know something. I could not have achieved this book without his freely-given support.

INTRODUCTION

"BETWEEN 1869 AND 1939 about 100,000 child immigrants, casualties of unemployment and poverty in Britain were sent to Canada. They were uprooted from their homes and families with hopes of giving them a better start to their lives. British agencies sent the children to receiving and distribution homes in different parts of Canada. A few of the younger children would be adopted into Canadian families but most were sent to farms as agricultural labourers and domestic labourers or to homes to work as domestic servants. Often deprived of education and the comforts of family life these children suffered loneliness and despair."

These words, written in both French and English, appear on a plaque erected in the garden of 51 Avon Street in Stratford, Ontario, by the Canadian Government on August 19, 2001. They describe the movement of disadvantaged children from all parts of Britain to Canada – an exodus that came to an end just before the Second World War.

Motivated by philanthropic and economic forces, more than 50 British organisations, including several in Bristol, sent orphaned, abandoned and pauper children to Canada. Many believed that these children would have a better chance for a healthy, moral life in rural Canada. However well-intentioned, the migration scheme was seriously flawed. In today's world, it is difficult to imagine the hardship and suffering that many of these children would have experienced.

Around four million Canadians are descended from a British Home Child, with an estimated 60,000 people descended from the more than 1,500 Bristol children sent to Canada. With an ever-increasing interest in genealogy, I am often asked to help a descendant find the family of their Home Child. During my talks on the subject, it is clear that few know about this mass movement of people and what lay behind the migration of pauper children from Bristol.

It is hoped that this account will help to tell another untold story from Bristol's past.

THE STREET CHILDREN OF BRISTOL

❖❖❖

BRISTOL CHILDREN WERE first sent to Canada in the late 1860's from the newly set up industrial schools. Bristol guardians – men and women elected by local parishes to run workhouses - sent their first group of children in 1870 and had the dubious honour of sending the last group in 1915. Approximately 1,500 Bristol children, who can be identified, were sent from the industrial schools, reformatories and the workhouses. An unknown number left from the Canadian Emigration Home for Little Girls based in the city, and some were even sent by their own parents. Most of these children landed in the port of St John in New Brunswick but others were sent to Quebec, Niagara-on-the-Lake and Belleville in Ontario.

Avon Street in Stratford, Ontario, and the plaque erected by the Canadian Government in 2001

The people who sent them thought they were doing a favour to the child. Life at that time was very uncertain for the poor; if the mother of a family died then the father, struggling to cope, may just give up the unequal struggle and desert his family. If a father died, leaving the mother with a large family, unless she took up a life of prostitution, the only place where a mother could be sure of finding food for her children was the workhouse. Neighbours sometimes stepped in to help but, because they had their own families to feed, wouldn't be able to continue and either the relieving officer from the local workhouse might step in or the children would take to the streets. These children often proved to be very resilient; they bedded down where they could and would beg, scrounge or steal food to survive.

When the plaque was erected in the garden in Stratford, Ontario, in 2001, many Canadians did not know about this massive wave of child migration, a movement which is, of course, an important part of their country's history. From the time that the descendants of the Home Children became aware of their ancestry, they have been asking questions about the lives of their parents or grandparents - even great grandparents - wanting to know their stories. After learning what had happened it seemed important to share their findings and they wrote articles for newspapers, journals and some published books. They told their stories to anyone who would listen using radio and television; unfortunately the information often stayed within a province and didn't spread across Canada. With the spread of the internet, descendants of children sent by Barnardo's (the charity founded by Thomas Barnardo in 1866) or by John Middlemore (who established a children's trust in 1872) were able to use Facebook to exchange information and tell their stories. The British Isles Family History Society, operating from Ottawa, has been responsible for collecting materials, setting up databases and providing information for the families and anyone who is interested. Today there are numerous websites which support descendants and help them in their quest to tell their stories and, importantly, to establish their family history.

CHILD MIGRATION WAS NOT NEW

In the 17th century the idea of emptying the gaols of England by sending the occupants to swell the numbers of colonial labourers was being considered and in 1606 a note suggested that idle vagrants might be sent to Virginia. In 1618 there was a report of a voyage to Virginia by a Captain Andrews and Jacob Braems, a merchant. They sailed in the vessel *Silver Falcon* from the City of London, with 100 orphaned and destitute children, who were starving in the streets, and took them to Richmond, Virginia to work as servants. Roger Kershaw and Janet Sacks, authors of *"New Lives for Old"* wrote that "they were a nuisance to the authorities, a burden to tax payers and were even suspected of spreading the plague". On February 27, 1619, the names of boys and wenches that were chosen were announced; they were held in Bridewell, a police station in London, before being shipped to Virginia. On January 10, 1620, the Lord Mayor of London ordered a collection of money in each parish for clothing, feeding and transportation of 100 poor children to Virginia. The City of London selected the children for transportation and granted £500 for the passage and outfits. On January 31, 1620, the children were "to be taken from the multitudes, however unwilling", and the Virginia Company was authorised to receive and transport them, and was given licence to punish any disorder.

With hindsight it could be said that this started a movement to send socially embarrassing and unwanted children that lasted until after the Second World War. The underlying reason appears to be purely economic; a huge increase in orphans, homeless waifs and foundlings became a burden on the rates of the cities and, in this case, London.

A Parliamentary Ordinance of May 9, 1645, ordered that officers and justices be diligent in apprehending persons engaged in kidnapping children for overseas. Marshals of the Admiralty and Cinque Ports were ordered to have ships searched to discover such children. An ordinance of the Common Council dated September 29, 1654, stated that in view of the many complaints of kidnapping and to prevent such mischief:

"It is this day agreed, ordained and enacted by the Maior, Aldermen and Common Councell, in Common Councell assembled, that all Boyes, Maides and other persons, which for the future shall be transported beyond the Seas as servants, shall, before their going a shipboard have their Covenants or Indentures of service and apprenticeship enrolled in the Tolzey Books as other Indentures of apprenticeship are and have used to be". (Tolzey Book means Council Book).

The church of St Mary Redcliffe overlooks the port of the city of Bristol and the River Avon.

It was further ordained that any master carrying a passenger not so enrolled was to be fined £20 for each offence (one quarter to go to the informer and the rest to the poor). The Water Bailiff of the port was also empowered to search all ships and vessels for non-indentured passengers.

In 1645 Parliament passed a law which, in effect, set out punishments for anyone who would sell, buy, convey or receive any child for profit. The Act should have stopped this trade. Sadly this law doesn't appear to have been considered important. Perhaps economics were regarded as more important than child care. Bristol was no different from London. Between 1654 and 1685 more than 10,000 servants sailed from Bristol to the West Indies. Amongst these servants were many pauper and foundling (abandoned) children, suggesting there was an organised trade of exporting children to New England and Virginia. It seems there was a practice at that time of kidnapping, inveigling and bribing youngsters onto ships bound for the labour-hungry colonies. Bristol City Council set up a system of enrolment to record the names of all the servants embarking from the port for service overseas but in spite of all precautions taken by the council, forcible shipment of servants continued. After the Parliamentary Order of 1645, Bristol City Council then required that

Welsh Back from Bristol Bridge. Warehouses line the banks of the river; the work of the port continues even in the heart of the city.

all boys and maids and other persons must have their indentures enrolled in the Tolzey Court Books before going aboard a ship which would take them beyond the seas as servants. All these entries were written up in rough books known as "Action and Apprentices". Altogether 10,000 names were recorded, most coming from the West Country and some from Wales. There appears a suggestion that parents or guardians might have packed errant children off to the colonies to serve their time. This doubtful concern shown by parents over their children's welfare was not just a part of those times but can be found in later years when the story of child emigration from Bristol is revealed. It was the children of the poor who were sent to Canada without friend or family, a move that aimed to give them a better start in life. While many people really believed this rationale, the less idealistic saw the financial and practical reasons which led to this movement. There is no evidence to suggest that the feelings of the children themselves were ever considered. The emigration of children from Britain mostly involved the orphaned and deserted children of the poor and although this is interesting it is also important to look at the efforts past governments have made to deal with this problem.

TRANSPORTATION AS PART OF PENAL POLICY

The question of what to do with pauper children seems to have developed into a pauper strategy of sending them away to another country without family or friends. The poor then have nothing; no money, no goods, nowhere to live and no expectation that things might change. They became reliant on others for food and lodging, begging or stealing to live. There may even be the ones who offended another, perhaps in a more influential position, and found themselves on the way to the Americas to be used as a servant.

This was the pauper strategy. To send children away and clear the streets of the poor and, in the years to come, it became a part of Britain's penal policy. Men, women and children who had been found guilty of a crime could be sentenced to transportation to another country for a set period; not being free to return to England until that time had passed. Many were transported for life, being forced to leave their families, and it was inevitable that the children of these convicts became a burden on the poor rate. Children were often found guilty of crimes that, in modern times, we would judge as minor misdemeanors. Henry, only 12 years old, was sent to Van Diemans Land, which we now call Tasmania, for seven years because he had been found guilty of stealing a pair of shoes. He was transferred to a prison hulk moored on the River Thames before he was put aboard a prison ship heading for Australia. Records show that he was well behaved both in the hulk and during the voyage, so not too much wrong with his behaviour then.

If it was that easy to send a 12-year-old boy to another country for stealing a pair of shoes then it became a short step to using emigration as a device to deal with an over large population of orphaned and destitute children. Members of the Government asked if this was the answer to streets seemingly full of children and concerns over the spiraling cost of workhouses, where one in three paupers were under the age of 16. Emigration was being seriously considered as an answer which would suit Britain and Australia; a forced separation of children from those who had shown themselves unable to care for them and those whose families were considered unworthy. The belief that this would offer the chance of a better life to the street children and the children of the poor became accepted by many Bristol citizens. Those who had businesses in the city would testify to the nuisance of ragged and filthy

The hulk storage vessel on the River Thames where child prisoners were held before their transfer to Van Diemen's Land (Tasmania)

children begging for food or coins, passing by children deformed by rickets and avoiding tiny girl prostitutes standing on the street corners.

HOW THE POOR WERE ORGANISED IN THE ELIZABETHAN ERA

In early times, monasteries and churches assumed responsibility for the poor amongst their congregations but as time passed, care of the poor also became part of the duties of the Lord or Squire of the Manor. From 1549, when church wardens were appointed by the Bishop to serve in each parish, the parishioners were expected to contribute towards the costs of helping the poor within their parish. By 1601, a rate was levied on all householders within each parish; overseers were appointed to levy the tax, distribute help to the poor and keep an account of all the monies. The Poor Rate was set at the annual vestry meeting by the Parish Council, members of this important body of people having been elected by the parishioners. Important changes to the law in 1662 gave each person born within a parish a lawful settlement in that place; they also had the right to rent or purchase property, hold church office, become apprenticed and claim support when reduced to hard times. This worked well for those who had settlement rights within a parish but there were some who, for different reasons, could not claim settlement in any parish and were reduced to begging or wandering the countryside. Many children were affected by these laws. If a child was born to an unmarried woman, and if the mother couldn't name the father to support her, then both mother and child were sent out of the parish. The Overseers (people who collected rates and distributed money) would not wish to use rates collected from the local people to raise an illegitimate child. Life became very hard for anyone without legal settlement. Most parishes provided for their own sick and elderly and by 1723 workhouses had begun to appear in parishes where paupers could live and be given work; however, settlement rules might still apply.

From Elizabethan times children were seen as a valuable commodity; they were able to earn money from an early age and so contribute to the finances of the family. With no acceptable method of birth control many families became very large. In most villages a system of apprenticing children of the poor at seven years of age would ensure they were not a burden on the Poor Rate.

This system lasted until 1834 when the New Poor Law Act grouped sometimes 30 or 40 parishes into Poor Law Unions, with each Union having an elected board of guardians. At the heart of this law was the well-regulated workhouse, one built for each union and made as wholly unattractive as possible. Paupers and their families were firmly discouraged from receiving the "out relief" of bread and money support and herded into the workhouses instead. It seems as though the people in authority felt that all paupers were feckless and didn't really want to work and therefore didn't try very hard to find work. It was reasoned that if their stay in a workhouse was unpleasant then all these people would want to move out as quickly as possible. Families were split and sometimes parents may only see their children once a week, sometimes over a wall and not even being allowed to hold them. The guardians of the unions were also required to set up schools so that pauper children did receive a basic education and training for employment, a good move on the part of the government but they then discouraged the parish apprenticeships.

At this time children were living and sometimes dying on the streets of the cities and in the fields of the countryside. The measures put in place and all the efforts made by voluntary bodies were just not equal to the problem. The new workhouses became very full. Calculations made by the Government at the time indicated that one in every three paupers living in workhouses was under 16. This became a huge problem for the Government. The problem of children living on the streets of the cities still existed and, if anything, was worse than in earlier times. It was expensive for the Government and took a substantial amount out of the local and national purse.

ORGANISATION OF POOR LAW IN BRISTOL

In Bristol the idea of grouping together parishes providing relief to the poor had existed since 1696 but some parishes had been struggling to support much larger numbers than others. Industrial growth in the parishes of St Philip and Jacob, Temple and St James supported an increase in the population and it became necessary to change the way the poor were supported. In 1696 an Act of Parliament combined or "incorporated" the 17 parishes and the ward of Castle Precincts into one body called the Corporation or the "Incorporation of the Poor". A group of people called the guardians were elected to carry out the day to day organisation of this new body. One of their first tasks was to provide a place where paupers might live and work for their keep. A building formerly used as a Mint and situated next door to St Peter's church was bought and named St Peter's Workhouse. This was to be a place where paupers could claim board and lodge and be given work to help support themselves.

The Guardians of the Incorporation of the Poor planned to have two workhouses; one for girls, which was set up next to a house in Bridewell; and one for boys, in the building at St Peter's. The children were to be taught spinning and weaving; the finished cloth was to be sold to support their finances. However, sales of this cloth were so poor that the children were put on to unskilled occupations such as pin making and oakum picking. Both proved to be more lucrative for the guardians. The high minded idea of teaching the children a trade seemed to have disappeared in the quest for more income. When the 1834 Poor Law Amendment Act was passed, Bristol - already a union of parishes - was able to retain the organisation of the Incorporation of the Poor as one of the new poor law unions and, in principle, all its management systems were allowed to remain. Bristol was one of the earliest cities to be incorporated by a local parliamentary act; now in the new Act, these 18 parishes were grouped into the union.

St Peter's Workhouse, formerly used as a Mint, stood close to Bristol Bridge.

The Clifton Poor Law Union was formed on April 9, 1836, to conform to the new Act. A board of guardians was elected to oversee the 12 parishes of Clifton, St James, St Paul and the part of St Philip and St Jacob within the City of Bristol. The parishes in the county of Gloucestershire of Compton Greenfield, Filton, Henbury, Horfield, Stapleton, St George, Stoke Gifford, Westbury-on-Trym and Warmley were also included. In the early days of the union the guardians planned to keep any parish workhouses already in use - Clifton Wood for the aged and sick, Pennywell Road for able bodied paupers and St George for the children. As these buildings were in a poor condition and pauper numbers were rising, the decision was eventually taken to build a new workhouse at Eastville. This workhouse opened in 1847 at 100 Fishponds Road and was designed to accommodate all classes of paupers. It is interesting to note that in the same year, residents living in the village of Clifton became unhappy that they shared the same name as a poor law union. After some considerable lobbying by Clifton parishioners and some spirited discussion in the weekly meetings of the guardians, the Clifton Poor Law Union was renamed Barton Regis Union on March 14, 1847, and so gave that name to the new workhouse.

Over the years the boundaries of the City of Bristol slowly expanded northwards taking over the civic administration of these areas. In 1897 the Bristol Board of Guardians took responsibility for the poor of some of the Barton Regis parishes and for the workhouse situated in Fishponds Road. Although now reduced in terms of the number of parishes for which it was responsible, the guardians of Barton Regis Union decided to build a new workhouse at Southmead. This ambitious project started in 1900 and was completed in 1902. At its centre was an infirmary and housing for an older population. By 1904 Barton Regis Union was wound up and Bristol Union managed the new workhouse which, in time, became the nucleus of Southmead Hospital. Some of the Barton Regis parishes were taken into the Bristol Union and the South Gloucestershire parishes into the Union of Chipping Sodbury.

Many of the registers and other records of both Barton Regis and Bristol Poor Law Unions were kept at St Peters Hospital in the central area of Bristol. When, in 1940, Bristol suffered what was to be its worst bombardment of the war, St Peters Hospital, one of our most spectacular buildings, suffered a direct hit. The building and all its contents, which included many important records, were regrettably destroyed. Fortunately a small number of records, which were stored elsewhere, survived and it is possible to find some information about the unions and learn something of the way they worked.

The Poor Law Amendment Act of 1834 seemed to be designed to provide support for the children of the poor. The pauper child would now receive an education, he would not be apprenticed at the early age of seven and, above all, no child was to be sent overseas without accompaniment by family or friend. Some boards of guardians did send their pauper children out to the colonies after 1834 arguing that as these children were destitute, the savings to the country were beneficial. Several factors influenced the Government to introduce changes through the 1850 Poor Law Act. The numbers of people living in the workhouse had risen dramatically; a third of these paupers were under the age of 16 and since the parishes had stopped taking on young boys to train as apprentices, these children now lived in the workhouses. Government policy had been designed to make conditions in the workhouses so bad that people would want to find work and not rely on the workhouse but out relief was also discouraged. Nowhere was it written what a family was to do if there was no work to be found. Workhouses became full and the rising costs of feeding and keeping these families and their children was taking a considerable amount from the Poor Law Relief Fund.

Concerns from the Poor Law Commissioners about costs led to changes which were set out in 1850 Act. Among the many provisions that affected the lives of paupers, those relating to children, during the next three quarters of a century, were totally life changing for thousands of children. The Act gave legal authority to the guardians to send children, under 16, to another country without family or friends although certain safeguards were set up at the time. Provided these controls were followed then permission would be given to the Poor Law Unions who were expected to be the only sending agencies. Orphans were adopted by the guardians who then took on the role of parent and the rights of the parents.

POOR LAW UNIONS WERE ADMINISTERED BY BODIES APPOINTED BY PARLIAMENT:

1834 - 1847 Poor Law Commissioners
1847 - 1871 Poor Law Board
1871 - 1919 Local Government
1919 - 1930 Poor Law abolished - taken over by the Ministry of Health

Documents referring to the work of these organisations are in the Home Office files and stored at the National Archives, Kew.

LIFE FOR THE POOR IN THE CITY OF BRISTOL

In the 19th century the centre of Bristol was a place of furnaces and factories, of ash-laden, smoke-filled, gritty air. The River Frome sluggishly wound its way through the city; all the effluent from the closets of the houses lining the

In Victorian times Bristol was a crowded industrial city.

bank fell straight into the river which was an open cess pit. Ships and boats made their way along the River Avon, tying up in the centre to unload and load passengers and freight. Docks, harbour and ships were all surrounded by a warren of alleys, courts, with twisting narrow passages leading through and around warehouses, tenement blocks and small businesses. The population of the city had risen quite dramatically; people from villages walked into the city to find work and needed a place to live. In the early part of the century, responding to the demands of industry, the railway was built, cutting through small houses and businesses to reach the docks and feed the ships.

Living space in the city became limited and expensive, which forced families to share the spaces available. For the poor it became a time of multi-occupation; one family, sometimes two, living in one room, and every room in a house occupied. The Public Health Act of 1848 stipulated that every house must have a toilet yet in one of the Bristol tenement buildings, there was just one toilet in the courtyard for as many as 60 people to use. In 1880 the Bristol Mercury newspaper ran a series of articles about the living conditions of the poor in the city. Whether this information surprised or shocked the general population of Bristol is not recorded, but it was a time when those with the means to do so moved out of the centre of the city into the new houses being

Jones Buildings Hotwell Road

Narrow lanes, crowded housing, cramped and constricting alleyways – as depicted in this sketch of Jones' Buildings in Hotwell Road

built in Clifton and Redland.

Many men worked as labourers, and they set out each day to find work. When the financial affairs of the country were good and trade was booming, work could be found and wages might be good. However, when trade was poor, work was hard to find and wages were low. There was no minimum wage agreement in the 19th century and an employer could manipulate rates according to the market. At times it was possible for a labouring man to work all week and still not have enough money to feed his family and keep a roof over their heads. It was a very fine balance for a poor family keeping everyone fed, finding a place to live and clothes to wear. With both father and often the mother out working, the children were left at home, the elder looking after the younger. It is easy to see how the children could roam the streets all day and be thought by the authorities to be without parental guidance. With the birth of another baby - there was no guaranteed birth control in those days - an elderly family member needing care, or a parent becoming ill maybe dying, that fine balance is lost and the family begins to fall apart.

Families dealt with this in different ways. Some might take the middle children in the family to an institution, the rationale being that those children would be fed and then there would be enough to feed their siblings at home. Children could find work from age 14, were encouraged to do so, and were expected to pass over the money earned. In the worst times the family might sell their furniture to buy food. Their clothing would also be sold to buy food which left the children dressed in rags, tied around them with string. Out on the streets, begging for food or money, these ragged children became part of the life of an industrial Victorian city. If either parent died, then the surviving parent would try to keep the family together. Wages for women at that time were about a third of those for men and, for some mothers, prostitution was the only way they could earn money and still care for their families. Working as a prostitute immediately took away their respectability as a parent, and then there was the danger that their children would be taken away from them. Sometimes another family member might care for them or a neighbour might take them in but this often broke down. Children were put out onto the street in the day while a parent worked and were often left alone at night. It is easy to see how some children moved onto the streets to live, begging for their food and stealing where necessary.

DEALING WITH THE VAGRANT CHILD

In 1850 the chief magistrate of London stated that the streets of London were too full of children and proposed emigration as a solution. With the workhouses full and the poor rate stretched, emigration began to be seen as an answer which would suit both Great Britain and Canada. The belief that this would offer to the street and pauper child the chance of a better life became accepted by many of the people who met them day after day as they walked through the streets of the city.

In the early 19th century schools were run by the churches, charitable organisations and private citizens. The Government had yet to decide whether

So many children on the streets!

it had a responsibility to offer education to all children. The better off citizen, the wealthy and the children supported by charities had access to education; the poor were offered classes on a Sunday. During Sunday school, teachers taught all who came to read, and possibly write, using the scriptures. The vagrant child who lived on the streets, the ragged and unwashed children of the poor, who struggled just to feed their families, were excluded from these establishments.

Many of the children living on the streets were orphans, some were deserted, others were runaways but all would be destitute. They scraped an existence begging for or stealing food and money where they could. Sometimes they were able to earn coins but they certainly got in the way of the people of Bristol going about their business.

Efforts by voluntary groups and the workhouse were not equal to the scale of the problem of children living and dying on the streets of the cities. One of the solutions proposed and acted upon was the Industrial School system where children were lodged, clothed and fed, educated and taught skills to enable them to get work.

SEND THE CHILDREN TO CANADA?

The people who promoted emigration to Canada were convinced that the children would find a better life there than if they stayed in the industrial cities of England. Other countries were considered. For example, children were sent to South Africa, Rhodesia, Bermuda and Australia, and it is important to consider why those looking for a place for these children looked towards Canada. Education was not considered to be important in this consideration of life for the street children in Britain but was used by those wishing to take the children to Canada, promising they would go to local schools alongside Canadian children. What was it about Canada that attracted those who wished to find homes for these children?

The Victorians were very proud of the British Empire and the Government was in favour of strengthening links between Great Britain and her colonies. Canada had become a Dominion in 1867 and the British Government, anxious to retain these links, was keen to send "good British Stock" to the country. Canadians looked upon Britain as the 'mother country' and welcomed this relationship. The new Canadian administration was very aware of the immigrants flooding into their country and became concerned about providing enough food for its ever growing population. Farmers, particularly in remote areas, struggled to produce enough crops and needed more labour but couldn't afford to pay adult wages.

The young men of Canada, not interested in hard farming work for small wages, preferred to work in the coastal cities where the wages were higher, and life was more interesting. The idea that the children who were crowding into the workhouses and living on the streets in Britain might be put to work on the farms of Canada, and so fulfil the needs of both countries, was welcomed by both governments. It became a question of supply and demand; the farmers of Canada needed labour to grow the food and Britain had a ready supply of manpower, or should we say child power, and could supply that need. It is also important to point out that the farmers were poor and overworked; they really thought they were doing a favour to the child. Nobody seems to have considered the needs of the children.

Farming homes would be found for these children when they arrived and it was anticipated that they would become part of the family. They could go to school with the children of the family and work on the farm as one of the family. It was reasoned that Canadian children worked on the farms, particularly during the summer months, and the British children would join them. During the winter months they attended the local school and it was expected that the British children would do the same. This seemed an ideal solution; it solved the labour problems for the farmers and gave a home and family to the children who were living on the streets and in the workhouses of Britain. In this country the idea was welcomed by many groups of people; the Victorians were very proud of their Empire and considered it important to support this newly formed Dominion.

Not everyone was convinced by the promise of a better life in Canada. George Cruickshank, illustrator of Dickens and Harriet Beecher Stowe, thought that "the transportation of innocent children was a disgrace to the Christian world". There were many people who agreed with his views.

The emigration of children to Canada was surrounded with good intentions; there was an honest belief that the children would have a better start in life. The children would be taken into homes and adopted, they would live on the farms, eat fresh farm food and go to school with the Canadian children. Newspapers printed drawings showing girls in pretty dresses holding a shepherd's crook and boys lying under a haystack chewing a piece of straw, seemingly showing what life would be like in Canada. Mr R H Pope, a visiting Canadian, wrote a letter to The Times in which he encouraged people to send their children to Canada. He wrote of the extraordinary beauty of the colony; the sun always shone when it was supposed to shine! When the cold weather came it killed all the fevers making Canada a healthy place for the children. They had snow in the winter and the children could have such a jolly time, throwing snowballs and tobogganing. He just forgot to say that the snow would be eight foot deep and the temperature might be minus 30.

The Ragged Schools Union Magazine wrote about the ragged children and the London Samaritan Society published in its journal, "*The Christian*" a comic

OUR GUTTER CHILDREN

Cruickshank's cartoon drawing, sketched in 1869, is set against a background of beer houses and signs advertising different alcohols and shows Maria Rye holding a whip.

Clergyman: According to the teachings of Jesus, all these little Gutter girls are our sisters, and therefore I feel it my duty as a Christian Minister to assist in this good work.

Lady with Whip (Maria Rye): I am greatly obliged to you Christian ladies and gentlemen for your help and as soon as you have filled the cart I'll drive off to pitch the little dears aboard a ship and take them thousands of miles away from their native land so that they may never see any of their relatives again.

First Child: Mother! Mother! I want my mother! Oh! Mother! Mother!

Second Child: I want my Father!

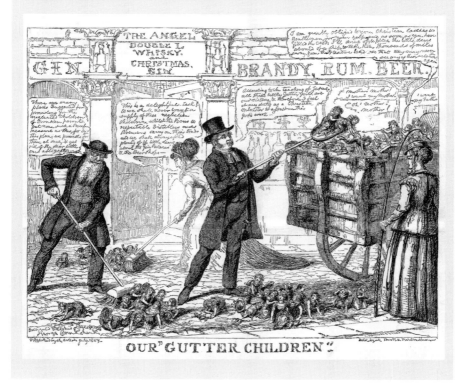

OUR "GUTTER CHILDREN"

type strip showing the advantages of emigration for the ragged child. It was as if the spin doctors of today had gathered together using all their cleverness to advertise these schemes. The newspapers of that time also ran articles about the country and the amazing opportunities just waiting for any who had the wisdom to move there. Advertisements were placed offering support and help for would-be emigrants to purchase land, even offers of free land but with no guarantees as to the quality. Societies offered financial help to would-be emigrants and many families were tempted to move and start afresh. Canada was considered the place to go.

Individual parents were known to send their own children because they also thought it would offer the chance of a better start in life. Perhaps these were unruly children out of control of their parents.

Many of the men and women who became involved with the emigration of children from Britain to Canada were people who had become concerned about the kind of life the children of the poor lived in the industrial cities of this country. Most had been through a profoundly religious experience which urged them into working for their God and in questioning themselves about what they could do, so they decided, using their words, "to save the children". They were going to save the children from destitution and starvation, to remove them from the corrupting influence of city life and, of course, from those unworthy families. This became their life's mission and they put all their resources and time into this evangelistic work, taking the children, as they thought, to a better life in Canada.

From our time it is perhaps easy to look back and wonder whether providing a widow's pension or ensuring men who couldn't get work received some monetary support, would have made life easier for the family and enforced emigration would not have been necessary.

The children - unforgettable in their ragged clothes - with their individual problems are the moving force behind the wish to tell their story.

BRISTOL RAGGED SCHOOLS

I T IS TIME to introduce Mary Carpenter (1807 – 1877), a woman who became involved with all aspects of Bristol's street children but more particularly with their education. It would be impossible to write about them without acknowledging her work. She knew these children well, seeing them every day of her life, as she walked from her home in Great George Street to the Unitarian Chapel in Lewin's Mead. She was the daughter of the minister, Dr Lant Carpenter, who, in 1817, moved his family from Plymouth when he was invited to preach there.

Dr Lant Carpenter was an educated man and a brilliant teacher. He set up a school for boys in his home and ran a caring and sympathetic establishment at a time when schools were known for their hard discipline and repressive routines. Mary appears to have been a very serious and thoughtful child. The story is often told that when, at the age of five, she was asked what she would like to do when she grew up, she replied that she would like to be useful. Her father had a high expectation of her usefulness and made arrangements for her to study with the boys in his school. Consequently Mary had the best education that any girl of her time might achieve. However, there was a downside to this; her father expected Mary to stay at home when her own schooling was over and help her mother to set up and run a school for girls. Mary adored her father, his wishes were sacred to her, and therefore any plans she may have formed for herself would be put on hold until she was free to control her own life. She longed for his approval but had to compete for his attention with everyone else who lived in their home. Once a week the whole of his extended family would sit around a large table with the newspapers. They were expected to examine and discuss their reading. For Mary this was excellent preparation

Mary Carpenter

for her future career in public speaking and certainly underlined the value of the written word. He also expected the entire household, the boys in the school and all members of the Carpenter family, to help the poor of the city, not just by providing financial support but also taking an active part, visiting homes and giving practical help. This training prepared Mary for what she called "her life's work" but first she had to fulfil her father's wishes and work with her mother in running a girl's school.

Mary was 40 when, at last, she was free to follow her own ideas and begin to put them into practice. Mary had learned much from her visits to Irish families who lived in a Bristol slum called Lewin's Mead; she knew the children who lived on the streets, she had seen them covered in sores and dressed in rags tied together with string. Jo Manton, biographer of Mary Carpenter, wrote in her book "*Children of the Streets*" that Mary leaving her home would see these children, "deformed by rickets, stunted in growth, tattered and filthy creeping barefoot along the pavement".

Mary was determined to open a school for them; although these schools carried the name "ragged" this type of education would not suit Mary. She began by opening her school in a dilapidated hall in Lewin's Mead; this school was to provide an education for the ragged children although Mary was determined that this should be a school with a difference. The education

The Unitarian Chapel at Lewin's Mead attended by Mary Carpenter. From here she gained much support for her work.

offered was not to be poor and tattered but full of richness with a variety of interest. Mary wanted to offer the same standard of education to the children of the streets as she had offered to the children of professional families. She had heard of the work of John Pounds and appreciated how his work took the children from the streets, taught them to read and write and so gave them a limited education. She appreciated that the ragged schools, as they became known, could fulfil a social need and, given government support, should be encouraged even though the standards of education were low.

THE OPENING OF RAGGED SCHOOLS

John Pounds was born January 17, 1766, the son of a sawyer in Portsmouth Dockyard, and was apprenticed at the age of 12 to a shipwright. In 1781, when 15, he fell into a dock and suffered serious injuries which crippled him for the rest of his life. John placed himself under the instruction of an elderly shoemaker and in 1803, started on his own account in St Mary's Street, Portsmouth. In 1818 he took charge of the two sons of his sailor-brother. He

JOHN POUNDS, OF PORTSMOUTH,
FOUNDER OF RAGGED SCHOOLS.
BORN 17TH JUNE. 1766.   DIED 1st JANUARY, 1839.

John Pounds (1766-1839) a Portsmouth shoemaker, teacher and philanthropist who, from 1818, provided free basic education for the poorest children in the town.

began giving them lessons and invited another boy, who spent every day on the streets while his mother was out at work, to join them. Being aware of other children wandering local streets, he persuaded them to join in and share the lessons, often using a promise of free food. He taught them to read, write, learn simple cookery, and how to mend their shoes and playthings. He became school master to Portsmouth's street children. He didn't receive a salary, but was supported by the Portsmouth Unitarian Congregation.

Another school was opened in Edinburgh by Thomas Guthrie and then one in Aberdeen through the efforts of Sheriff Watson. All schools were for boys; it wasn't until 1843 that a girls school was opened and two years later a mixed school. The Ragged Schools Union was founded in 1844 with Lord Shaftesbury

LORD SHAFTESBURY

When making a speech in Parliament, Lord Shaftesbury explained that of the 1,600 children in 15 ragged schools, 162 had been in prison; 116 had run away from home because of ill treatment; 170 slept in common lodging houses; 253 lived by begging; 216 had no shoes or stockings; 101 had no underlinen; 68 children were the children of convicts; 219 had never slept in a bed and 306 had lost one or both parents. This was a huge problem for members of a Government yet to fully understand the complexity of their responsibility.

Lord Shaftesbury at the Ragged Schools Union Jubilee April 1894

as president and over the next 20 years more than 200 schools were opened to offer free education to the poorest children.

Many of the children living on the streets in Bristol during the latter part of the 19th century were orphans. Some had been deserted, others abandoned but all were destitute. They scraped an existence by begging or stealing food and money where they could, sometimes they were able to earn coins which

Street Children captured on camera in around 1862

would buy them food but they lived and died in corners and doorways of the streets of the city. They would certainly be noticed as they got in the way of Bristol citizens going about their daily business.

Mary Carpenter's Ragged School opened in Lewin's Mead on August 1, 1846, and although it was backed by the Bristol Unitarian Congregation, there was not enough money to employ a certified teacher. A temperance missionary called Phelps volunteered to run the school and this proved to be more difficult than either Mary or Mr Phelps had realised. Mary's mother, being very practical about her support for Mary's school, provided soap, towels and combs. She was so worried for Mary and felt that clean children might be easier to teach. She also described the first day in very clear language, describing how 20 boys came in on the first day and one said "let's fight" and so they did! Mr Phelps treated the boys with great kindness but was unable to do very much with them. Then Mary came into the school and started to

Large families and multi-occupation of houses. The streets became a living space for many as seen in these 1906 scenes, courtesy of Bristol Municipal Charities.

teach. She was a natural teacher, starting from what the children knew and building on that knowledge. The children loved her stories and by Christmas the school was so successful that larger premises were needed.

Mary rented a disused chapel in St James Back, an alley known as a notorious thief's kitchen and slum, an area where hardened policemen would only patrol in pairs. After much cleaning, and with the support of the local police who appreciated that Mary was keeping the children away from the streets, the area became quieter. Those causing trouble moved elsewhere and the school became popular. In 1847 a qualified teacher, Mr Andrews, accompanied by his sister, took charge. The school prospered and it was considered that the continuing success was largely due to their work. Joseph Fletcher, Her Majesty's Inspector (HMI) for the Government visited the school in 1848 and 1849 and, being impressed by Mary's achievements, encouraged her to write about her ideas. After only 18 months of experience she drew up a set of rules which she thought should apply to all ragged schools. She set out her strongly held belief that education should be as rich and as varied as possible and not reflect the title of ragged school. In 1850 Mary bought the hall and the whole of the slum court. Her intention was to run the school until there was no longer any need to do so.

Then, with the expectation of schooling for all from the Education Act of 1870, Mary closed the St James Back School with the understanding that the street children would be welcomed by the new School Board.

Questions about religion became of prime importance when setting up or running a school in Victorian times. For instance some schools declared they would only accept children of one particular faith. However, many of the schools set up to educate the street children based their education on Christian principles, using stories from the Bible to teach a Christian way of life rather than follow any one faith. Mary experienced problems with the parents of the Roman Catholic children who came to the ragged school in St James Back. The children were kept away from the school and she was accused of trying to convert the children away from their family religion. Mary, very aware of this prejudice, worked hard to explain how she used the stories from the Bible in her teaching and how much they were enjoyed by the children. Religious prejudice was not new to Mary. She knew, from personal experience, that the

Ragged Schools Union would not admit any school funded by the Unitarian Church so the St James Back School, supported by her own church, was not included in the union. In 1855 it was declared that all teachers in schools must be members of the Church of England and girls, in their third year, were used to deliver a Christian Education to the younger pupils.

THE BRISTOL EDUCATIONAL AND INDUSTRIAL RAGGED SCHOOL COMMITTEE

Mary Carpenter was not the only person in Bristol to be concerned about the children on the streets of the city. In 1848 the Bristol Educational and Industrial Ragged School Committee was set up as a charity. Money would be collected from interested Bristol citizens and a list of subscribers formed. The first meeting for the Society for "Establishing ragged schools in Bristol and its vicinity" was held on February 4, 1849, in the Victoria Rooms. Although setting up these schools was part of a philanthropic plan it was still seen as "an experiment to civilise and educate the destitute child whose deplorable condition can no longer be overlooked". The objectives of these ragged schools included cleanliness, submission and regularity, and teachers had to pay attention to the moral and religious teaching until all claims to the name of ragged had been lost. A discussion also took place about the achievements of the school opened two years previously by Mary Carpenter in St James Parish - still considered one of the worst areas of the city. The meeting heard about the living conditions for some of the children living in the city:

- One child, her mother is dead, her father locks her out of the house in the morning. She wanders the streets all day. There is no bed, she only has the clothes she wears, nothing to pull over her at night.

- Two children, whose mother had died, were left alone night after night by their father. The only fire they had was a heap of coals they had picked up in the street. Their bed was a heap of rags. They would have starved had a neighbour not given them some food. Their father got six weeks hard labour for neglect.

The committee decided to set up four schools - Lime Kiln Lane in Hotwells, Bread Street in St Philips, Church Passage in Temple and one in St George, Brandon Hill. Each school would be run by a committee which needed to include the local minister and, because all schools would need local patronage, each required to have its own set of subscribers. Space was needed; it was thought that perhaps school rooms could be used and then it was suggested that three sessions a day would be a good starting point. Girls and boys under the age of eight would attend in the mornings, girls over the age of eight in the afternoons and boys over the age of eight in the evenings. It would also be left to the committees to consider payment for each child and to decide which of the families were deserving of support; it was ordered that those considered to suffer from neglect and depravity within the family would not be supported.

The committee issued this high sounding and somewhat pompous statement: "The Ragged Schools promotion of order, of cleanliness, of good habits, of moral conduct, of Religious Knowledge and conduct among the destitute must form part of a complicated system of moral machinery by which each individual of the dense mass of the population of our cities is or ought to be trained in habits of order, industry and religion from the cradle to the grave".

With these solemn and stern words it was clear that the committee comprised a very serious group of people committed to the education of the street children as long as they had good families. The first days of these schools coincided with the opening of certain shows in the city which promised entertainment, amusement and gambling, all thought, by the committee, to be very demoralising!

The children flocked into the schools when they were opened, perhaps out of curiosity, but for whatever reason the daily attendance was good. A report from the school in Church Passage, Temple, revealed that it was crowded on the day the school opened and even after three months 150 children attended on a daily basis. A report written at the time underlined that the general characteristic of all children was of great poverty, with many having no shoes or socks. The report also contained the news that nine boys from Temple had been taken into prison for theft. There was also a report that the Government was considering extending the emigration of the ragged children to the

A WAIF.   RECLAIMED.

This change in a child was the aim of those who pledged a subscription and those who served on the committee.

colonies but it is not known what the committees thought about that news. Knitting and needlework were also introduced into the school curriculum and it proved to be a year of hard work for all within these schools.

Industrial employment also became a part of the school day, the children being employed in some productive labour such as oakum picking, tailoring or shoemaking. The boys were able to save money and were buying copy books from their earnings. As the children were beginning to learn reading and writing skills, the classes were becoming quieter, and behaviour was improving and the children were provided with clothes as a reward for good conduct.

One school reported that boys were now washing their faces and hands before they came to school "if they have the time," remarked one teacher, and in St Philips, the neighbours reported that the streets were quieter. Mothers came into the schools to ask the teachers if they could come to school because if they could learn to read, then they could help their children. Some very positive reactions came from families and friends.

An analysis from the different schools run by the Ragged Schools Society stated that of the girls, 74 were fatherless, 32 motherless and nine were orphans. Of the boys, 68 awere fatherless, 40 motherless and 13 were orphans.

After three months the staff at Temple School reported that 300 children attended regularly. Attendance in the St Philips School over a period of three months for girls was 74, 63 and 62, but for the boys it dropped from 165 to 43 in the three months from October to December 1849.

Attendance in Temple School over a period of three months for girls was 28, 25 and 19, but for the boys attending in the evening it numbered 74, 104 and 84. At the end of six months, charts were published showing attendance figures for all the schools.

In the early days a committee of men, chaired by Lord Teignmouth, was appointed to manage the Industrial Department of these schools. Its first meeting was held on December 23, 1848, when it agreed to the picking of oakum in the day for the boys. The master of St Phillips, Mr Littlebury, was to be asked to superintend such labour. At a later meeting it was suggested that money would not be part of the remuneration but boys who worked regularly, between the hours of 12 to four in the winter and 12 to five in the summer, would receive two meals daily. Nothing was written to tell us what the boys thought of this news. It was unlikely to have been well-received. Although picking oakum would occupy the boys, it would not offer them any training towards finding employment when they were older. In fact it was the St Philips School, which was to become one of the first Industrial Schools in the city, that went out to find work for the boys which might give them some training for the future. They found and organised work on mending nets for Cornish fishermen and mending and making shoes and slippers. However, when it was hard to find work for men, it became very difficult to find work for boys.

The ragged school opened by Sheriff Watson in Aberdeen in 1841 became the first industrial school in Great Britain. It was reported that within a short space of time the streets had been cleared of begging and destitute children. The involvement of the local police, who were given the power to arrest the children found living on the streets and take them to the new industrial school, had made the enterprise very successful. This was acknowledged by the Bristol committee which became interested in this move to set up an industrial school. Alexander Thompson, who was involved with the Aberdeen project, was invited to Bristol to discuss his experiences. Bristol was compared to Aberdeen; both were trading cities with busy ports which would give them an advantage over other cities. Thompson explained that they gave the children three meals a day. Each child had three to four hours of instruction and they spent a few hours at manual work each day. At first the costs of feeding the children were high. Initially, it cost £8 per year but cost savings and better efficiency reduced costs to £6 and then, by the time of his visit to Bristol, costs stood at £4.10 per year. The high costs in the first year were due to some blunders.

He commented on the actions of the police when taking the children off the streets, as he didn't believe in being too kind to them. He told them about 345 children living on the streets of Aberdeen being apprehended by the police the year before the school had opened. After one year the number dropped to 126 children, after two years 14 children and after three years only six children were taken from the streets. It appears that, as the nuisance value of these children had been contained, there was little concern about their welfare.

The committee running the Bread Street School in St Philips was moved to take up the challenge because so many of the boys attending the school did not have a home and were returning to the streets each night to find a place to sleep. Initially the committee provided food for the boys and then realised there was a need to organise cheap lodgings for them. After listening to Alexander Thompson the committee rented the former Clifton Workhouse in Pennywell Lane, and from December 31, 1849, ran what effectively became one of the first industrial schools in Bristol. Their aims were to lodge, board, educate, teach trades and find the boys employment on leaving school. It had room for 38 boys but accepted 47, these boys being among the most destitute. Of this number 24 had no parents, seven with a father who was sick, in prison, deserted or crippled, and of the 90 coming into the whole school, 20 had been in gaol.

By 1850, the year when cholera swept through the city, the Bread Street School was called an industrial school where no homeless child remained and everyone at the school was provided with lodging at the society's expense. One report described their inmates as children of a class notorious for vagrancy, lawlessness and dissoluteness of habits. This school became known as the

Bristol Industrial School for Boys, and was the first of its kind in the city and possibly in the South West of the country.

Cholera claimed many victims from the families of the children attending these schools. It was not unusual for multiple deaths to occur in one family.

NUMBERS OF GIRLS AND BOYS ATTENDING SINCE 1849 – RECORD OF ATTENDANCE TAKEN IN 1850

	Girls	Boys	Girls	Boys	Girls	Boys	Girls	Boys
	morning	morning	afternoon	afternoon	evening	evening	Sunday	Sunday
St George	80	82	43	49	33	34	51	35
St Michael	25	38	24	39	26	41	6	0
St Philips	167	118	84	80	69	51	60	30
Temple	74	56	27	26	54	51	28	19

Teachers from St George told of a five-year-old girl attending on what was to be her last day at school. She had been marked by her eagerness to repeat all the texts and verses she had been taught. She died the next day, her widowed mother survived her by just one day, leaving surviving children. Apparently the Orphans Asylum found money and clothes for these children.

Mrs Emma Davis, mistress at the St Philips School, wrote to the committee on behalf of Ann Phelps who wished to thank them for their assistance during the illness of her daughter. Sarah had died but in the time leading to her death had sung the hymns and prayers which she had learned at school; she knew she was going to Jesus and the angels were waiting for her. The Reverend Meredith, Minister of St Luke's Church, had visited the school and talked to all the children.

Comments from neighbours in the areas where these schools were opened were generally supportive; they said the streets were much quieter now that the ragged schools were opened. Teachers at the Clifton National School reported that their numbers had increased; this was due to the numbers of children having attended a ragged school who now wished to move on to "proper school". The committee minutes noted that the general characteristic of the children was of great poverty, but the children were more orderly and parents had expressed their gratitude. Knitting and needlework had been introduced into the curriculum.

In 1852, after four years of work, a report produced by the manager of these schools indicated that the prejudice they had encountered at the beginning was disappearing. Results of examinations taken in reading, spelling, geography and arithmetic indicated improvements; a library had been opened for the use of parents and there had been good feedback from the parents about the progress of their children. Making nets for the pilchard fishermen had been suspended because a market could not be found but making paper bags, slipper making and sewing upper leathers for boots for export continued. Finding industrial work for the boys had become difficult; it was at a time when if men could not find work it was not surprising that the schools were struggling. The boys were employed at gardening, and even went onto the streets to clean shoes.

The number of children attending the ragged schools totalled 1,128 but the committees were still struggling to find enough income. Even so, five educational schools and two industrial schools had now been established.

In order to impress subscribers that their work was achieving positive results and, of course, to keep the subscriptions flowing in, the committee wrote reports about the successful intervention into the lives of some of the children. Here are a few examples:

- In 1852 John came to school in Pennywell Road; he could read a little, could not write and had little knowledge of Christianity. His father was a journeyman hatter, unemployed, of bad conduct and often drunk for a week; he beat his wife and his children. Mother was consumptive and too weak to do heavy work. In May 1855 the father took John out of school to run errands and took the money that John earned to buy drink. John's teacher fetched the boy back to school. John did well in school and is now working for a boot manufactory. The teacher acted with some bravery here as there was no rule or law that compelled the children to attend school.

- Two brothers came into Temple school; they were quite destitute and this was the only school they had ever attended. The report showed they had learned to read and write well and, with their united earnings, were able to support their widowed mother. The report didn't mention how they earned their money only that it must have been with the approval of the teachers.

- An interesting comment was written by one of the teachers at the St Phillips School about a small girl. She had been some time in the school and the teacher noticed that she was better clothed than in the past and asked her about it. The girl explained that her father now brought all his money home and didn't get drunk or beat her mother like he used to. "He will even listen to us read when we borrow books from you and Ma says it is all due to us coming to this school."

- Perhaps the most life changing incident came from Temple School when a boy, no name given, whispered to a master that he would like to speak to him alone, and on being taken aside said that he had done something very wicked that day. He had passed by an eating shop; no one was in it, so he had run in and prigged a silver spoon and knife. Now he was sorry. If he fetched them would the teacher take them back? We don't know what the teacher actually said but apparently they were returned.

At the end of every year, reports were published on the progress of the schools and the financial accounts of each establishment. The main committee report was more general and concentrated on the finance and general news on the schools. In 1857 it was reported that the school in St Michaels had closed as the hall was too dilapidated. The children were sent to the Bread Street School which appeared to be thriving. The report mentioned they were now training some children to become pupil teachers in the school and noted that many of their pupils were getting good jobs. The Temple School, which organised a Maternal Association to support mothers who wanted to learn for themselves, also reported to the committee. Of the 98 mothers who joined at the beginning of 1857, only 74 were still members. They met on alternate Monday evenings, with the average attendance being 40 to 50 mothers.

The report stressed that much of the support given was of a religious nature and that this might account for the fall in attendance. The teachers of St George School at Brandon Hill also wrote of children learning and making good progress. Some children had done so well in the school and, with support available from their homes, were now able to attend the Clifton National School.

The report noted that children of a higher class were coming to the schools. These schools were not intended for these children, who had gained a foothold into the school in Bread Street because no other schools were open to them in the area. The report then discussed payment, and how that a low rate could be established for these children as they clearly didn't want to turn them away.

There were only five school reports for 1857 and some indication that the Ragged School Association had done such a good job improving the life of many children and their families that they were working themselves out of their appointed role. The 1859 Industrial Schools Act gave Mary Carpenter the opportunity to set up Park Row Industrial School for Boys, so offering different opportunities for the street children.

On April 18, 1852, a girl's industrial school known as "The Home" was set up by a committee of ladies from Clifton in the area of St James, Hotwells. Six girls aged 14 were taken in at the start and numbers increased to eight and then to 14. It was intended that these girls would qualify to fill the situation of domestic servants. The matron described her charges when they entered the school as having "uncombed locks and unclean rags" and proudly contrasted their present "neat, cheerful appearance" to show how well they had settled and the value of what the home was trying to do. The only comment from the Ragged Schools Committee about this school came in 1855, when it was announced that five girls were suffering from a fever which was an additional expense for the school. Twenty girls were now in the school; one girl had left having found a position with a lady. This school was not part of the work of the Ragged Schools Society and had its own subscription list and organising committee. It may have been set up at 14 Dowry Terrace and could be the school listed in the 1861 census and three following census reports. It is believed that the term "ladies" is applied to women with some status because they are daughters or wives of professional men such as doctors or lawyers.

By 1854 anxiety about the income available to run these schools increased and it was becoming difficult for these schools to continue with their work. The school in St Philips was asking for donations of cloth to make clothing and old carpet for shoe making; finding work for the boys had become impossible. The committee discussed the need for teachers to be gifted with more than ordinary patience and firmness and to have the skill to convey instructions. In its ninth annual report in 1856 the committee outlined the need to train teachers and agreed that pupil teachers would be accepted in the schools. It was also announced that no child had been committed for theft that year which was entirely due to the early training given to children rescued by the society. Thanks were expressed for the generous support given over the year.

THE FIRST INDUSTRIAL SCHOOL IN BRISTOL

In February 1856 the school, now called the Bristol Industrial School, employed a teacher called Mr Hibbins who became the master of the evening school. He was well thought of and, in 1856, the HMI requested that he be made superintendent of the school. On May 20, 1858, the annual report of the Bristol Certificated Industrial School for Boys in Pennywell Lane was produced. The aims of the school were "to reclaim the abandoned and to rescue those whose unhappy circumstances would inevitably lead to crime and profligacy". The committee responsible for running the school explained the poor financial situation. It managed to keep out of debt but the school could not survive on voluntary contributions. It had become hard to find industrial work for the boys, when men were unable to find work. This was a recurring theme.

A petition was to be sent to the Government for the school to be certified under the 1856 Victoria Acts 20 & 21. This would give them half the rent, one third of the cost of tools and materials, and see an augmentation of the teachers' salaries. All this would be paid by the Government. For every boy sent by the magistrates they would receive five shillings a year. They also reported that the magistrates had ordered some parents to pay towards the schooling of their boys. The school had been told that it was the duty of the managers to collect that money, but it was understood that the managers were not willing to do this. An inspection was carried out and, on May 7, 1859, the certification was received.

In the annual general meeting in May 1861 an announcement was made that the school had been registered under the Industrial Schools Act of 1859 and ten boys were committed to the school by Bristol Magistrates. The point was made that the parents of these boys were unable to contribute towards the costs of the school, even though the Act allowed the schools to charge parents. By this time 16 boys had left the school; three went into the Royal Navy; one into the Merchant Navy; four were apprenticed shoemakers; three became errand boys and two just left, with no reason given. A vote of confidence in Mr Hibbins was taken and boys were reported to be growing their own vegetables and potatoes, learning the art of tailoring and a drum and fife band had been set up in the school.

On January 1, 1863, a printed report from the Bristol Industrial School for Boys gave readers an insight into the progress of the school which still occupied the building in Pennywell Lane:

a) There were 53 boys in the school and during the year 14 had left and 24 had been admitted. However, 63 pairs of boots had been needed! Obviously some boots were kept in reserve!

b) Disposed: - Three sent to sea, nine gained employment and two were sent to friends. Of these, 10 were doing well, one had died, one was convicted of petty pilfering, one had been lost sight of and one had enlisted.

c) Fatherless nine, motherless one, orphaned one, 10 were sons of drunken and profligate parents, and three were utterly neglected. Only two could read or write fairly, and 22 were unable to read or write at all.

d) Reporting on the industry in the school; they had procured a sewing machine and made a profit of £79-3-6 from clothing sold and repaired. The tailoring and shoe work rooms had supplied to the boys 120 jackets, 120 pairs of trousers, 45 caps, and 139 pairs of boots.

e) The garden produced 80 sacks of potatoes that made £40-10-0, 12 bushels of onions that made £3-0-0, and cabbages, turnips and parsnips that brought

The band became an important part of school life; they were so good they were hired out for special events. Many boys, on leaving school, became bandsmen in the army.

in another £10-0-0 - a grand total of £53-10-0.

f) By the close of 1863 the balance was £275-8-8 and the debt had been largely reduced.

The drum and fife band had now been allowed to attend the parades of the Volunteer Artillery Corps on Saturday afternoons and to march with them to Durdham Down, accompanied by Mr Hibbins. This was a great honour for the band and the school, which was appreciated by boys and staff.

In 1866 the old workhouse in Pennywell Lane, still being used by the school, was required for a cholera hospital and the managers were obliged to find new premises. The school moved to Cliftonwood Crescent, Clifton Wood, on October 23, 1866. It was re-certified and became known as Clifton Day Industrial School.

Having developed from the ragged school, taking boys straight from the streets, the Clifton School continued to take Bristol children for the day, sending them home at night to their families. This was unusual; day boys were considered to be "at risk" because they were free at night to mess with the criminal element just waiting for them on the streets of Bristol. Then, of course, there was the influence of their unworthy families to be considered. The Government did not recognise schools that took in day boys and didn't give any monetary support to these schools until the Industrial Day Schools Act was passed in 1876.

Many of the children had found themselves living on the streets having lost their families through illness, death and desertion - but for some it was a chance to leave abusive families. A child being sent to an industrial school had to stay there until the age of 16, and contact with the home or family discouraged; family members could visit but only on a monthly basis and no one under the age of 14 was allowed. Many children did not receive a visit - they were orphans or had been abandoned and if their family was not considered respectable then visits to them would also be discouraged. All of the industrial schools in Bristol used emigration to Canada as part of their drive to remove the children from what was considered the damaging influence of unworthy families and because they sincerely believed the child would receive a better start in life if sent away.

In the 1869 annual report, the managers of Clifton Day Industrial School wrote that they were prepared to consider emigration to Canada for the boys "whose families would exert a strong influence over them to draw them back to a disreputable life". It was thought that a well-considered scheme in connection with emigration would be fruitful. In the 1870 annual report the committee noted that two boys were sent to America and five boys to Canada. In the 1871 annual report the committee announced it had found a trustworthy agent, a Mr Shipperley, who was well known to Bristolians. He lived in Quebec County and would ensure that boys sent from Clifton were found suitable employment.

DEVELOPMENT OF INDUSTRIAL SCHOOLS IN BRISTOL

IN THE SECOND half of the 19th century Bristol was an industrial city ranking alongside Birmingham, Manchester and London. Ships carrying cargo and bringing people from many places in the world sailed into the River Avon, passed through the gorge and moored in the centre of the city. With the ships came cases and boxes carrying the known, the unknown, the strange and the commonplace, all to be stacked and stored in warehouses. The harbour was a busy place which would attract curious children from many parts of the city, most eager to earn a coin or rescue stray cargo which might fetch a price later. The River Frome passed through the city centre receiving more than its fair share of effluent from the middens of the city so it became little more than a moving cess pit.

Narrow streets surrounded the port with cramped courtyards and narrow footpaths, all dark and damp as the sunlight struggled to reach the paving stones. In small workshops men tended fires in small furnaces and as they laboured, spark, grit and ashes dispersed into the air. It was amongst these streets and in this atmosphere that the street children found a place to live and survive. Large numbers were living and some even dying on the streets of the industrial cities at this time; it was a huge problem that needed to be addressed by local and central Government. The Local Government Board responsible for the workhouses was unable to offer shelter for all the children needing somewhere to live; individuals struggled to fill the gaps and all were looking for solutions.

Mary Carpenter was still actively campaigning for the establishment of

Taken some time in the 1870's, this photograph of the docks shows how easy it was for the street children to hide, find sleeping places and so become a nuisance to the citizens of Bristol.

industrial schools for vagrant children even as she was running Red Lodge, her reformatory school for girls. She had met with members of the Government and fiercely explained about the children who lived on the streets. She had also written letters to anyone with influence, even writing to Queen Victoria, to explain her ideas on education. At first Mary was a novelty; women were not expected to campaign for change, men were responsible for all decision making and Mary was just seen as a nuisance. In 1836 Mary tried to enter a conference hall to listen to the speakers but was turned away, simply because she was a woman. Mary, not a woman who was easily put down, was supported by Joseph Fletcher, Inspector of Schools. He was impressed with her ideas on education, encouraging her to write them down and publish pamphlets. As Mary's work became known, she was invited to these conferences to explain why she felt it was so important not just to educate the street children, but to offer them an education of quality. When attending these important occasions she dressed with care, always wearing black and carrying an umbrella; her speech prepared with great care was delivered with firm conviction. Jo Manton, her biographer, wrote, "wherever the needs of deprived children are recognised one may imagine a ghost, umbrella and blue book in hand, eye and tongue devastatingly sharp, the approving ghost of Mary Carpenter".

Manton also described what Mary would have seen as she walked the city streets: "You would see them, huddled in shop doorways to escape the icy winds. Beggars and gangs of children lived by scavenging like rats and living like rats." Children crippled with rickets would be seen begging and getting in the way of passers-by and, shocking to our eyes and minds, tiny girl prostitutes standing on street corners in our city.

Charles Adderley MP, a friend and supporter of Mary, who represented North Staffordshire in Parliament, was described by some as having radical Tory common sense! He had made a study of the transportation of convicts and supported Mary in her determination to set up reformatory education. He now turned his energy towards finding a solution to the huge problem of children living on the streets. Education and industrial training were to be at the heart of his proposals but he needed the support of the Government.

In 1857 the bill to set up and support industrial schools was put before Parliament by Charles Adderley. He had been impressed by the work already carried out by Mary Carpenter; he had listened to her ideas, consulted with others interested in the street children; and this bill was the result. He proposed that magistrates would have the power to sentence any child between the ages of seven and 14, with no means of subsistence, without family or a place to live, to be sent to an industrial school for educational and industrial training. Once certified by an inspector the school would then be able to get financial help from the Government; half the rent, money towards teachers' salaries and school meals. Although the bill was passed and became the Industrial Schools Act of 1857, little happened. The wording used to set out the reasons why children may be taken into these schools was ambiguous and there was little response. However, the committee of the newly named Bristol Industrial School in Pennywell Lane applied for certification and was able to benefit from this Government support.

PARK ROW INDUSTRIAL SCHOOL FOR BOYS

Mary Carpenter, though, was not someone who could stand by while decisions were made - she set about making arrangements to open an industrial school for boys in Bristol. A Liverpool business man, Frederick Chappell, impressed with the success Mary had achieved with those Liverpool girls who had been sent to Red Lodge Reformatory, bought Lunsdale House in Park Row so that she might open an industrial school for boys. Her first hurdle was achieved, she had a building; but more money was needed to make it ready to receive the children. Mary approached her long suffering friends. Only £15 had been received when a surprise donation arrived from a Mrs Evans, a total stranger to Mary and her friends. At last Mary was able to open this new industrial school.

Eleven boys were brought in by the police. They had been picked up from the streets around the docks as the police were concerned that these boys were in danger of being taking into professional gangs. A teacher called William Skinner, with his wife, moved into the house and Mary had this vision of a happy family life for these boys, eating their supper round a fire in the kitchen with the master and his wife. An impossible dream perhaps but it does appear that the boys settled well into this new life. A certificated teacher, John Langabeer, with his wife and family, also moved into the Park Row School. He was a man who was skilled at working with wood and seemed to have the patience necessary to supervise these boys. For Mary, this was one of her most successful ventures; the boys went out for picnics, visited places like the zoo and the circus, and it is claimed that, in those first ten years, no boy made any attempt to abscond. Jo Manton wrote that the school was genuinely offering the boys a better life than scavenging in the streets, so in those first few years, the boys were happy to stay. Mary's insistence on family life meant that, for many boys, this was the first home they had ever known. She set up separate banks for each boy; they could earn pocket money and were allowed to handle the schools' petty cash which, she said, they did with complete honesty. A physician was also called in to examine the boys and, at the end of two years, reported an improvement in their health and growth.

What is interesting is that, in 1870, Mary Carpenter also reported that several boys were already doing very well in Canada, working as pioneer farmers. This indicates that the school must have been one of the first Bristol institutions to send children to Canada. Unfortunately their names were not recorded when they left the school. At a later date the committee minutes

The Docks on the sides of the river were a great attraction to the children; goods to be found and money to be made!

noted the progress of these boys, as they wrote to the school, to tell of their lives and of other Park Row boys they had met.

Mary Carpenter ran the school by herself for four years and then, in 1862, set up a board of managers with her brother-in-law, Herbert Thomas, in the chair. She also took her place on the board as correspondence secretary, a position she retained until her death in 1877. Apart from making decisions about how the school would be organised, in most of the first committee meetings, the managers spent a considerable time discussing the vexing problem of drains. It seems they were in a very bad condition and it became clear that some considerable expenditure was necessary and that involved the managers in some serious decisions. Mary must have been aware of all these problems and chose a good time in deciding to hand over control to a board of managers.

William Skinner left and, in 1862, Mary appointed John Langabeer as the new superintendent. This appeared to have been a good choice; he was a patient man with a good understanding of young boys and he raised his family of four boys and five girls in the school; three of his children possibly being born in the school. He was, however, subject to the decisions of the committee that had control over all aspects of the school. In December 1866 the committee decided to increase his salary, but, as there was not any ready money, school rations were provided for him and his family. We don't know what he, or possibly his wife, thought about this, but it could well be seen as a downside to living on school premises. Later on, when gas lighting was put into the classrooms, John Langabeer had to ask for this to be put into his bedroom, so not so easy for him to be subject to the decisions of the managers.

A review of the working of the 1857 Industrial Schools Act came before Parliament in 1866 which clarified the type of child to be admitted to an industrial school under the terms of the Act:

"By means of the police of that place or, if necessary by an officer of their own, put in force the 14th section of the Act and every School Board where there is an industrial school if possible and kept there under the terms of that act.

Cause children under 14 years of age found begging or wandering with no settled abode or proper guardianship, or visible means of subsidence, or found to be destitute to be brought before a magistrate in order that they may be sent to an industrial school if possible and kept there under the terms of that Act."

Now it had been made clear that any child under the age of 14 and over the age of nine, found begging, receiving charity, wandering or homeless with no means of support, were to be sent to a magistrate. Similarly a child who was keeping company with thieves, was beyond the control of parents or, if under the age of seven, or who was thought to be guilty of a crime, would also find themselves in front of a magistrate. The police who had been given the power to find these children were often joined by concerned citizens who went out on the streets looking for children they might save! These people were often the men and women involved in running these schools; convinced that the life offered to a child in one of these schools was better than a life on the streets. They believed it was their Christian duty to save these children from a life of degradation and despair and really did believe that there were criminals gangs just waiting on every street corner, ready to entice the children into a life of crime. When gathered up, the children were taken to a magistrate who would charge each child with one of the offences or whatever would fit on that occasion.

Most of the boys sent to Park Row Industrial School were charged with "not having proper guardianship", but others might be charged with begging or being without a home. The son of a Welsh tinker was charged with singing in the street! The Bristol children were sent to the workhouse at Stapleton, and children from outside the city to Barton Regis Workhouse until enquiries had been made about family circumstances. Street children were kept apart from the workhouse children as the guardians viewed these street children as being substandard to their own charges. The Bristol Workhouse used a small room for the street boys; the street girls were housed in the ordinary women's ward but neither was admitted into the school for fear of contaminating the regular children of the workhouse. In Barton Regis Workhouse they were kept in an upstairs room and not allowed to mix with the other children or attend the school. After the child had been charged and lodged in the workhouse, then enquiries would be made about their home circumstances. When brought back to court the child would usually be sentenced to live in an industrial school until he or she reached the age of 16. Much would depend on the home circumstances.

The guardians of both workhouses were so concerned about the possible contamination of the workhouse children by the street children that, during a Conference of the Children's Aid Union in Bristol, April 1887, it was suggested that a detention house be attached to a police station to hold these children. It was stated by Catherine Woollam, a Guardian for Barton Regis Workhouse, that many people thought that street children did harm to the workhouse children and were harmed themselves as the workhouse was seen as an undesirable place for them. It is relevant to point out that there were times when the committees running an industrial school were struggling to support a boy who seemed unable to settle, so they would send him to the workhouse! They reported that he was not of the right standard for an industrial school and saw the workhouse as a more suitable place for him!

The 1866 Act gave much needed clarification on which child might be detained, how the schools would be supported financially and what might

Park Row Industrial School, now called Lunsdale House in Park Row

happen when each child reached 16. It was also made clear that any person wishing to open an industrial school must apply for certification from the Home Office. This would be followed by an inspectors visit and, if the school passed, then certification was granted.

Very early in their tenure the new management board running Park Row School learned about the problems faced by the children who needed a place in their school.

In June 1862 Michael came to Park Row School a little before tea time to see his brothers. He was in a sad plight; filthy rags pinned around him for clothes, face and head very dirty and no shoes on his feet. He had had nothing to eat since the morning before when a man had given him a new penny loaf and an old coat, which he now wore. He asked John Langabeer, superintendent, if he could stay with his brothers if he gave him three brass buttons. He had no home now, his father had killed his mother and the policeman had taken his father to Gloucester Gaol. The brothers took Michael, found him food and clothes, and the next morning the superintendent took him to the magistrate who charged him with having no home and officially sent him to live in Park Row School. The magistrate acknowledged the value of an industrial school and promised

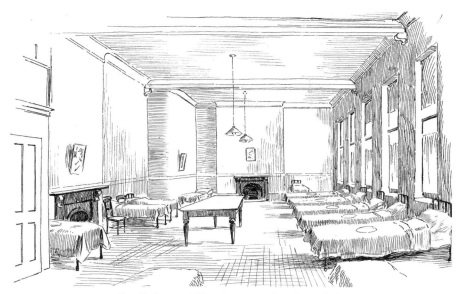

The 1869 Act stated, "Every inmate must have his own bed"

to do all he could to support the work being carried out. The father, also called Michael and a cab driver, was remanded in custody in Gloucester Gaol on June 5, 1862, while awaiting trial. He was convicted of manslaughter and jailed for two years.

This is just one story of a neglected child; there are many others told throughout the years of this school.

These schools were for the neglected, orphaned or abandoned children and, certainly in the early days, were to equip children with industrial skills rather than academic achievement. Such skills that might be needed in the trades of shoemaking, mending shoes and slippers, tailoring, making nets for fishermen, chopping firewood, and making bread, thus providing a skills service to underpin the Industrial Revolution. They were also to be lodged, clothed, fed and taught.

Sometimes children were discharged earlier than the age of 16 but permission from the Secretary of State had to be given in writing and it seems that this permission was only given for two reasons. One, the child was to be released for emigration purposes or two, the child had been diagnosed with a serious illness, possibly leading to an early death. The 1866 Act did not bind

Making and mending boots, shoes and slippers was an important part of the boys industrial training

the managers to provide any special provision for the children but they had the power to place children out on licence so that they might work outside the school, or to put a child into an apprenticeship. They also had the power to consider emigration for a child providing they followed the law and made every effort to gain permission from family or friends.

At first the schools were overseen by the Home Office although later there was a move to give this responsibility to the School Boards. HMIs were appointed by the Home Office and became responsible for visiting and inspecting new schools, agreeing the number of children and providing the certification which would enable the schools to accept children. Notices of the certification of schools were sent to the Gazette. Returns were made annually by each school to the Secretary of State, to show the situation of employment and character of all children discharged during the preceding three years. All schools were inspected annually with the inspectors submitting their reports in writing and commenting on the appearance, manners, behaviour and health of the pupils. Reports about the educational achievements of the children were very general and unstructured at first but, as the schools settled and general expectation of what the children might achieve improved, results of given tests were reported.

The same inspector appeared to visit all the schools in Bristol and did so until he retired and another took his place. It was possible for the superintendent of a school and the inspector to get to know each other quite well, in some cases improving the quality of care being offered to the children. The Rev. Sydney Turner was able to intervene and improve the management of Red Lodge Reformatory because he was aware of the qualities of Mary Carpenter and understood how she wanted to work.

The 1866 Act also expected contributions from parents which were to be paid into the Bank of England or Her Majesty's Paymaster General; the law gave managers the task of collecting these contributions and since they were not happy about it, there was some suggestion that they did not work very hard at collecting the money. Parents were to contribute unless the police reported that they were paupers or were unable to pay. It wasn't until 1876 that the managers were allowed to appoint an agent who would collect those monies.

By 1860 Bristol could boast two industrial schools for boys; Clifton Day Industrial School, formerly The Bristol Industrial School, and the school set up in 1859 by Mary Carpenter, known as the Park Row Industrial School for Boys.

CLIFTON DAY INDUSTRIAL SCHOOL

The Bristol Industrial School for Boys began its life in the old workhouse in Pennywell Lane as a ragged school run entirely by voluntary contributions, responding to the needs of the boys living on the streets. The school developed into an industrial school which was certificated in 1856 in order to take advantage of the new Act allowing grants of government money. In 1866, when their building was required for a cholera hospital, the managers needed to find new premises; they rented the Clifton Poorhouse in Clifton Wood and moved the boys on October 23, 1866; the school was re-certified and became known as Clifton Day Industrial School. Mardyke House, adjoining the Clifton Poorhouse, was taken on a long lease in 1872; the committee finally purchased the house along with number 102 Hotwell Road in 1887. The school

From the ragged to the respectable. The objectives of the Clifton Day Industrial School were clearly visible in its emblem that proudly adorned its official documents.

eventually became known as the Mardyke School and closed in August 1924. From its inception the Clifton Day Industrial School had always taken in day pupils; children who came in for school every morning and left at the end of the school day. When the school moved to Clifton the managers continued with the practice even though no funding was available for day boys. Many people considered that day boys would just return at night to the streets where criminal gangs were just waiting to teach them bad habits. It wasn't until 1876 that the Government allowed the schools to receive money for their day pupils.

STANHOPE HOUSE INDUSTRIAL SCHOOL FOR GIRLS

The 1866 Industrial Schools Act clearly defined what child may be taken into these schools and how they would be funded which, unsurprisingly, encouraged the opening of more schools. It certainly prompted Mary Carpenter to question the lack of an industrial school for girls in Bristol. She made her feelings known at the main committee meeting of the Park Row School for Boys in March 1866 and, being quite a forceful character, persuaded the other managers to support her. As always, when trying to raise money, she went to her long suffering friends to ask for their help to set up a school for girls in the city. As always, they agreed to help. In the past they found money to support her setting up her ragged school and then again found money when she opened the Park Row School and here was Mary, again looking for support. This time she was not only asking for money but active help in finding premises and setting up this new school; she explained about the girls living on the streets of the city, often earning money by prostitution, and they agreed to help.

If you were a friend of Mary Carpenter then you really needed to have deep pockets! She explained that she was booked to go to India at the end of the week so could she leave this all to them! Her friends didn't seem to mind being left with all this work; they found the money and in 1866 the first industrial school for girls in Bristol, and possibly in the South West of England, opened in a small house in Fort Road, St Michaels. It was certified on November 7, 1866, but, one year later, the house being too small for the number of girls needing a home, moved to Stanhope House in Portland Square. It was re-certified on October 23, 1867, and became known as Stanhope House Industrial School for Girls and was for the reception and treatment of destitute and vagrant girls of the Protestant persuasion who had been sentenced; girls who were neglected and tutored in crime!

This was the first school to ask for the children to follow a specific religion; all other Bristol industrial schools appeared to take children according to their need and didn't specify a religion. As far as one can tell, this insistence was not questioned but since all records relating to the running of this school have been lost then it is impossible to tell. However, there was no shortage of pupils. In four years the numbers had risen from six to 46, and any applications from other parts of the country had to be declined.

Industrial training was offered in the form of laundry work, plain needlework and knitting but three hours a day had to be devoted to education. The laundry girls were to have instruction before breakfast and after tea. The other girls would go to the school room in the morning and afternoon; afterwards they would follow the Holy Scriptures and learn about Christianity. Subjects followed were reading, writing, ciphering, geography and history but they were also to read books. The girls were expected to make their own clothes,

The girls of Stanhope House Industrial School. All the younger girls are holding a cuddly toy.

also all bed linen, house linen, do the washing as well as take in washing and, if that were not enough, bake their own bread!

From 1870 to 1876 numbers rose from 45 to 53 and the managers were asked to take in the truant children. Feeling unhappy about this they joined with other schools in sending a memorial to the Government. They seemed genuinely concerned about the effect of truant children on the other inmates, and the clause was withdrawn from the proposed Education Bill.

At the time the report was written it became desirable to look for new premises. The dining room and school room were too small, they had seven bedrooms but there were eight beds in each one. The school moved to a larger house in Somerset Street on October 31, 1884, and was re-certified for 60 girls. Now they were able to receive girls from all parts of the country. An inspection report commented on the appearance of the girls; apparently they looked clean and seemed happy, and they walked about the school in an orderly fashion which was clearly approved by the inspectors. Records for this school have not survived but they continued to take girls until the school closed in 1918; this information can be found in directories and from reports found in newspapers.

A report written in the Western Daily Press in 1883 does give some information about emigration from this school. Since the school had opened,

190 children had left, 25 had found situations abroad and most had done well. Three had gone to Africa, one to Queensland, and some to America. Letters had been exchanged and the girls had not been lost sight of after their period of detention had ended. They knew they could return if they were in trouble and some came back on a weekly basis to attend an evening class. The matron also received many visits on a Sunday. Unfortunately little is known about the running of this school but what we do know seems to indicate that it was a stable working establishment where the girls thrived.

THE *FORMIDABLE* - A SCHOOL ON A SHIP

In 1869 a trust was set up by a group of Bristol gentlemen, led by Mr Henry Fedden JP, in order to open an industrial school on board a ship. On December 1, 1869, the ship *Formidable*, which was moored at Portishead Roads, received 50 boys. The school was first certified in November 1867 and then again in 1869 for 350 boys. The school closed in 1906, the ship was sold and the boys moved on to the land and into a new building which became known as the National Nautical School. The committee running *Formidable* wanted to keep strong connections with Bristol, and the ship became well known to Bristol citizens. The school had a special relationship with the people of Portishead; pupils took part in local regattas, sailing and swimming competitions and local people used the grounds for village events. This was one of the most interesting industrial schools to open in Bristol and has a chapter all to itself in this book.

CARLTON HOUSE INDUSTRIAL SCHOOL FOR GIRLS

In 1874 a second industrial school for girls was opened in Southwell Street, St Michaels Hill in Kingsdown; it was called Carlton House Industrial School for Girls and it was certified in 1874 for 55 girls and closed on March 13, 1924. There are good records for this school.

ST JAMES DAY INDUSTRIAL SCHOOL

The ragged school in St James Back which was opened by Mary Carpenter in 1849 was still successfully taking in the street children, feeding them but also giving them an education. The Education Act of 1870 should have put the

This building was formerly the Carlton House Industrial School for Girls - later used for Bristol Maternity Hospital situated in Southwell Street

Ragged Schools out of business and Mary Carpenter hopefully closed down the school at St James Back, anticipating that all children would now be offered a free education in a day school, something she had always worked hard to achieve. It was always difficult to find sufficient funds for education, a fact which often got in the way of progress. The money available for education was fixed at such a low rate that it was the disorderly and neglected children, those who might need extra care, who were not catered for in these new schools. Many people objected strongly to the presence of the ragged street children in state aided schools and the certificated teachers were struggling to deal with them. They reported that the children were so poor, they were dirty, smelly, and added the comment that, at the end of the day, the classroom smelt like a "ferret's cage".

Some girls were almost naked except for an old gown and in one school, some attacked the teacher with sticks and stones and the police had to be called. Mary Carpenter was back on the attack again; she wrote to the Bristol School Board urging it to establish feeding in industrial day schools but with compulsory attendance. She even wrote to W.E.Forster, the creator of the 1870 Education Act in protest, explaining how the Act really left the children of the poor on the streets. Apparently he was not moved by her appeal.

On New Year's Day 1872 she re-opened the school in St James Back as a day industrial school and, as before, the children flooded in. She organised a hot dinner of pea soup and dumplings or bread and, because they were hungry when they came to school, she organised a cheap hot breakfast with dripping toast or bread and cheese with hot cocoa. It was free to the children so Mary now needed to organise a public subscription list to pay for the school and the school meals. No doubt Mary's friends were there to help her again. She demanded help from the Education Board which eventually agreed to certify the day industrial school for children who could not attend other schools and gave 1½ shillings a week for each child.

Attendance at this school was reported as follows:
1873 - 87 children on register, an average of 63 attended
1874 - 108 children on register, with an average attendance of 63
1877 - 63 attended but attendance was irregular
1879 - 92 attended.

In May 1876 an Education Act made education compulsory for all children and set penalties for parents who did not send their children to school. On October 3, 1877, resignation of the certificate, by the Committee of Bristol Day Industrial School, was accepted and the school was transferred to the Bristol School Board as a day industrial school for the purpose of the Elementary Education Act of 1876.

The school moved to Silver Street, Temple Back and was re-certified in 1883 for 40 children. The school was re-certified a number of times until it closed in 1917. In the 1897 annual report, 168 boys and 67 girls were noted to be present at the school. Girls learned needlework and worked at laundry and boys worked at carpentry. There was also a swimming pool and the children went regularly into the countryside and sometimes camped out for a few nights. Health problems were listed as diabetes, lung problems, rheumatic fever, anaemia, ringworm and infections of the skin and eyes. According to the report, all were due to dirt and malnutrition. It was decided to increase the amount of jam the children received because it was thought they didn't get much at home!

In 1883 it was reported that the two Hammond boys had gone to Canada and in 1884 the boys Hunt and Barrington followed them. Mr Mark Whitwill (manager at the Park Row school) visited the school and told the children they were doing well.

THE TRUANT SCHOOL

It had been suggested by the Bristol Education Committee that persistent truants should be sent to the industrial schools for training and education. After much discussion among the managers of the industrial schools, who were very unhappy about this idea, they reported that they felt these children would create difficulties which would deter their efforts to train the boys sent by the magistrate. It appears that the Bristol Education Committee listened to these concerns as it established a separate school.

A truant school was opened in Kingsdown on August 4, 1883, and it closed in 1898, lasting just 15 years. Records are limited but are very clear about the difficulties experienced by the staff of the school. The boys were described as dirty, verminous, covered in sores and dressed in rags. At the beginning of every day they went first to the matron who checked and treated their health problems. She used Jeyes Fluid to deal with the ringworm, dealt with boils and strange skin rashes, but was not able to remove the dirt that seemed to be ground into the skin. The children also suffered from boils, something we hear little about these days. It is not surprising to find that after only one term, the matron took a week off on account of her own health!

Food became a subject of much discussion. In order to save money it was decided that half of the food should come from the Carlton House Industrial School. The girls cooked pies in their cookery classes and the pies were duly sent to the truant school. Unfortunately the crusts were so hard, the pies couldn't be eaten! School started at 6 o'clock in the morning with breakfast at 8.30, dinner at 12.30 and tea at 6.30.

The headmaster wrote about the school. He had taken in two boys who didn't know their own names and had no reading or writing skills. The girls did needlework, kitchen and washing, the boys cleaned and chopped sticks. It was hard to discipline the children as they didn't attend regularly; the minutes tell of one boy who had to wear a placard around his neck with the words "liar" and "thief" written on it. It was doubtful he attended the next day. The Head commented that he didn't think the boys liked being in school because they were always anxious to get away early. This was clearly not the easiest teaching job in Bristol.

When the truant school closed it had worked with 244 children of whom 20 had left Bristol, 45 were still in the school, 12 were in the workhouse, 75 had left the school, and 91 had gone into the certified industrial schools.

MANAGEMENT OF THE INDUSTRIAL SCHOOLS

Each industrial school was run by a committee of managers - men who ran businesses or were professional people, possibly lawyers, doctors, men of the church, in fact people of a certain position in society. The women were the daughters and wives of professional men quite determined to do what they could for these children. In some schools they only met once a month, but when setting up the school on the *Formidable*, the committee needed to meet once a week. Once the Clifton Day Industrial School was established the committee only met twice a month. It was Clifton managers who emphasised that the objectives of an industrial school were to reclaim the abandoned, and rescue those whose unhappy circumstances would inevitably lead to crime and profligacy.

Noted below is the routine for a typical committee meeting at the Clifton School which followed the pattern used by most industrial schools in the Bristol area:

1. The master's journal was read. Then three lists of boys names were presented; those for entry to the school, those who were due to be discharged and those who were to be punished.
2. Illness and death lists.
3. List of all punishments
4. Any representations from the Secretary of State were read out.
5. Grants of licenses for boys due to go for work.
6. The accounts of the school.
7. Any comments received from any of the boards of magistrates who sent children to the school. Children were received from Bristol, Derby, Oxford,

London and Cirencester and from the counties of Somerset and Devon.

Although the industrial schools were funded from a number of sources such as the Treasury, the rates, the school boards, parents and voluntary subscriptions, it did not mean that these schools could always pay their way. It seemed that any individual support for boys in finding suitable work might suffer. In 1863, the wife of a shoemaker came into the Park Row School looking for a suitable boy to register as an apprentice for her husband; the managers were unable to find the £10 required for this transaction.

In 1883 the Western Daily Press reported on the development of the industrial schools in the country. The article set out the numbers. By the end of 1881 there were 133 such schools in England and Wales and 34 in Scotland. 109 of these took children of the Protestant religion and 24 of the Roman Catholic. The schools were funded from various sources.

£16,855 came from parents
£170,107 from the Treasury
£48,780 from the rates
£56,809 from the school boards
£34,727 from subscriptions
Any money paid by parents went to recoup money paid by the Treasury.

By December 31, 1883, the following statistics had been released:
51,418 children had been through the schools
14,717 had found employment or service
9,224 placed out with their friends
670 had emigrated
4,263 had gone to sea
689 enlisted
1,009 discharged because of disease and other ailments
930 to reformatories
1,784 had died
1,898 had absconded and not been recovered.

LIFE IN AN INDUSTRIAL SCHOOL

THERE WAS QUITE a ritual to be observed when a child entered an industrial school, starting with a bath, hair to be cut and washed, all old clothes to be taken away and new clothes to be worn, (all Bristol schools had decided that their pupils would wear a uniform). This was an important part of the philosophy that everything belonging to the old life must be left behind and nothing from their past would be taken into the school. Each boy or girl was starting on a new life which was to be one of usefulness and industry and every child must, as far as possible, forget the evil of their past life.

They were expected to obey all of God's commandments in order to prepare them to become honest and industrious men of society and to prepare them for another and a better life. The rules of the school would be made known to them on many occasions and would also be pasted on the wall in every room of the school. This was a serious commitment that every child had to make on entry and this was repeated in all industrial schools.

In most of these schools emphasis was put on living and working to Christian principles and an emphasis was underlined that teaching was strictly non-sectarian. The rules of most schools included a statement that categorically underlined that all sectarian teaching was forbidden. In 1866 the Government was seriously considering a new industrial schools bill which would allow ministers of all religious persuasions, to come into these schools to preach or teach. All Bristol schools, except for Kingswood Reformatory, signed a memorandum which stated, very clearly, their opposition to such a bill. They claimed it would be impossible to cater for the religious needs of all the children but the argument was strongly on anti-Catholic grounds. The

John was sent to Park Row Industrial School in June 1881 at the age of nine; the charge was truancy. His parents lived in St Peter Street with their five children; father was a labourer who would need to go out every day to find work. Aged 14, John left Swansea on the ship *Warwick* and arrived in New York in May 1885. He was sent to a farmer in Silver Creek, Merrick County, Nebraska, but sadly died of influenza before his 20th birthday. John is shown wearing the uniform of the Park Row Industrial School. Government rules did not require a uniform but all Bristol industrial schools made that expensive commitment.

Catholic Church opened its own industrial school in Cannington, Somerset, and all boys of the Catholic faith were transferred from other schools, regardless of the boys or the parents' wishes.

At Park Row, Mr Langabeer recorded a visit from a Mrs. Richardson who asked for a Catholic priest to be allowed to come into the school to give instruction to her son, James. She became very distraught explaining that the priest had kept her from confession and the Sacrament for months because her son was there, and she couldn't bear it any longer. If she were to die then God would punish her for disobedience to her minister and at her death the minister would not visit her. Had Mr Langabeer noticed the melancholy cast of her character? Also her boy lately had gone into a sullen mood and that could be the reason. In the morning after this visit the boy ran home and had to be brought back to school.

The school day was very structured, with a timetable that offered stability to children who had lived very disorganised lives. Every child would spend three hours a day, except Sundays, on their education. Subjects being taught were maths, English, scripture, history and geography, and only teachers who had passed the usual exams to gain their parchment were to be employed in these schools. Other subjects such as needlework, embroidery, knitting and poetry were introduced at a later date. All pupils were expected to write clearly. When Augusta was taken into Carlton House School for Girls at the age of 11 she was unable to write. Her letters written four years later, when she was in the tuberculosis hospital in Torquay, were clearly written. Her writing was well formed and entirely readable; she could express her thoughts and wishes so that we know what she was thinking.

AN EARLY TIMETABLE USED FOR THE PARK ROW SCHOOL

06.00 - Rise and Wash
06.30 to 08.00 - 1st Division School Room, 2nd Division Industrial Work
08.00 - Breakfast, Roll Call, Prayers
08.35 - Drill
09.00 to 10.30 - Work all Hands
10.30 to 12.45 - 1st Division Industrial Work, 2nd Division School Room
12.45 to 13.00 - Wash
13.00 to 14.00 - Dinner & Play
14.00 to 17.00 - Work all Hands Shoemaking, Wood, Garden work
17.00 to 18.00 - Supper & Play
18.00 to 20.00 - Schoolroom All Hands
20.00 - Roll Call, Prayers and Bed

The school at Clifton followed a very similar timetable but Wednesday and Saturday were half-day holidays and if the weather was satisfactory the boys would go out. Most schools allowed time for their pupils to walk out with supervision. Drill was taken for a half-an-hour every week day and some boys schools ran a band which practiced for an hour every day. Some became very proficient and were hired for special occasions. This was an opportunity for the school to recap some of the money spent on expensive instruments and many of these boys became bandsmen in the army when they left school.

Tests were held to check the progress of the children. In the early days of

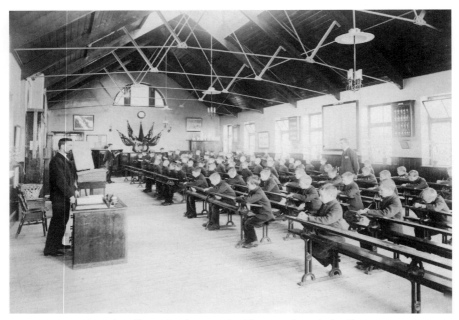

A large class of boys taking lessons in the Clifton Day Industrial School for Boys

Exercise class in a rather small gymnasium for the Clifton boys

the schools the records gave simple details about the progress of the children but as the schools evolved, the tests became regular and the results were published in the annual reports. The managers wished to know the outcome of the results and in the Park Row school they also became involved in the supervision of the tests:

Class I was examined by Mr Thomas (manager)

21 boys presented

Passes in four subjects	5	Passes in Reading	15
Passes in three subjects	3	Passes in Spelling	15
Passes in two subjects	2	Passes in Dictation	21
Passes in one subject	5	Passes in Arithmetic	7

Class 2 was examined by Mr Whitwill (manager)

17 boys presented

Passes in four subjects	0	Passes in Reading	5
Passes in three subjects	1	Passes in Spelling	12
Passes in two subjects	5	Passes in Dictation	1
Passes in one subjects	8	Passes in Arithmetic	3
Passes in zero subjects	3		

The youngest group was examined by Mr Terrell,(manager)
In reading two passed, two were tolerable and one bad.
Spelling was very low, fair in a very low standard.

In the examinations taken on January 25, 1880, 19 boys in class 1 were examined by Mr Thomas, and they achieved 100% in spelling, 89.5% in reading, and 95% in dictation.

All these schools appeared to submit work for the Mrs Alice Coles Scholarship and if considered worthy then money prizes were awarded; £5 and £10 appear to be normal; many boys and girls from the industrial schools were successful throughout the years that these schools were open.

If education took place in the morning then three hours in the afternoon was taken up with industrial work, or the timetable could mean that it worked in reverse. Industrial schools gave the boys and girls the opportunity to work at some form of industry and learn the skills involved. It was hoped that this practical experience would help the boys to find employment after leaving school but it also gave them the chance to earn money for their savings banks. All children in an industrial school were able to own a personal savings bank; this was held for them by the school until they left when any remaining money was paid out to them. There was an added incentive which worked well for staff and inmates; money could be added for good behaviour or improved work performance; equally, staff could fine those personal banks for bad behaviour or poor work.

In the early days they might attach soles to shoes for export; made slippers or mended clothes; grown vegetables and fruit or made bread for sale. When the school on the ship *Formidable* was set up in 1869, the committee made enquiries of the Clifton school asking if they would supply the ship with bread. The boys of Park Row collected wood and chopped it up to make bundles of firewood. They were then allowed to go out into the streets to sell these bundles. It was considered good training for the boys. However, the opportunity to make some money for themselves became too good to resist; the daily journal written by the master revealed that the two boys caught in the act were fined and received two handers in punishment. This was a relatively mild punishment. Mr Langabeer probably appreciated their ingenuity!

Clifton Industrial School set up a workshop in the school and the boys were taught how to work with wood, making small items of furniture which were used within the school. Clifton and Park Row schools also expected the boys to learn tailoring and to make their own uniforms. Many boys became very proficient at this and were able to take up the trade when they left the schools. Park Row management became particularly skilful at finding odd bolts of cloth that were just the right colour for the boy's suits and didn't cost them any money.

Brush making was also taught in the Clifton school, the boys became so accomplished that the officials of the Brush Makers Union became concerned. The boys were unskilled workers so the brushes made in the school were selling

All school uniform was made by the boys in both industrial schools. Some became proficient tailors

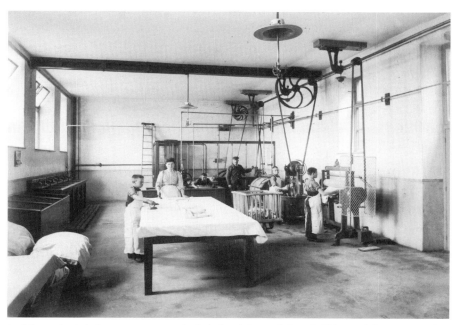

In all these schools the inmates were expected to look after their own clothes. All children took their turn to work in the laundry.

at a much lower price than those made by the fully qualified brush makers. The brushes made in the school were selling well and the brush makers were feeling very threatened. Strikes were threatened unless the school ceased their brush making activities. The managers tried to explain how they were trying to support these children and teach them a trade. Long negotiations between the union and the managers of the school took place until the conflict was eventually resolved and the boys could get on with learning the brush making trade.

Although the managers expected the inmates to work, they also recognised the value of recreation time, so on Saturdays and Sundays visits were made to places like the zoo or the circus, or perhaps a visiting group of players. Clifton boys were taken to see a show called "The Panorama of America" courtesy of the owner and Park Row boys took part in the opening of the Clifton Suspension Bridge in 1866. Regular visits were also made to places such as Clevedon and Weston-super-Mare. Park Row boys and Carlton House girls were regularly taken to New Passage for a week; this was treated as a holiday.

On one of the first Saturdays after Park Row School had opened Mr Langabeer decided it would be good to take all the boys for a day on Durdham Down. When they returned he wrote in his daily diary that everyone had enjoyed their day and all had behaved well but on reaching home, three boys were missing. The police were contacted and the three boys were returned to school. They were each were fined three pennies from their personal banks thus making the point that this was a serious matter. Absconding was a serious offence; anyone found helping one of the pupils of an industrial school to leave would be charged and find themselves in court.

The first case to come into court was reported in the Bristol Mercury and concerned a boy from Park Row Industrial School called Thomas Lovell. Thomas was a boy of 11 who ran away from school and went home, where his mother hid him under the table! The school called the police who visited the home and, of course, the first place the policeman looked was under the table. Both parents were charged with assisting Thomas to abscond; his father was cleared of the charges but his mother was found guilty. She was fined 10 shillings with costs or fourteen days in jail. The maximum punishment was a £20 fine or two months hard labour.

HARBOURING AN INDUSTRIAL SCHOOL LAD.

Thomas Lovell and Elizabeth Lovell, of St. Philip's, were summoned for unlawfully preventing, on the 20th November, a child named Thomas Lovell, who had escaped from Park-row Industrial school, from returning to the said school. Under the 34th section of the Industrial Schools Act, any person guilty of this offence is liable to a penalty of £20, or two months' hard labour. Mr. Knight, the schoolmaster, and Mr. Langabeer, the superintendent of the school, proved the absence of the child on the date named, and the former went to the house of prisoners, when the mother denied that the lad was there, but he was found concealed in a dark place under a table. P.C. Phillips, who also went to the house, saw the female prisoner, but the man was not at home. He asked the woman if her son, Thomas Lovell, was there, and she said "No." On his asking if he had been there she said he had, but had gone. On searching the house they found the lad. The magistrates dismissed the case against the father, but fined the mother 10s. and costs or fourteen days, this being the first case of the kind in Bristol. They intimated that similar cases would in future be more severely dealt with.

The first account of an industrial school boy absconding to go into the newspaper was in Bristol on December 6, 1879

William White, an inmate of Park Row, absconded from the school 14 times until the managers decided that enough was enough and he was transferred to the ship *Formidable*. They considered, quite rightly, that it would be difficult to abscond from a ship moored out on water but they also recorded that they thought that William wanted to go to sea when he left school. It would have been interesting to hear from William about what he thought!

Industrial schools always called the police when an inmate absconded and in the early days in Bristol, they appeared to find most of the children quite quickly. Later on it seemed to become harder and some boys managed to disappear altogether. Several names appeared in the Police Gazette with the police seeking information on boys from Park Row. During the last years of the school's life, the installation of the telephone in 1911 must have made it easier to summon the police.

For children who had been living on the streets, relying on hand outs or

The playground at Park Row School

food snatched when the shop keeper was looking the other way, the three meals a day being served in the schools must have been appreciated. The food was rather stodgy, much of it was bread, suet pudding and potatoes but a roast beef dinner with vegetables was served once a week. All the schools served a similar menu except on the *Formidable*, where the committee ensured that the boys had meat every day. When the Park Row boys who had left the school returned for a visit they brought with them apples, oranges, eggs and cake - treats for the boys still in the school.

The diet of the majority of people in the country at that time included large amounts of bread. It was not surprising that these children also received a high proportion in their food. Until 1916 in the Park Row School and 1910 in Carlton House School, food was portioned out onto plates by the adults. Then it was decided to allow the children to help themselves!

The general health of the children sent to the industrial schools was poor and some children were suffering from very serious conditions. All Bristol industrial schools needed to provide an infirmary within the school and to arrange for a doctor to be on call. Eye problems were recorded in all the schools

THE DIETARY TABLE OF CLIFTON BOYS INDUSTRIAL SCHOOL

Breakfast 08.00
Pint of hot milk with 4 ozs of bread
Pint porridge, half a pint of milk and 4 ozs bread

Dinner 13.00
Sunday: Corned beef 6 ozs Potatoes 8 ozs
Monday: Pea Soup 1 pint Bread 4 ozs
Tuesday: Irish Stew 1 pint Bread 4 ozs
Wednesday: Roast Beef 6 ozs Potatoes 8 ozs with Cabbage or another
             vegetable
Thursday: Boiled Suet Pudding 2 ozs with Stewed Fruit sweetened etc.
             Bread 4 ozs
Friday: Irish Stew 1 pint Bread 4 ozs
Saturday: Bread 8 ozs Cheese 2 ozs Cocoa 1 pint

Supper 17.40
Bread 8 or 6 ozs Cocoa 1 pint Butter Jam or Dripping ½oz
Boys over 12 years of age 8 ozs Bread - under 12 years 6ozs Bread
N.B. Extra bread was available at any meal, if required

but girls appeared to need more treatment than the boys. Regular outbreaks of measles were recorded and this was a very serious illness at that time. The schools also recorded cases of ringworm and skin infections; similarly the more serious diseases of tuberculosis, pneumonia, bronchitis, asthma, and all illnesses involving lungs, were recorded in each school. Children were sent to the local hospitals - Clifton School sent their boys to a sanatorium at Weston-super-Mare and Carlton House sent their girls to the Bristol Royal Infirmary. These illnesses were serious and often led to the death of a child.

Augusta was admitted to Carlton House Industrial School on December 22, 1875.

These details were entered into the register for that date:

"There is a father and a step mother both in prison, the father for assaulting the police, the latter for being drunk and disorderly and robbing a lady of her watch and chain. They are two of the most disreputable characters known. Augusta presented a half starved appearance and was in a most filthy condition. She does not know her letters."

She had been discovered by a policeman who had been sent to check the one room in which they lived. There was nothing in the room except a pile of rags on the floor. The police constable recorded that he was just about to leave when the pile of rags moved and he found Augusta. They did not know how old she was but decided she must be about 11-years-old. Augusta was not a well child and in August 1878 it was discovered that she had consumption in the left lung. The school made arrangements for her to be admitted to a hospital in Torquay; the matron at the school being friends with the matron at the hospital, it was thought the sea air might help. Augusta did well and there was talk of her taking on some work but, in 1880, the decision was taken to send her to Australia, a warmer climate was thought to be helpful. After a short time she developed full blown tuberculosis and died in a nursing home in Picton on February 2, 1882. Augusta was befriended by the Rev. Stanley Howard and his wife who had lived in Winterbourne before emigrating themselves. We know much about Augusta and her life; she wrote quite descriptive letters to the matron at Carlton House and it appears that the matron wrote back to her quite regularly.

The story of Augusta helps us to understand the difficulties experienced not only by the children but also by the staff. Augusta presents as a very pleasant child who, in spite of her illness, learned to read and write at Carlton House. The matron had to make quite serious decisions about this child - decisions which would normally be taken by the parents.

When, in 1884, "Louisa died after great suffering", one of the managers, Mark Whitwill, bought a grave for the girls and 12 girls went with Louisa to Arnos Vale to say goodbye. Death and illness were a part of their lives and it does seem to have been treated with care and compassion by the managers and staff of the school. In 1870 John Scandling, a pupil at the Park Row school, was diagnosed with consumption; staff were able to look after him themselves but after just a month he became worse so they sent for his sister who travelled from London to see him. Sadly, he died just before she arrived. All deaths were recorded in the committee minutes and schools were to inform the inspectors at the Home Office. There is evidence that the school managers paid for the funerals themselves. If it was possible children who were diagnosed with an incurable or serious illness were allowed to go back to live with their families; this decision was taken by the managers and had to be endorsed by the Home Office. This, of course, would depend on the home circumstances of the child. Mark Whitwill owned a convalescent home in Portishead and allowed the matron of Carlton House to send sick and weak girls there for a rest. A similar convalescent home in Shirehampton was used but the girls were expected to provide some general help while they were there.

Rules about discipline were written into the 1869 Industrial Schools Act. Usually the superintendent in a boys school or the matron in a girls school were the only ones authorised to give corporal punishment. All punishments were written into a book specially retained for the purpose. The book had to be available for the managers to read and it appeared general practice that recent entries in the book were read out at every committee meeting. Government guidelines were set for these schools to follow although individual schools did vary on how closely they kept to the letter or the spirit of the prescribed punishments. Food was used as a punishment - either the quantity of food was reduced or the quality but not both. The regulations stated that no child could be deprived of food for more than two meals in succession and a child kept in confinement could not have less than one pound of bread and gruel or milk and water daily. The Act stated, "that no child shall be confined in a room or light cell for no more than three days", and although this statement also adds that personal correction must be moderate, this was not clearly defined. No other method or form of correction could be administered unless it was with the permission of the Secretary of State.

In the early days of these schools correction was harsh and certainly did not always conform to the principles laid out in the Industrial Schools Act. At Clifton Industrial School the managers made it clear that anyone stealing would be severely flogged and deprived of all treats for three months and not be allowed to earn money. One boy who had stolen money in 1871 had his head shaved for three months and put on short rations for that time. In

Bar Bell Drill. A repetitive set of exercises carried out to shouted orders was a feature of life in Victorian schools. The Clifton boys are seen here going through their paces.

1872 a boy convicted of stealing received 12 strokes of the cane in front of the whole school and in the same year a boy was put on bread and water for three days for stealing bread. A master who took it upon himself to administer the cane was dismissed because corporal punishment could only be carried out by the superintendent and, more often than not, in front of a manager. In the early years the punishments set would seem very harsh to us. Caning was one of the most used punishments. Boys who wet the bed were caned; boys who used vulgar language were caned. These punishments were carried out by the superintendent and were supposed to be recorded although the punishment books have not survived. Flogging was a punishment given for the more serious offences but being deprived of privileges ranked alongside - for example a boy was not allowed to wear his Sunday clothes for three months.

At the Park Row school the superintendent seemed to administer justice as it happened. He kept a daily journal. He appeared to use "handers" as and when necessary. Handers were believed to be a clip around the ear. He wrote:

"A boy committing an indecency at the table - two handers

A boy playing a trick in church, the first boy punished for a disorder in church - six handers

Telling lies - two handers

Wickedness in the wash house - six handers."

Quarrelling and fighting brought sharp handers while Joseph Fudge, who decoyed a dog and secreted it in the house, received a dozen handers. It is interesting to note that for a boy found picking and eating broccoli in the garden for a second time, they felt it was worth using the cane, whereas dirty tricks in the dormitory (best not to imagine what that was) was worth six handers.

A boy who was sent to Clifton to sell firewood for the school but decided to go into business for himself was fined two shillings – a rather heavy handed approach to punish such initiative. A superintendent had some very challenging meetings with parents which he always recorded after the event.

Discipline in the girls school appeared to be more difficult to enforce. The matron would often call in one of the managers to help administer any punishment. She seemed to use the lighted cell more than a cane but there was no doubt that some of the girls were extremely difficult to discipline. In the early days of Red Lodge Reformatory, when Mary Carpenter was the superintendent, she found it difficult to enforce the rules. She was so aware of the girls' troubled pasts that she hesitated before punishing them. On the lower floor there was a single cell with bars instead of a solid door. This was the punishment cell, a very gloomy place even with a lighted candle in place. If one of the girls was sentenced to spend time there, Mary would sit outside the door and read stories to the imprisoned girl. One very serious punishment which might be handed out in any girls school concerned their long hair. If the rules were broken, the child might suffer the indignity of having her hair cut short. When the matron of the girls who were resident in Kingswood Reformatory cut the hair of three of the girls as a punishment, all the girls threw their bonnets and cloaks in the bushes and ran off to the bright lights of Bristol. Their long hair was that important to them.

Mary Carpenter was involved in the management and the life of many of these schools which was acknowledged in many ways. On her birthday the boys at Park Row were allowed to have currants in their buns for that day.

The relationship between the parents and the managers of an industrial school was one of distrust; for example:

- a parent who didn't take their child to church or chapel
- the parents who married after their child was born out of wedlock
- any parent who came to school the worse for drink

....all would be considered unworthy and not respectable. These were parents thought not fit to raise their children. These parents would not be encouraged to visit, some actively discouraged and some actually banned. Parents who visited the school making demands that their child be released to them could find out that their child had been emigrated to Canada instead. Two girls from Carlton House were sent to Canada. The matron allowed one of the girls to go home to say goodbye to her mother but the second girl could not because her mother was thought unworthy. Monthly visits from families were allowed. Children under the age of 14 were banned from visiting and only about a quarter of the girls were visited. See table of visits below:

In September 1881 11 girls were visited out of 52
In October 1883 13 girls were visited out of 51
In January 1887 17 girls were visited out of 52

The Carlton House matron received a visit from Margaret's mother who had been to the local hostelry first, probably to give herself courage to face the matron. She was rather abusive and shouted out that she would not give permission for her Margaret to go to Canada and they were not to send her. In reading the minutes it became clear that Margaret's mother had done the worst thing she could possibly do. It was not surprising to find, three pages later, that all the girls were sewing clothes ready for Margaret to go to Canada. As soon as Margaret became 16, a place was found for her and she was put on a ship to Canada.

In all of these schools the word respectable was used to distinguish between the parents who were acceptable and those who failed to come up to the expected standard. All inmates of industrial schools were bound to stay in the school until they were 16, when they were allowed to leave. Many 14-year-olds were sent out on license to work outside the school. Boys worked as pages or as servants in large houses, girls as house servants. If they were to be "live in" servants they were overlooked by the matron who visited the master or mistress regularly. Those who went out to work and returned to the school every day were given very strict time keeping. Any complaint about their work or behaviour would be brought back to the school. They would be removed from the job and may not be allowed to go out again. It was expected that these jobs would continue until they were 16. Some of the girls from Carlton House were sent to the Girls Guardian agency where they learned how to be a servant. To train in this agency the girls had to be sponsored and be "good" girls. Some of the girls were sent to the Maudlin Street Agency when they left Carlton House, where they were offered cheap lodgings, found employment and, provided they behaved, they might do well.

When the day boys left Clifton Industrial School the managers were very concerned about allowing day boys to go back onto the streets of Bristol. It was considered that these boys would go back to their old disreputable lives so a determined effort was made to find jobs for them far away from their home city. Some were sent to the farms of South Wales while others went to work on the fishing boats of the Grimsby Trawlers.

In 1874 the schools were able to appoint an "outdoor agent" who would supervise all boys after their discharge from school and ensure they were in suitable employment. The agent was also to offer advice and keep a friendly interest in the young people, writing letters to those who worked in a different part of the country. This agent also had to be available for discussion with the superintendent of the school and for all this earned the princely sum of £20 per year. Looking back this seems a sensible move which perhaps could be used today.

CLOSURE OF THE SCHOOLS

After the turn of the century all industrial schools were small in comparison to the elementary schools now receiving children in Bristol. The Government was expecting all schools to offer games and physical activities but industrial schools did not have the space within the school or the playground space

AN ANALYSIS OF 258 BOYS WHO LEFT CLIFTON INDUSTRIAL SCHOOL FROM JANUARY 1895 TO DECEMBER 1898

Mechanics	29	Cow Men	1	Coal Hawkers	2
Farm Service	51	Working in Brewery	1	Butchers	2
Soldiers (Bandsmen 11)	24	Working in Saw Mill	2	Blacksmiths	2
Sailors R.N. (Band 2)	10	Working in Quarry	1	Coachmen	2
Sailors (Army 1)	8	Working in Colour Works	1	Working in Lace Factory	2
Shoemakers	6	Working in Timber Yard	1	Under Manager at Club	1
Drivers etc	9	Working in Wall Paper Works	1	Groom	1
Labourers (various)	9	Working in Woollen Factory	1	Cooks Assistant on Steam Ship	1
Working in Skin Yard	5	Working in Plastering Trade	1	Engraver	1
Ostlers etc	5	Working in MIneral Water Works	1	Office Boy	1
Errand Boys etc	11	Navvy	1	Casual Employment	3
House Boys	4	Postman	1	Out of Work	7
Shop Assistants	4	Telegraph Boy	1	Unknown	6
Working in Printing Trade	4	Brick Layer	1	Convicted	10
Working in Mill	3	Painter	1		258
Milkmen	3	Cattleman	1		
Barmen etc	3	Confectioner	1		
Van Boys	3	Sadler	1		
Cabinet Makers	3	Collier	1		
Malsters	2	Fisherman	1		

All of the seven boys reported out of work were of good character and the six reported as unknown were assumed to be doing well. Two of the 10 boys convicted were reported as doing very well and three were in reformatories. The information contained in this portion of the report was as follows:-
Boys visited: 198, By letter: 54, Unknown: 6, Altogether: 258

outside. Girls were expected to take part in cookery lessons so schools needed to provide access to sinks, suitable tables and cookers. It was difficult to find the space in a small school but even harder to find the necessary money. New health regulations required schools to organise a dentist's examination for each child at a cost of five shillings per child per year; the money was quite simply not available. All these government demands forced managers of all industrial schools to review their options and make some difficult decisions.

A report dated 1919 - 1920 written about Park Row Industrial School set out the position for these schools and underlined the increase in maintenance costs and the higher standards of education needed to meet the requirements of the Home Office and the new Education Act. Negotiations had been opened with the Bristol Education Committee with a view to the transfer of this school and all its endowments to the local authority. The change of management took effect at the close of the year on March 31, 1920. The Western Daily Press of March 23, 1922, recorded the closing of Park Row Industrial School and noted that it was the first industrial school to be opened in the country.

Carlton House School resigned its certificate on February 29, 1925, to take effect on August 28, 1925, but was told to complete not later than June 30, 1925. There were 22 girls still at the school and some were sent to the Walcot Girls Home in Bath. An "After Care" agent, Mrs Smith, was appointed to support girls on licence who entered Carlton House between 1916 and 1924. She also had responsibility for the girls still under supervision orders - four were still in Bristol and two of whom needed help.

These schools took the children from the streets, gave them an education and taught them skills they would need as an adult. They gave them a chance to learn industrial work and supported them after they had left. Many of the children had found themselves living on the streets having lost their families through illness, death, desertion but for some it was a personal decision, they were the "runaways". To the Victorian citizen these families were seen as unworthy, not respectable and certainly not considered capable of bringing up their own children to become hard working adults. Taking these children and sending them into the care of the adults running the local industrial schools was seen as a solution to this problem. As in all institutions much depended on the management and the individuals within the school; on one level the inmates received food, clothes and a bed to sleep in as well as some kind of industrial training. On another level the difficulties in their early lives, and the authorities' attitude towards their families, will have left many of these children struggling with organising their lives and their personal relationships.

THE STORY OF
THE *FORMIDABLE*

FROM THE RAGGED schools in Bristol grew the industrial schools; Clifton Day Industrial School and Park Row Industrial School taking the boys, and for girls came Stanhope House and later Carlton House. They all opened to offer these children a life free from vice and crime. From a belief that taking boys away from the city and giving them the life of a sailor would save them from such a fate, came the founding of a school on board a ship.

PLANS TO SET UP A SCHOOL ON BOARD A SHIP

On March 23, 1866, at the weekly meeting of the managers of the Park Row Industrial School for boys, the chairman, Mark Whitwill, told the meeting that he believed it a great advantage for boys to become sailors. Boys who lived on the streets of Bristol were often influenced by the gangs of criminals who roamed the streets. Training such boys to learn the discipline of life on board a ship would take them away from the corrupting influence of city life. It would complete the successful reformatory training that was carried out in industrial schools.

He felt that many a boy was longing for this move in life and urged the managers to take steps to obtain from the Government a suitable ship which might become a certified industrial school. Boys might be drafted in from other schools to complete their training; he also felt that this ship might be moored at King Road, near Portishead. It was agreed to form a committee of six people from the managers and their task was to enquire into the cost and management of such a ship. The committee, which included Mary Carpenter, reported back to the managers meeting in April 1866 but they were not very positive about their findings. A hulk may be moored in Bristol harbour; the

Ragged boy to Navy boy. Each lad was to leave his old life behind and to bring nothing with him so as to prepare him for a new and more useful life.

cost of finding a hulk would be £600 and add on the running costs, which would be £300 a year, it would be an expensive project. They also reported that the harbour master was not happy about such a ship being moored in the harbour. They had looked at the possibility of a mooring in King Road, but this was not considered suitable. To provide staff for this ship would involve a higher cost than a similar school on land and as the labour of the boys would be unproductive of money then costs of food and clothing would be high. It seemed clear to the managers that it might be difficult to raise the money needed and no further discussions took place in the meeting.

Nothing is recorded after this meeting but it is probable that information about these proceedings were discussed amongst the businessmen of the city. We do know that Henry Fedden, a Justice of the Peace and chairman of the Board of Magistrates in a poor district of Bristol, had become very concerned about the large numbers of destitute boys appearing regularly before him in the courts. He wanted to save these boys who had been contaminated by association with vice and crime and actively supported the idea of setting up a ship dedicated to training boys for life on the sea.

When, in 1867, one year later, "a provisional committee was set up for the purpose of endeavouring to establish a training ship for homeless and destitute boys for the port of Bristol", Henry Fedden became very involved. His rooms in St Stephens Chambers, Baldwin Street, Bristol, became the official address for the ship. The Western Daily Press recalled how the idea for a training ship came about:

"It was on 16 March 1867 that certain gentlemen of the city met and formed themselves into a provisional executive committee for the purpose of endeavouring to establish a training ship for homeless and destitute boys for the city of Bristol. The Government had favourably received their application for a vessel and a large number of leading citizens had promised their support; it was now time to set out their plans. The committee was to meet once a week at the committee room of the Commercial Rooms in Corn Street and straightaway set about securing financial support through promised subscriptions. They considered an approach to the Society of Merchant Venturers as essential and Mr Woodward was asked to visit; he returned with a promise of support but no actual money, this was disappointing. They consulted the Poor Law Guardians, magistrates, H.M.I.'s, the police and made some serious decisions about how the ship should be run. They believed that it was important for the boys to live a life of duty and usefulness so there would be strict discipline on Christian principles, religion would be non-sectarian. The following noblemen to be asked to become patrons of the Institution His Grace the Duke of Beaufort, The Right Honourable Earl Ducie, the Right Hon Earl of Cork, Sir William Miles and Mt T Morley M.P; and all were in agreement."

Plans were made, staff selected but no ship had been found. However the committee decided to hold a public meeting as it wished to set up a Trust to run the ship. It was considered important to keep the people of Bristol fully informed of progress. The committee favoured the use of public meetings and invited reporters to each one. An advertisement was placed in the newspapers to find a commander to run the ship. By May 14, 1867, 32 candidates had applied for the post. Six were selected for interview and Captain Edward Poulden, by a unanimous decision, was selected. He accepted the position of Commander Superintendent and became very involved in all of the preparations and organisation.

INTRODUCING THE BRISTOL PUBLIC TO THE IDEA OF AN INDUSTRIAL SCHOOL ON BOARD A SHIP

A public meeting was called for March 23, 1868. The Lord Mayor agreed to preside but the Town Clerk stated that a requisition to his Lordship was necessary. Consequently a form had to be drawn up and signed by a large number of influential citizens. The inaugural meeting didn't take place until March 23, 1869, a delay of one year. A large room was hired at the Athenaeum at a cost of one guinea; large numbers of Bristol citizens were invited by a committee, anxious to bring to the public the need for such a ship and to gather financial support. Reporters from the local newspapers were invited and given every facility to enable them to report all details.

A report in Western Daily Press of this public meeting held at the Athenaeum on April 8, 1869, was long and detailed. The Bristol public was able to read about the plans and aspirations of the supporters of the project. Henry Fedden read out letters of support, Viscount Sidmouth pointed out that there was no place quite as good for ships as Bristol and explained about the three types of training ships already present in the country. Ten ships were supported entirely by voluntary contributions such as the *Chichester* on the Thames and the *Indefatigable* on the Mersey, but these ships required £2,000 to £3,000 a year to support them. Two reformatory ships, the *Cornwall* on the Thames and the *Akbar* on the Mersey supported boys who had been convicted of a crime and three training ships had been placed under the Certified Industrial Act of 1866. It was also proposed to place the *Wellesley* on the Tyne under the latter conditions. The benefit of this was that the Government would provide five shillings per week for every boy so that they could be kept long enough to do them some permanent good. This avoided the idea that crime was followed with punishment, a way of working which was associated with reformatories.

The meeting was told that the religion must be sectarian and services would be conducted by the captain and the crew. They could not say what size ship would be used but that would decide how many boys they would be able to take when a ship had been found. A decision had been made to moor the ship in Portishead Roads, a mooring which was considered both healthy and convenient but the committee really wanted to keep the links with Bristol. Discussions took place about the annual costs and the figure of 100 boys was used as a basis for the calculation, and using what was known about the other training ships, it would cost around £20 per boy. Here the point was made that all boys would be expected to join the navy.

Captain Pocock of the *Wellesley* spoke of his ship and wished he could invite all present to visit the vessel as he could show them what a difference was made to the life of the boys. Those present were told that the provisional committee had visited some of the ships.

Mr Nash then proposed that an immediate effort would be made to establish a training ship in connection with Bristol for the reception of homeless and destitute boys under the Certified Industrial Act of 1866. He explained that the two industrial schools already set up in Bristol, and the reformatory at Kingswood, were currently full. He said we had poor boys in Bristol who were untaught and uncared for, through no fault of their own and the meeting was asked to look at the problem from an economic point of view - the criminal class was largely recruited from the ranks of these poor boys and criminals were a great expense for the country.

Reverend Percival echoed his own understanding by stating that he knew about the dangerous classes but doubted that anyone there realised that the dangerous classes began as boys! Boys needed training of good habit and discipline in addition to enlargement of their mental capacity. It was known that the Government felt its responsibility in this matter. British shipping had increased by 25% and a quarter of all seamen working on British ships were foreign, therefore underlining the need to train young men. He thought that boys, as a rule, wanted to go to sea but they lacked the necessary training. The Reverend Turner, Inspector of Industrial Schools for the Government, explained how industrial schools were set up and explained that the Government gave five shillings for each child to the school but parents were expected to contribute with whatever they could afford. However, he was concerned that the magistrates did not enforce this. This was not surprising because it was the managers who had been given the task of collecting the money, but didn't think it was their responsibility. It wasn't until 1879 that a collector was appointed.

A very practical speech was given by Mark Whitwill, manager of the Park Row Industrial School for Boys. He said there were 116,000 professional thieves in the country who earned their living by thieving; 100,000 were turned out of jail every year. About one third of them were habitual criminals and he calculated that, in Bristol, a very large number of sons and daughters of misery were the raw material from which such criminals were made. Of the 1,800 sent to these schools, 99 were illegitimate, 322 had lost both parents, 1,000 had lost one parent and 322 were deserted or their parents were in prison.

One important decision made at the meeting eased the way for volunteers to be accepted for training on board the ship. They would pay for their own training at a cost of £223 per annum; this was £23 more than a boy being sent by a magistrate. Uniforms were to be supplied and situations would be found at the age of 18 years. Advertisements to this effect were placed later in the local directories.

After all these speeches supporting the resolution with none against, it is no surprise that the resolution was carried. A Trust was formed to set up a ship to train boys for the navy and the head of the Trust became Henry Fedden J.P. of St Stephens Chambers, Bristol.

FINDING A SUITABLE SHIP

With the speeches over it was time for the committee to get down to the practicalities of finding a suitable ship of 1,600 to 2,000 tons for the purpose. The committee did not want to wait for a ship to be assigned to them by the Admiralty as that vessel may not be suitable, but sent Captain Poulden and the Bristol harbour master, Mr Drew, to visit ports such as Devonport, Portsmouth and Sheerness to search for a suitable ship.

They inspected the ships *Centurion* and *Implacable* at Devonport and then travelled to Sheerness and inspected the *Formidable*. They agreed that she was in good condition, considered her suitable for use as a school and applied to the Admiralty for permission to use her. The Admiralty refused to let her go and offered the *Ajax* instead – agreeing that repairs to the *Ajax* were needed and gave the committee its considered estimate of £350. The committee was unwilling to trust this sum and sent a shipwright to inspect the vessel. He returned with his own estimate of £2,742 for repairs. The committee declined the Admiralty's offer and Henry Fedden went back to the Admiralty and successfully negotiated for the *Formidable,* which sailed from Sheerness on

The *Formidable* seen on the left on her permanent mooring. An ideal place for teaching the boys to row and sail the *Polly*, seen on the right

The boys line and wave from the rails in this unusual view of the *Formidable*

Tuesday September 7, 1869, reaching Portishead Roads on September 11. On board were Henry Fedden, Captain Poulden, his wife and several committee members. However, money was still urgently needed. The committee had already paid £400 in fees for the pilot and the 40 or 50 men it took to sail her to her new home.

It was at this point that the Bristol Mercury paid tribute to their choice when, in September 1869, the newspaper published an article on the reception of the *Formidable* at Portishead. Part of the article is reproduced below:

"Captain Poulden, late of H.M.S. Excellent *at Portsmouth, was appointed to command and we feel we should commend them on their choice. Captain Poulden has 20 years experience in the navy; in addition to this are impressed by his unassuming thought, polished manners and the invariable courtesy with which he received all who approached him. The humane, Christian feeling which is evidently one of his ruling characteristics must have favourably impressed all who accompanied him on the voyage from Sheerness to our roadstead."*

Formidable was built in Chatham Dockyard and was laid down in October 1819 and launched May 19, 1825. She was a wooden two-decker warship, pierced for 100 guns but actually only carrying 80. Her sister ship, the *Ganges*, later became a training school for cadets and its mast remains on land near Ipswich. Much work was needed before the *Formidable* was ready to receive the boys. A new steam galley was fitted and alongside that baths were installed for washing but doubling up as a swimming bath – the boys were expected to learn to swim. A fire engine was to be bought - an essential purchase as wooden ships were very combustible and, since she was jury rigged, Captain Poulden was given the task of changing the rigging to one more suitable for the boys to handle.

FORMIDABLE FACTS
Width 322 feet
Beam 50 feet
Draught 16 feet
Length 193 feet 10 ins
Depth 27 feet

Examples of the different uniforms provided for every boy. No expense spared!

Outfits were to be purchased for the boys and as the managers thought it important for them to feel good in their uniforms they insisted on gold thread to sew the name of their ship *Formidable* on their caps. Each boy received two outfits of best uniform, work clothes and rainwear, one pair of shoes, haversack, knife, lanyard, brush, comb and cap.

All this was very expensive and the committee had to work hard to keep the money coming in. Being astute managers they invited the great and good of Bristol, and hopefully those who might take out a subscription, to a lunch on board ship on October 1, 1869. Tickets cost ten shillings for men and seven shillings and sixpence for women; this also included their fare from Bristol. Interesting that perhaps they thought that women didn't eat as much as men! Two hundred and fifty guests arrived by steamer, setting off from Cumberland Basin to take part in this significant occasion. It was so important to keep this project in the hearts and minds of Bristol people and to that end newspaper reporters were welcomed to visit on all occasions. From these reports it appeared that all invited enjoyed their lunch, most seemed to have a chance to raise a toast to the new school and clearly returned to Bristol in a happy frame of mind.

The view of the *Formidable* taken from the end of the pier owned by the Portishead Pier and Railway Company.

FINDING A PERMANENT MOORING FOR THE SHIP

Through the month of October 1869, while the ship was made ready for the boys, the committee worked hard to establish a permanent mooring for the ship that would be acceptable to the Admiralty. The Portishead Pier and Railway Company, which had built a pier for the lighters bringing in coal for the new power station, was involved in discussions with the *Formidable* committee. They were unhappy with some of the proposed arrangements being made to find a mooring for the ship. They argued that the ship would be in the way of the lighters bringing the coal, and other small ships needing to pass backwards and forwards. Putting her on the mud caused her to roll and if the mud was dredged then she would be in the way of smaller vessels. Eventually, after weeks of discussion, she was anchored further out using four sea anchors. The Admiralty approved the site for a permanent mooring and the *Formidable* continued to occupy that mooring until she was scrapped in 1906.

When the ship was opened for the boys the managers agreed that she would also be open to visitors on any day of the week except Saturday and Sunday. All visitors were requested to use the boats from the pier to reach the ship. The Pier and Railway Company, now content with the arrangements, was charging one shilling per passenger for the use of the pier to reach the *Formidable*. In the end the arrangements worked well for the ship and the Company.

The following notice was inserted into local papers and appeared in the pages of the local directories:

"This ship was certified under the Industrial Schools Act for boys between 10 & 14 are received under this act XVI, XV, XVI also under the Elementary Education Act Sec XII Sub Section 2. Under these Acts the authorities who send boys provide part of the required payment. Any boy suitable for a seafaring life may also be sent as a voluntary inmate on payment of £223 per annum. Boys are trained for the Royal Navy and Merchant Service are provided and situations found on discharge generally at the age of 16."

THE SUPERINTENDENT GENERAL IN CHARGE OF THE SHIP.

Captain Poulden worked with the committee on every aspect of the preparation of the ship as the arrangements to prepare her for the boys to live on board continued. His family lived on board with him, a condition of his appointment, and on March 31, 1875, he celebrated the birth of a daughter on board the *Formidable*. Staff were selected by the superintendent and were subject to his authority. In the 1871 census there were four officers on board, two seamanship instructors, one school master, a tailor, nurse, cook and steward. In the 1901 census there were three instructors and school masters, a band master, carpenter, watchman as well as cooks, stewards and a nurse. Captain Poulden resigned in 1877 and the committee announced that a Captain Nicholetts, R N had been appointed November 26, 1877, to run the ship. At this time there were 18 staff. At the yearly prize giving on July 31, 1894, the retirement of Captain Nicholetts was announced to the assembled company and they introduced Captain Still as the next Superintendent General. These three men held an important position on board ship and were held responsible for everything that took place.

They supervised all recordings such as the registers, log books, cash books, and the general order book which all visitors signed as they arrived. The Superintendent General was also responsible for all punishments which were recorded meticulously in the appropriate register. Punishments were set out in government guidelines and approved by the committee. They included deprivation of privileges; degradation from a place in the ship; time in a light cell although not more than 48 hours; reduction in rations and corporal punishment though not exceeding 18 strokes from a cane. He could also cancel any leave to which the boys may be entitled, and any visit from a parent. No one could leave the ship for any reason without permission from the Captain. He had total authority over the running of the ship. Outside the Captain's cabin was a box in which, it was hoped, visitors would deposit donations. This was the only money allowed on the ship.

LIFE ON BOARD SHIP FOR THE BOYS

The school on the ship was certified as an industrial school in November 1867 and was officially opened by Charles Kingsley on December 1, 1869, with 50 boys arriving that day. People learned this from the newspaper reports, but the committee minutes record that the first boys to arrive numbered nine and they came from Park Row Industrial School. These lads had shown an interest in joining the navy and had been accepted as the first boys in the new school. Visitors were encouraged for all of that first week which must have made it very difficult for the staff to settle those first boys into their new school. As Christmas approached the committee decided not to allow any boys to go home on that first Christmas as they felt that, "many good boys come from the worst homes", and decided to buy the boys a good Christmas dinner instead. Christmas was not one of the activities which appeared regularly in the managers' reports but in 1869 each boy received a basket of sweets and a Union Jack handkerchief.

Some of the boys were sent to the ship by the magistrates for the following reasons.

- James, his parents were dead, a woman in the street took in the children but couldn't continue.
- George was found begging in Park Street.
- Jimmy, neglected, was found wandering in the streets with nowhere to go.
- Joseph, a vagrant child, utterly destitute.
- William was found wandering with no visible means of support, father was dead and mother drank.

This photograph was taken in 1871 on board the *Formidable* two years after the opening ceremony; some of the boys will have been on board for a very short time.

Reporters from the Western Daily Press told their readers that: "The qualifications for taking a place on the *Formidable* are poverty, parental neglect, vagrancy and danger of being contaminated by association with vice and crime."

When the boys first joined the ship they were sent to the tailor to learn how to wash and mend their clothes and then sent to learn to blow the bugle and pipe calls used on board ship. We don't know how long these lessons took but can presume they continued until the boy was proficient. A band was established early in the life of the school and was used to march boys to lessons, roll call and prayers. Boys were summoned to their duties and to mess by calls on the pipe exactly as if they were sailors working on board a ship at sea. The newspapers reported that, "the boys carry out seamanship training, learning such feats as 'clap on a jigger', 'make a turks head', or 'box the compass' and perform other mysterious feats with strange sounding names". This sounded very interesting and highly nautical, but when the school had been open for a short while, a visit was made by Her Majesty's Inspector. He was not pleased when he found that the prescribed three hours education did not form part of the daily arrangements. From that point the boys were taught scripture, reading, writing, arithmetic, geography, history and poetry for three hours per day on each week day. To this curriculum was added sword training, gun drill, rowing skills and all kinds of practical seamanship lessons with the clear intention that all boys would join the Royal Navy.

School days followed a strict pattern so that all boys would know exactly what they should be doing and where they should be at any time in the day. Here was the typical timetable:

- Rise at 6.00 am in summer, 6.30 am in winter. Hammocks stowed, mess tables put out, decks washed for the day. Hands to dress.
- 8.30 Toilet Inspection & Prayers - the band plays as the boys march to the top deck for prayers followed by school or seamanship instruction.
- 10.30 Stand easy, five minute break. Stroke of Bell
- 11.45 Clear for dinner - Pipe to Mess.
- 12.00 Eat Dinner in silence. Boys are organised into Mess teams with one as a leader. Start Afternoon School in silence.
- 4.00 Finish. Decks are swept. Mess cans of sweet cocoa and bread.
- 9.00 Hammocks.

Sunday was a quieter day.

Industrial work was part of the pattern on life on board ship; the boys mended and made shoes, and worked as tailors. All finished articles were taken ashore and sold. An individual account was kept for each boy, as was the pattern in all industrial schools. Money would be added to their account so they could benefit from the work they did. No boy was allowed to have money on his person.

By July 1872, 235 boys had left the ship; 40 had just left, six had gone into the Royal Navy, 188 had gone into the Merchant Service, two had gone as ships boys, and three had emigrated to America.

Discipline in industrial schools was prescribed by government which could be followed to the letter or practiced with some discretion. The committee set the discipline regime for the ship which was similar to that being practiced by other schools. The boys could receive not exceeding 18 strokes of a cane or rod which must take place in the presence of the Superintendent General. The committee discussed using a rope end which was usual at that time but

The boys are shown demonstrating the industrial work and the naval skills they are learning on board the ship

decided on a cane or rod. Absconding was considered a very serious breach. Any time a boy left the school without permission the police would be asked to fetch them back. It actually was very difficult to abscond from a ship moored out on the water but on October 14, 1877, 13 boys took one of the boats and rowed down the Bristol Channel. They were followed by a small group of officers who caught up with them while they were on a food break at Kingston Seymour. All were taken back to the *Formidable* for punishment. Stealing was also regarded as a serious offence so when one boy stole some money, he was charged and sent to the courts. The judge thought that he was already in the

SAMPLE MENU
- Breakfast and Supper - Sweet Cocoa and Bread, more for supper.
- Beef Steak Pie, Potatoes, Bread.
- Salt Pork, Mixed Vegetables, Pea Soup, Bread.
- Cold Meat, Plum Pudding, Bread.
- Meat, Vegetables, Bread.
- Boiled Pork, Pea Soup, Bread.
- Meat, Plum Pudding, Bread.

Preparing to join the Navy

right place and sent him back to the *Formidable*. The managers refused to take him back so the judge had no option but to send him to the reformatory at Kingwood.

Right from the start the managers had decided that the boys would be well fed; meat or fish would be served every day with bread or vegetables and the meals would be substantial. Petty officers and monitors were allowed butter every day.

A Doctor Davis was employed to examine the boys at least once a year and to report on their progress. The Navy would only take boys who were a good size, were strong, and had good teeth. Many of the boys who had lived on the streets had often gone hungry and those whose families had struggled to feed them would not pass for the Royal Navy, so many joined the Merchant Navy instead. It soon became clear to the managers that not all boys could qualify for working at sea and they were forced to seek other employment for these lads.

THE HAZARDS OF BOYS LIVING ON A SHIP

The number of boys increased from the initial 50 to 300 and although swimming lessons were given, a serious number of boys died after falling into the River Severn. They couldn't swim or even keep themselves afloat. It wasn't until 1881 before the managers bought a floating bath, measuring 18 feet by seven feet (5.38 metres by 2.15 metres), which would be attached to the side of the *Formidable* every summer but removed during the winter. Efforts increased to teach the boys to swim but even then there were a number of incidents where boys fell into the water, couldn't keep themselves afloat and, because of the strong tides, were carried away from the ship. Captain Poulden himself jumped into the water to save a boy who had fallen and in his turn was struggling to stay close to the ship; he was helped to safety by Mr Dyer with a long hook. A presentation was made by the High Sheriff of Bristol to thank him for his actions. On July 7, 1878, Charles Burdon got into serious trouble in the water quite close to the ship. One of the other lads, Aubrey McGuire, dived to the rescue and saved his life. He was awarded the Bristol Humane Society Bronze Medal. Apparently Captain Nicholetts contacted the Royal Humane Society as he thought Aubrey should be awarded their Silver Medal but nothing seemed to happen. In 1899 a swimming bath was created in Portishead Docks. Before it was used the school had 73 swimmers but by the end of September of that year the school could boast 300 swimmers.

For young boys living on a ship on the River Severn, swimming was not the only hazard. Many accidents occurred; a number of the boys fell or slipped on the ship suffering injuries, some minor but some very serious and some boys died. William wrote about a boy who fell off the ship, but as he knew enough to keep himself afloat, he was saved by an officer. He described two accidents; one boy fell off the mast, hurt his head and was taken to the on-shore hospital and another fell down the hatch, broke his neck and died from his injuries. The Western Daily Press of July 28, 1897, reported that Henry Kelland was working in the rigging; he fell from the crosstrees onto the main deck injuring himself so badly that he died about 45 minutes later, sadly just before a medical man arrived. The inquest was held at the General Drapers in Hotwells. William wrote to his mother, telling her that he had a nasty accident and now had a scar on his face but he didn't describe what happened. It is easy to imagine the feelings of his mother; she must have worried about him but she would also have been pleased to read his news.

The sick bay on board the ship was small and was used for short term

Many of the boys who died while they were on the *Formidable* were buried in Portishead Churchyard, others were taken home by friends.

illnesses, so in 1881 the wives of the officers on board set up a hospital on shore. A cottage, quite close to the ship, was adapted and used both for long term illness and serious accidents.

Many of the boys came from the streets or from poverty-stricken families. Most were under weight and lacked real strength so it is not surprising that a number suffered from the illnesses common at that time. Boys suffered and often died from conditions such as consumption, lung and brain diseases, heart failure and blood poisoning so the hospital was well used; boys were nursed there until they returned to full health or died. It was possible for families to collect the bodies and some did; otherwise the boys were buried in the churchyard of St Peters, Portishead, where a stone has been raised over their graves. Some bodies were taken to the pauper section of Arnos Vale Cemetery, no stone has been raised but it is possible to check the burial books.

Seven letters survive. They were written by a boy called William to his mother starting in April 1879 and the last is dated March 1880. The letters are written on printed sheets, collected from the captain, and headed with the name of the ship; it sets out rules about writing home, presents and when leave may be taken. William's writing is neat and well formed. He tells his mother that he is working hard and because he was top in an exam he was

Prize Giving held at the Zoological Gardens in Clifton; members of the public were welcomed to admire the work of the school

allowed to go ashore with the petty officers. He is now a monitor, he has good reports but now he asks if he should be a clerk and not go to sea. Life on board was not always so good for William, he stole some bread and now he can't come home on leave; he promises his mother never to do that again. In every letter he asks for his mother to come to see him but only once does he ask after his father; William always asks after his brothers and sisters. He writes of some easy times; they had a good feed at Christmas and he talks of a puppet show and offers her one joke. He asks his mother, why is a public house like a counterfeit coin? The answer is "because you can't pass it". We don't know if she was able to supply the answer or even what she might think.

Early in the life of the school the managers engaged a Clifton photographer to take photographs of the school on different occasions. It was partly a way of advertising the good work they were doing but was also used as another way of making money. These photographs were sold for five shillings, quite expensive at that time, but they were also designed to show Bristol citizens that the boys were learning skills and the school training was preparing boys for a useful life. Prize day, held every Spring, at first on the ship but later at the zoo, was another event when Bristol people were invited to see for themselves how the boys were progressing and to admire the good work achieved by the school.

The *Polly*, a training ship used to teach the boys to sail. Seen here under full sail

Once a year the Annual General Meeting, held at the Victoria Rooms, attracted Bristol people who would be presented with a report, in the form of a booklet, which would explain the good progress made in that year. A number of the pages listed the people who subscribed to this worthy cause; it also asked for donations of goods such as books, rope paint, tar etc. The managers of the *Formidable* were good at raising money, a very necessary skill when running such an expensive establishment. Henry Fedden, who led these meetings every year, became a well-known figure in Bristol, always associated with the ship and the boys who lived and trained on board. For him, the life of a poor boy was a sacred trust. For every visit he made to the ship, a specially chosen group of boys would meet him and row him out to the ship in the captain's gig.

An important purchase was the *Polly*, a ship used to teach the boys about sailing.

In 1875 the managers made yet another expensive decision; they decided that a real sailing boat was needed in order to teach the boys to sail. Using a toy boat was perhaps better than nothing but it was not good enough for the purpose. Gaining permission from the inspectors at the Home Office they bought a wooden Brixham Schooner of 88 tons called the *Polly*. She was built

When the *Polly* sailed into the centre of Bristol to collect supplies, she was always the centre of attention

by Dugdale and Company, cost £15,000, and with a change in sails became an important part of the boys' training. Between 30 and 40 boys were taken out for a week or two weeks at a time sailing sometimes towards Ilfracombe and sometimes to Bristol. William wrote to his mother and told her he had sailed on the *Polly* into the harbour at Bristol as they were to fetch a new tender. One of the old postcards of Bristol shows the *Polly* by the steps on St Augustines Reach, boys on board but a large number of people on the Centre looking on. A small but bold advertising feature in the Western Daily Press of April 25, 1884, promised the Polly would be moored by the drawbridge and would be open for inspection. Then the writer adds that contributions towards her expenses were urgently needed.

The *Polly* attracted a great deal of interest wherever she went and that would please the managers of the school. This interest did make it easier to collect donations towards her expenses. On August 29, 1902, the *Polly* became part of the Naval Review at Spithead. It was said that *Formidable* stood at the head of all training ships in proportion down to training from the *Polly*.

Every year the school organised a regatta day. There is a full report in the Western Daily Press of August 26, 1878, and the paper also prints the results of rowing competitions, swimming races and various nautical competitions.

RECORDS SURVIVE THAT EXPLAIN WHAT HAPPENED TO THE BOYS WHEN THEY LEFT THE SHIP

By the end of 1872:

- 235 boys had been educated on the ship
- 40 had left
- 66 went into the Royal Navy
- 188 were apprenticed to the Royal Navy
- Two had gone as ship's boys
- Three had emigrated to America.

A report from June 30, 1875 stated that 350 lads had been placed in honourable and useful professions but no details were given.

By the end of 1881 the total admission was 1,251 boys:

- 561 had gone to sea
- 52 into the Royal Navy
- 116 gone to other employment
- 73 gone to friends
- 17 into other institutions
- 14 into the Army
- 13 had emigrated
- 24 had died and
- 351 still on board.

Two years later it was recorded that three boys had emigrated to Canada.

Teams from other institutions and places, particularly from Portishead, competed and there was no doubt that the boys from *Formidable* could compete and hold their own against the other teams. The *Formidable* teams also took part in other regattas in the region.

Visits by HMI's were made to inspect the school at least once a year and reports were written about their findings:

- In 1876 the report stated the inspector found excellent sound discipline, the boys looked bright and cheerful, it gets better every year and the tone of the ship is excellent.
- In 1880 the inspectors wrote about sound discipline with more done by encouragement than punishment.
- By 1901 the tone of the report had altered to listing the worst offences such as insolence, pilfering, use of tobacco, bullying, offences common to every school. Add to that charges of laziness, disorder, and general slovenliness, and there appears to be a problem at the end of the life of the school.

EMIGRATION

Several boys did emigrate when they left the ship although the numbers were small considering that a total of 3,500 boys were inmates over the years. Most of them were either 15 or 16 when they sailed and although some were named, it has not been possible to identify all of them. Most of the boys went to St John, New Brunswick, Canada, sailing in small groups with the Bristol Emigration Society, organised by Mark Whitwill who was acting as an emigration agent. Sometimes they sailed with him in one of his ships as he was the owner of the Great Western Steamship Company.

The Reverend Shipperly, who was used as the emigration agent for the Clifton Industrial School, took a small number of boys to live in Quebec County where he lived and he brought one into Halifax. Two boys emigrated to join a parent already living in Canada; another boy joined a parent in the United States; and one boy wishing to emigrate to Australia left in 1885 and arrived safely in Brisbane. A number of these boys were born in different parts of Britain and only a small number were born and lived in Bristol, yet they were all sent from the city.

The records don't give any feedback from either the groups or the individuals who organised their journey or their placements; this doesn't mean that this information wasn't received, just that it wasn't noted or the records have been lost. We do know that two of the boys sent to Canada from the *Formidable* were boys who were in the charge of solicitors; they had not been sent to the school by the magistrates.

On July 14, 1904, Her Royal Highness the Princess of Battenberg laid the foundation stone of the new school.

DECISIONS TAKEN TO MOVE THE SCHOOL INTO A BUILDING ON LAND

The gales during the winter of 1901 damaged the ship. Some of her timbers were rotting and the managers became concerned that she would not be safe for the boys to stay on board for another winter. They considered moving the ship into a harbour but neither the Portishead nor Bristol harbour master would agree to take her and although Chepstow offered to give her space, the managers wanted to keep their links with Bristol. It was considered that the boys might transfer to the Feltham Farm School but that was rejected, and eventually it was agreed to hire the steam tug *Iris* to moor by the side of the *Formidable* throughout the winter.

Bristol School Board bought land in Nore Road, Portishead, and the managers and the people of Bristol were now committed to raise at least £20,000 to build a school on land. Once again the managers of the Formidable Trust committed to raise yet another large sum of money. They called a meeting, invited reporters of the local press and Henry Fedden took the Chair. He needed all his persuasive powers as the estimated costs soon rose to £30,000. Officials at the Home Office insisted that each boy must have the space of 36 feet in area which, he explained, seemed odd compared to the small amount of space each boy had when on the ship. There was nothing they

This new building built on land in Nore Road, Portishead, was designed by Edward Gabriel and became the National Nautical School

could do about it and just had to accept the ruling. He pointed out that he had seen boys in rags, very dejected, clothes tied with string in a filthy condition, absolutely hopeless and miserable. They come on board and within a few days they were pulling boats in a brave and manly way following an honest, good and wholesome life.

With the support of other prominent Bristolians such as the Wills and Fry families, enough money was raised and the architect Edward Gabriel was engaged to produce plans for the new building. Certainly it does seem that building started within a short time and continued without hindrance.

On July 14, 1904, Her Royal Highness the Princess of Battenberg was asked to lay the foundation stone of the new school. The ceremony was attended by many prominent citizens of Bristol and during the ceremony she presented prizes to some of the boys.

On April 26, 1906, the managers discussed the arrangements for the opening ceremony of the new school which was to be performed by Princess Christian of Schleswig Holstein, daughter of Queen Victoria. The chosen day was May 5, 1906. It was to be a great occasion, with a guard of honour and a lunch at a cost of £1 17s od per person.

Portishead Council wrote to the managers asking for a donation towards providing suitable decorations in the town. The managers were not very

On May 5, 1906, the new school was officially opened by Princess Christian of Schleswig Holstein. She is shown here arriving at Portishead Railway Station

impressed by this, and a suitable reply was sent. With due pomp and ceremony, as recorded by the many newspaper reporters of the day, Princess Christian arrived at Portishead Railway Station and was escorted by the North Somerset Yeomanry. She was accompanied by carriages of the local gentry and arrived at the newly built National Nautical School.

On being presented with a key, designed by a group of artists from the Bromsgrove Guild, which featured emblems of the sea and a symbolic boy's head wearing a laurel wreath, she opened the large door into the school. It was a successful day and for Henry Fedden it was quite special. He was able to see his life's work set to continue in a splendid new building. Princess Christian presented him with a painting of HMS *Formidable* by G Noble Barlow in recognition of his dedication towards establishing a nautical school in Portishead. The princess toured the building, tea was served and she was accompanied back to the station.

THE LIFE OF THE INDUSTRIAL SCHOOL *FORMIDABLE* COMES TO AN END

On December 19, 1905, a new certificate was issued by the Home office for an industrial school on land for 350 boys. On January 25, 1906, all the boys transferred to the school on land. One month later, on February 27, 1906, the ship *Formidable* was taken back by the Admiralty. This was a very emotional moment for all who had been associated with the ship and reporters were there to describe the occasion.

The Gloucester Citizen of September 12, 1906, painted a moving scene as the tug *Oceanna* pulled her away from the spot she had occupied for so long, and as she passed, the dredger moored by the pier gave three hoots to which *Oceanna* replied. Crowds lined the banks and all the boys from the school were assembled to see her pass; hundreds of voices singing "Auld Land Syne" followed her across the water. Three hearty cheers followed her as she passed out of sight 38 years to the very day since she arrived in Portishead. The *Formidable* had been sold by public auction and she was now on her way to London to be broken up for scrap.

After 38 years on March 10, 1906, The *Formidable* Training Ship passed out of the control of the Trust formed in March 1869 and on May 22, 1906, the first meeting of the Incorporation of the National Nautical School, Somerset, was held.

Henry Fedden, after 40 years being involved with the life of this school, was determined that the new school should have a chapel and a chaplain. Once again the money raising efforts commenced and, in 1911, the foundation stone of St Nicholas, the patron saint of sailors, was laid by the Bishop of Bath and Wells. Sadly the photograph of the procession is in a very poor state of repair but it is possible to see that this was another important occasion for the school. The Right Reverend Henry Kennion was appointed to care for the church and the boys.

The numbers from 1869 - 1909 appear in the final minutes. It is noticeable that only the boys who went into the naval services after leaving school are shown; 1,196 boys followed a different course and are excluded from the minutes:

- 3,700 boys were discharged
- 2,312 went into the Merchant service
- 192 went into the Royal navy
- 80% went into the Naval Mercantile Service or became as bandsmen.

After the National Nautical School was built, Henry Fedden raised the money through the Wills
family and other benefactors to build St Nicholas Church for the boys. This window in the church,
depicting the *Formidable*, was given by Fedden in memory of his son.

"*Formidable* played an important role in the social and historical development
of the Bristol area. It became the receptacle for the street arabs and urchins of
Bristol doing a two fold job, clearing the streets of these children and providing
a partly trained labour force for the Royal and Merchant Navy."

The National Nautical School for Homeless and Destitute Boys, Portishead,
was re-certified in 1931 for 225 boys' but from 1933 it became a senior approved
school.

In 1983 the National Nautical School closed its doors for the last time and
was sold. The grade one listed building was refurbished and became residential
flats. It became private property and was named Fedden House. The money
from the sale of the land and property was used to set up The Portishead
Nautical Trust. This is still being used to help young people today, the aims
sounding a haunting echo from the past:

"*The Trust aims to relieve and assist young people under the age of 25 who suffer
deprivation, poverty, financial hardship or difficulty, parental neglect, lack of control
or other misfortune. At the discretion of the committee funds can be made available
for worthwhile causes that will further the interests of young people.*"

REFORMATORY EDUCATION

THE RAGGED SCHOOL in St James Back, opened in 1846, was very successful. Joseph Fletcher, inspector, was so impressed that he asked Mary Carpenter to write down her ideas and then ensured they were published. He said he had never seen anything like it before and praised the good order, pleasing manners and gentle tone of the school.

Sadly it wasn't all good news; during the first year of the new school, several boys were sent to prison for stealing. When Mary Carpenter paid them a visit, her first hurdle was to get past the prison warder. He informed her quite forcibly that this was not the place for a lady and he simply could not understand why she wished to visit the boys. Horrified at the living conditions in the prison she questioned the warder quite closely. For his part he was genuinely puzzled about why she was so concerned about the children's welfare. At that time any child found breaking the law was brought before a judge. If found guilty, he or she would be sent to the same prison as an adult criminal. Mary was concerned that children, who were sent to prison and shared the same space as adult criminals, were open to their influence and more likely to become like them. She resumed her campaign to change the law whereby children who had been found guilty of breaking the law would be sent to a reformatory school and not to prison.

Mary Carpenter

This was the Victorian age, a time when children were expected to be good and were punished to drive into their minds the need to be good. Mary Carpenter held unusual beliefs for this time; she thought that these children needed love and the experience of a happy family life, not hard punishment. She campaigned for special schools called reformatories, where children could eat three meals a day, have toys to play with and pets to look after. She wished for them to experience a happy family life.

KINGSWOOD REFORMATORY

In 1852, while Mary Carpenter was campaigning for reformatory schools for the children who had been found guilty of a crime, she was approached by Russell Scott, a wealthy Bath businessman, who was very interested in reformatory education and anxious to set up a school. He had paid £1,000 for the old school buildings in Kingswood, recently vacated by John Wesley, who moved his school for children of the clergy to Bath. Russell Scott invited Mary Carpenter to work with him in the new reformatory school and she was delighted, because here was a chance to put all her ideas into practice. Scott and Mary Carpenter took on the superintendents work of the Kingswood school between them and when, on September 11, 1852, a master and mistress were installed the new reformatory began to take in children.

Both boys and girls were admitted in those early days. At first they took children from their guardians and some from parents who were experiencing difficulties in controlling them. The children didn't want to be there, resented being sent by their parents and did their best to be as disruptive as possible. Unfortunately Russell Scott and Mary Carpenter differed in their approach; Scott was for a much more disciplined approach with boys and girls learning industrial work, while Mary Carpenter wanted to offer them the chance to live as a family. Matters came to a head on a number of occasions when basic discipline broke down.

There was the time when matron cut the hair of six girls as a punishment. In an act of outrage they flung their bonnets and cloaks into the bushes and ran off to the bright lights of Bristol. Fortunately one of their mothers informed the police who were waiting for them and bundled them all into the local jail until a teacher could come to take them back to school. When Mary Carpenter

Kingswood Reformatory showing the Wesley Tree

reached the police station she discovered that the girls had been causing such a riot that even the constabulary could not calm them down. It was reported that when Mary Carpenter walked in, the girls quietened immediately, they kept telling her how sorry they were and promised to behave in future, which sounds as though they were not sorry at all. They had had quite an outing and Mary Carpenter was left wondering how she was going to get them back to the school. She wanted to walk them to the nearest cab stand but, on being advised that this was a really rough neighbourhood, she was obliged to borrow bonnets and shawls before it was felt safe to walk them along the road.

On another occasion, when two boys who misbehaved in prayers were forcibly sent out, the whole school decided to support them. Everyone ran out into the surrounding fields defying the teachers to come out and get them. It took the combined efforts of the local population and the teachers before they were able to get the children back into the buildings. It was a difficult time and when the 1854 Schools Reformatory Act came into force, Mary Carpenter decided to open a separate establishment for the girls.

The 1854 Act allowed the courts to impose a 14-day prison term for a convicted boy or girl under the age of 16, followed by two to five years in a reformatory school. Anyone absconding from such a school might face three months imprisonment. An Amendment to the Act was passed a year later that set a weekly contribution of five shillings from parents in support of their children. Mary Carpenter was very unhappy to find that children still faced two weeks in prison. She imagined how that child might feel when locked in a cell, and never ceased campaigning to get that clause lifted.

Looking back from the 21st century it seems extraordinary that children who had been found guilty of a crime were now able to get a free education, which was more than 15 years before the children who came from poor families. This was a great achievement for Mary Carpenter who had worked tirelessly for an education for these children.

RED LODGE REFORMATORY FOR GIRLS

The 1854 Act made money available from the Government towards the rent of a building, teachers' salaries and the costs of tools. Mary Carpenter realised that she could now set up a reformatory for the girls and with that in mind she searched for a suitable house. She found an Elizabethan house called Red Lodge situated in Park Row and thought it would be ideal. She set about raising the money to buy it, but her great friend, Lady Noel Byron, stepped in and bought the house and then rented it back to Mary Carpenter at an extremely low rent - proudly taking possession on October 10, 1854. The first girl to arrive was called Annie Woolham. Annie and the new matron arrived on the same day to find the house in a poor condition and very dirty. It was Mary Carpenter herself, with Annie and the matron, who scrubbed, washed and swept two rooms, just enough to live in until the house was ready. From this point Mary spent much time chasing the builders until after weeks of hard work the place was scrubbed and polished ready for her work to commence. Six new girls followed and then the girls from Kingswood transferred to their new school.

The school was examined by the Inspector of Prisons and on December 9, 1854, the certificate which stated that Red Lodge was fit to be a reformatory school, arrived from the Home Office signed by Lord Palmerston himself. The certificate was framed and took pride of place on the walls of her office; it remained there until the school closed. Mary Carpenter remained superintendent of Red Lodge Reformatory until her death in 1877. When the

RED LODGE REFORMATORY
Opened October 10ᵗʰ 1854.

decision was taken to close the school in July 1919, all surviving records, which included the framed certificate, were sent to the Bristol City Archives for safekeeping.

Jo Manton wrote about these first pupils in her book, "Mary Carpenter and The Children of the Streets" and commented that there was nothing about these girls to appeal to a conventional child lover. She described their flattened misshapen heads, their rotting teeth, and their blear-eyed scrofulous faces, writing of them as pitiful marks of neglect. Some were orphans, some illegitimate, some lived in fear of a parent or step parent, many carried burdens of responsibility on their shoulders and while some were withdrawn, others were always noisy and clamoured for attention. Of the first 27 girls across a range of ages, only seven could read and all of them slept in their clothes. None had ever taken a bath. Most of the children were covered with impetigo (sores or blisters). One had never been fed by her mother and had been driven to steal by hunger and another had been locked in a dark cupboard because no one could control her wild rages. Most of the adolescents had already served six or eight prison sentences. These were the children Mary Carpenter grew to love although the casual visitor would not find them attractive in any way.

Mary Carpenter wrote a journal of the first six years of the life of this school and in it she recorded the problems and the difficulties working with the teachers and matron, as well as the girls. She had a position of great power as the management of Red Lodge was entirely in her hands and because she was determined to control all aspects of school life, she did become too involved in the minutiae of the school. It became difficult for her to "stand back" and examine the progression of the school. She had written a set of rules named "The Principles, Rules and Regulations of Red Lodge" which set out not only how the children should behave but also the staff! Jo Manton commented, "A staff of angels could hardly have carried out Miss Carpenter's rules."

Mary Carpenter suffered a serious illness at the start of 1854 and was absent from the school for three months. When she returned she wrote that she found everything in "serious disorder". There had been many problems with the girls; Agnes had set fire to the house thinking that they would then be sent home. Margaret, having been released to a servant's position, burgled her employer's house, and Eliza, using most immodest language, had encouraged the little girls to prostitution!

It had become clear that since many of the older girls had been used to living a rough life with men while they were on the roads, they would never settle to life at a school. Emily flew into a rage and smashed all the crockery and Susan broke a window and screamed to the passers-by in the street that she would never come out alive and, "when I am dead I shall tell everyone that Red Lodge killed me". It all came to a head in 1858 when Eliza, a girl rather mature for her age, had absconded, was found and then locked up in the gaol. When Mary went to fetch her, she noticed that the Governor had come to say goodbye, an unusual act which surprised her. After returning home with Eliza the atmosphere in the school became rather disturbed when Eliza declared she was pregnant. When she pointed at the Governor of the prison as the father, Mary remembered the farewell gesture. Very reluctantly, Mary appealed to Sydney Turner, Inspector for Schools, for support and with his help the three girls involved were removed from Red Lodge with an order from the magistrates who met secretly in Red Lodge. In this way a public scandal had been averted; not one report of the proceedings made it into the newspapers.

The problems of looking after difficult and disturbed adolescents continued and there were other failures but there were many achievements. As Mary herself felt, the majority of the girls were not delinquent but simply neglected and responded to the attention and love they were given. However, the order and control which was really needed in the school was not in evidence. It was difficult to achieve as the teachers kept changing and there was no one who was capable of taking effective charge when Mary was absent. When a child needed to be disciplined Mary Carpenter insisted that she must do this herself; she was the superintendent and therefore in charge. The teachers felt that she was undermining their control; they complained that they didn't get a chance to set their own boundaries and just didn't stay in the job for any length of time.

Sydney Turner, an inspector, and a supporter of all that Mary had been doing, was concerned about the atmosphere in the school and the lack of control when Mary was absent. In August 1859 Mrs. Johnson arrived to take the position of matron; she took control immediately and was well liked by the children. Since Mary thought that she herself must be in control and felt threatened, it was not in her nature to accept that Mrs Johnson had the necessary authority to be effective. There was some disagreement between them; Mrs Johnson was quite determined to work without interference from Mary and asked for Sydney Turner to visit. She explained that she must have more independence in her work or she would leave. A painful interview with Mary followed as she offered to resign the certificate and all Sydney's powers of persuasion were needed; but Mrs Johnson remained and Mary gradually withdrew from the everyday management of Red Lodge.

"I must be free to develop my principles!!" Like every good administrator Mary Carpenter had worked herself out of a job.

When Sydney Turner visited in 1862 he noticed an improvement and wrote that Miss Carpenter was very fortunate in having a very efficient matron and school mistress. In 1863 he noted a decline in the number of punishments underlined by an improvement in school work and behaviour. He made similar comments in 1864 when he noted that the girls' answers to questions showed much intelligence and knowledge. Leaving Red Lodge in the capable hands of Mrs Johnson and Sydney Turner, Mary Carpenter turned to other concerns.

An inspection in the summer of 1877 reported the premises to be "very

The back of Red Lodge showing the garden

clean and well arranged", with the 58 girls in good health. The inspector remarked that he was perfectly satisfied with the appearance of the school. He declared that the education was satisfactory, reading very good, no serious misconduct to report, there had been no attempt to abscond, and the order and behaviour in class was very good.

Mary Carpenter died on June 15, 1877.

In her Will she set out the arrangements for how Red Lodge should be run after her death and such was her faith in her organisation, that was exactly what happened. A trust was formed to be responsible for the school but no member of the committee was allowed to be a member of the trust or to have anything to do with it. Committee members were required to sign the minutes to this effect and there was an insistence that they follow the guiding principles of Mary Carpenter.

The chairman of the new committee was Herbert Thomas, brother-in-law to Mary, and when one of the new members asked about the financial arrangements for the school, he was able to say that Mary had found the payments from the Government quite sufficient. She believed that they could

A peaceful picture of the sewing class; Red Lodge girls mended the clothes of the boys of Park Row and made coverlets for the boys who were emigrating

carry on without asking for subscriptions from the public. Mary had organised the school monies; she had been scrupulous about accounting for every farthing and nothing was wasted. It was going to take a good accountant to follow her example.

A new Superintendent Matron, Elizabeth Langabeer, was appointed in January 1880. She was the daughter of John Langabeer who was still the superintendent of Park Row Industrial School. Another daughter took the post of teacher and both remained at Red Lodge until it closed on December 11, 1918. Between these two women, and the fact that Langabeer family was still involved with Park Row School, it ensured that Red Lodge was run to the guiding principles laid down by Mary Carpenter.

As the years passed the way that similar institutions were managed changed; styles of teaching changed; but unfortunately styles of management and teaching in Red Lodge stayed the same. Jo Manton wrote that the Langabeer family "ran the school as a pious memorial to its founder, consulting the rules she laid down 1854 and even applying them 60 years later".

Doll dressed in the uniform of a Red Lodge girl

The committee found different ways to raise money, one of which was to dress dolls in the uniform of Red Lodge and sell to any who would buy them; one such doll can be found in Blaise Castle House Museum in Bristol.

In 1916 the school faced a deficit of funds. Additional costs resulted from inspectors asking for hot water in the bathrooms, swimming lessons, seaside holidays, organised games and the Home Office had also established new salary scales. Finally, on July 9, 1919, it was decided to close the school. The 44 remaining girls were moved to other institutions and Red Lodge closed after 65 years of caring for the troubled.

SOME OF THE RED LODGE GIRLS WHO EMIGRATED

The first girls to go to another country from Red Lodge were V. Lawrence and a girl called Goddard (Christian names unknown), who went to America in March 1856. They were followed by Annie Northam, who left just before Christmas. They left quite early in the life of the school and there was the view that they went out independently to work as servants rather than being sent with an organisation. When their emigration was approved by the Secretary of State, the girls in the school subscribed to buy them a writing case and Mary Carpenter gave each of them a warm cloak. There is no doubt that Mary Carpenter approved of emigration. During her visit to Canada in 1873 she visited her brother Philip in Montreal and was able to see for herself what had happened to the children. She was told that many children from reformatories in England had been settled into farms on virgin land with the help of the Children's Aid Society. For the farmers and the children the work was hard, yet Mary learned that many of the children now owned pieces of land for themselves and had done well. For her this was proof of her long held belief that it was urban society that was the problem, not the children themselves.

In February 1882, Elizabeth Thorne travelled to a home in Montreal run by a Rev Renaud. Mary Carpenter's brother found places for the girls sent out from Red Lodge. These arrangements appeared to work well; when the girls arrived in Montreal they went into the home run by Rev Renaud and positions, such as servants, were found for them. When the girls left these jobs or found themselves dismissed they seemed to find their way back to Rev Renaud.

Girls were encouraged to write to the matron at Red Lodge as if they were writing home; she always wrote back although they may have to wait a couple of months for her reply. Some wrote fairly consistently, some wrote once and there were others who wrote only when they were in trouble. A book was kept and all letters were given a date and a number. For some letters, comments were added and thanks to this system it was possible to learn about their lives after school.

Mary Ann Holcombe, discharged in 1888, wrote in 1890 that she had had a child by a man with whom she was keeping company and asked if she should return from America. The matron replied concisely to say she would do better to stay in America. Mary Ann replied in 1891 to tell the matron that the baby had died and that she was getting married and gave her married name.

One of the girls, who gave only her married name, wrote to say that she had lost her daughter of nine years, was now a widow but was in a good situation. She had another child with her and she asked if matron would say a prayer for her in the old oak room. Margaret Jane Hughes had settled in Washington; she was married and sent a photo. She was very settled. Then a very muddled situation about a girl called Parker who was sent to prison and then married but she needed money as both of them were in the workhouse. The letter was written by another woman.

Elizabeth Allsopp wrote several letters from Port Arthur and Emily Lilse was a cook in the Valkenberg Asylum in Port Elizabeth. It seems that the girls from Red Lodge found homes in many different countries. Sometimes they returned to England, as did Eliza Buckingham, who wrote letters from New York and then wrote to say she had returned to England. Her husband had been appointed to a position in Brentwood Asylum in Kent and she sent a photo.

The story of Susan Williams, born 1879, who was sent to Red Lodge by the magistrates in 1892, gives a clear picture of just how difficult it could be looking after these girls. Susan first appeared in the records on July 4, 1892. She had been insubordinate and would not be allowed to go on a visit. Then on July 26, 1894, she had absconded, walked to Clevedon and Weston from Bristol but had tired of walking; she had been found by the police at St George and was brought back the same day. In February 1895 we read that Susan had been put into the cell for noisy singing and shouting at night, keeping everyone in her room awake. A comment that she had been good for some time was made in the record. On May 22, 1895, Susan was in custody. She had appeared before the magistrates on charges of insubordination many times. The Matron was obliged to send for a policeman to take her away and she was remanded for a week. The magistrates decided that she must go to prison for three weeks and then go to another reformatory and it was the responsibility of the Bristol Police Courts to find a reformatory that was prepared to take her. Eventually it was agreed to send her to the East Chapelton Reformatory, Bearsden, in Glasgow. One year later on February 5, 1896, the matron of East Chapelton Reformatory wrote and asked for information about Susan's parents because they were getting her discharged. Then on February 22, 1896, a Miss Hunning travelled from Glasgow to bring Susan home, and stayed at Red Lodge for two nights. Susan was not a bad girl, she did not steal or hurt people, but she clearly was very disturbed and perhaps had mental health issues. There was no agency able to help and support her at that time. The best that could be done was giving out punishment which made matters worse and, from a modern perspective, we are left to speculate about what might have happened to her.

It is unclear how many girls left Red Lodge for Canada. After 1882 one or two girls left each year until E Gadd left in 1899. Most went to the Andrews Home in Montreal but some appear to have been found positions in the United States and sailed directly there. No details are given about who found them their positions and how it was settled. The supervisor and the committee could decide to send a girl, or one of the girls might ask to go. Once that was decided there was a matter of costs to be settled before permission from the Secretary of State could be sought. This was only necessary for girls under the age of 16 who were still serving their time in the reformatory. It was only possible to identify 14 girls to place on the database.

KINGSWOOD REFORMATORY SCHOOL FOR BOYS

Kingswood School for Boys was founded by Russell Scott in September 1852. It was certified for 150 boys on October 4, 1854, and re-certified July 1892 for 120 boys.

Russell Scott bought the buildings in Kingwood in 1852 for £1,000, and when Mary Carpenter visited she became excited at the thought of what she might be able to do for the children but didn't fully understand the work involved. The school had no fixed income and because it was a private venture there was no official recognition of the school and therefore no public funds were available. An appeal by Mary Carpenter brought in enough funds to prepare and make ready the school for the children, but even so there was no gas, and water had to be carried from a source two miles away. The boys were to have industrial training and to learn shoemaking, carpentry, farming, brick making and the work of a blacksmith.

The first in-take of boys and girls came from parents who could not control them or did not like them, and from boys and girls who had been to prison. These young people were difficult to control and exhibited very disturbed behaviour. Gradually the children settled into life at Kingwood. A drum and fife band was set up and boys could be trusted to go on errands into the village. The girls, however, seemed to take longer to settle - they were always slipping out of school to go back to their old lives. The Young Offenders Act proposed by Mary's friend Charles Adderley became law on August 10, 1854. This is now commonly called the "Reformatory Schools Act" and gave Mary Carpenter the

Boys from Kingswood Reformatory lining up outside the chapel

opportunity to establish the Red Lodge Reformatory discussed earlier.

A report of the first annual meeting of Kingwood Reformatory was printed on November 17, 1855, in the Bristol Mercury where managers described Kingwood as an asylum for young persons who had either become amenable to the law or were evidently about to fall into crime. Readers were informed of the statistics for juvenile crime for the years 1846 - 1851.

Convicted at the assizes and quarter sessions in those six years:-

- Under 12 years - 1,023 males, 166 females
- Above 12 years and under 14 years - 11,294 males, 416 females
- From 14 years to 17 years - 11,294 males, 2,258 females.

The message was quite simple; the school was worthy of support.

The report went on to say that, unfortunately, Mr Scott had moved abroad and Miss Carpenter had been very ill; the interim superintendent had to move away and suddenly it seemed that the school might be in serious trouble. A Mr. Barker was appointed to take on the job of superintendent and things settled down again. Looking back down the passage of time this must have been a very difficult school to supervise – with most Victorians seemingly keener to

KINGSWOOD REFORMATORY REPORT FROM 1857

In 1857 the school looked closely at the parents and their children and while they seemed to make decisions on open-ended information, it is interesting to examine their findings.

Of the boys, 19 had no education, 17 could read and write a little, two could do more than that, one was an orphan, three only had a father, nine only had a mother, eight had one step parent, 17 had both parents.

Circumstances and Character of Parents in connection with crime.
Respectable and capable 0
Temptation and natural propensity only 13
Incapable 15
Criminal and Indifferent 9
In want or orphaned 1

Training
Accustomed to work 35
Never at work 3

Convictions
Never 12
Once only 17
Twice only 1
Three times 7
Four to eight times 9

punish rather than educate children who broke the law.

Kingswood school continued working with boys only but Mary Carpenter still appeared to be involved in visiting and teaching. The Western Daily Press report of 1857 acknowledged her support and reported that eight boys had emigrated to Canada and taken up positions secured for them by Mary Carpenter. Nothing had yet been heard from them.

The report included the following detail:

A wood working class in Kingswood Reformatory; industrial training was an important part of school life

- Two boys were placed out in England,
- Two had returned to friends,
- One had been transferred to other schools,
- One was incorrigible,
- One had been dismissed on medical grounds,
- Two had absconded and not been recovered
- One had died.

On Mary Carpenter's first visit back to Kingswood she was delighted that the boys seemed pleased to see her again. On November 1, 1861, she returned for the annual meeting and Harvest Home in company with many interested people from Bristol and Gloucestershire. The Bristol Times and Mirror published a full report of the proceedings and reported that 90 inmates had been fully occupied the previous year as brick makers, gardeners, tailors, shoemakers, quarry-men, carpenters and masons - so much so it was surprising they had any time for education. Not only had 300,000 bricks been made and sold but a large number of suits produced, boots made and repaired, 15 acres of garden well laid out, and 70 sacks of wheat ground by hand and made into bread.

The whole premises had been repaired and painted and lastly 100 dozen heads of cabbage grown and taken to market. The report assured readers that they had also been working at reading, writing, ciphering, geography and knowledge of the common things of life, involving a total of 21 hours of instruction every week. One wonders if the inmates were given any time for themselves!

The intake of boys during 1861 came from:

- Bristol 14
- Birmingham 6
- Derbyshire 5
- Plymouth 1
- Manchester 1
- Wales 2.

Of the boys who were discharged - 25 to Somerset, one to Liverpool, 3 to London, two to Bristol, two to Derbyshire, five to Gloucester, one to sea, and six had emigrated to Canada. All others were doing well and living by honest industry, only three had lapsed into crime.

There was a presentation of prizes which consisted of handkerchiefs, books and pocket knives. Perhaps the boys who received the latter had been carefully chosen.

After meeting the boys at their meal, Mary Carpenter wrote, "potatoes vanished wholesale and meat followed suit, nor did each little pair of jaws cease their motion till every plate was as though it had just been washed!"

During 1861, Mary visited Kingswood regularly and took the opportunity to teach the boys. She walked four miles each way, in all kinds of weather, to work with the boys. She was inspired by her work with these boys and justified her journey to her anxious family by reminding them how much she loved the work. Mr Turner, inspector, noted that the boys worked in the garden that year and there wasn't a single attempt to abscond. The managers bought a steam press for brick making, hoping that this would help to restore the financial situation of the school. All boys worked on the brick making and were soon producing 4,000 every day. It was physically heavy and demanding work. At

Kingswood Reformatory Band; many of the boys joined the army and became bandsmen

the next inspection Mr Turner appeared very concerned that the boys would be too tired for their education work and, in 1862, Mary Carpenter resigned in protest. There was a change of committee, a new superintendent was appointed and although Mary Carpenter started to visit again, her influence on Kingswood was over.

The Western Daily Press for March 15, 1872, reported that boys numbered 140, and during the previous year, 30 had been admitted and 22 discharged, 12 had returned to friends, two had emigrated, one had gone to sea and one had died. It was emphasised that during each day, periods of rest and work were fairly portioned out, and the financial position of the school was improving after bearing the cost of the brick machine.

The work continued and all seemed well until 14 years later the Bristol Mercury newspaper of May 29, 1886, reported that an emergency meeting was held by those involved in the life of the school. In spite of government subsidy, the school was nearly bankrupt. Mr Herbert Thomas, brother in law to Mary Carpenter, made an appeal for financial help and reminded readers that the boys were sent to the school for a total reform of character which prevented an increase in the permanent criminal class. It seemed that this appeal was successful as donations were received and subscriptions promised.

The financial position of the school must have improved considerably as the Bristol Mercury of September 15, 1892, reported the opening of a new building for the school; this was exactly 40 years after Mary Carpenter performed the original opening ceremony. The opening speech gave some interesting information on the number of reformatories across the country. Fifteen years earlier there had been 62 reformatories; ten had since closed and people might question why a new building was needed. Supporters of reformatory education needed to understand that the new school would be a special reformatory for the young boys who lived in the counties of Somerset, Gloucestershire and across the South West. The speech was followed with the remark that although this school was in Gloucestershire, the managers noted that no donation had yet been received from that county. They also wished to add that £1,600 was still needed.

In 1894 George Whitwell, the current superintendent of Kingwood commented in an article in the Western Daily Press of 20 February on the changes in the new Reformatory Act of 1893. The age for boys to be sent to a reformatory was now 12 whereas it used to be ten and inmates must leave by the age of 19. Boys and similarly girls may now be received without an initial term of imprisonment. This was an important part of Mary Carpenter's campaign more than 40 years earlier and one she never relinquished.

The Bristol Mercury of March 3, 1899, reported on an inspection of Kingwood with some very positive remarks. Old boys were serving in the forces with great distinction, breaking away from undesirable home circumstances. There had been a development of industrial training and the desirability of emigration for specially selected boys was limited by the want of funds.

Boys admitted in the previous year were noted as: six over the age of 12 years, three over the age of 15, of these boys four could read and write well, 29 imperfectly, nine unable to do so.

Twenty two were on their first conviction. Of 33 discharged, 19 returned home, three enlisted, one discharged with disease, one absconded (in school one week only). At this time the managers wished to state that they believed that 90 to 95% of boys had turned out well.

The annual report of 1916 printed in the Western Daily Press, June 16, 1916, underlined the work being achieved by their ex-pupils towards the war effort.

- 337 were in the fighting line; since 1914
- 31 had enlisted
- 12 had died at the front
- Some were doing munitions work
- Eight were working in a factory where guns were being made
- 16 lads, still in school, were making mail bags for the Government and had completed 1,000 so far.

The managers publicly announced their pride in the achievements of their young pupils both past and present. We now know that many of these young men won medals for their bravery and fighting skills from military medals to the Victoria Cross.

In 1933 The Children's and Young Persons Act was passed; now all reformatory and industrial schools were abolished in favour of Senior and Junior Approved Schools which would come under the jurisdiction of the Home Office. Kingswood eventually became a centre of excellence to inspire young people through the arts and called the Kingwood Foundation Creative Youth Network.

EMIGRATION

It was clear from the annual reports that a large number of boys were sent to Canada during the life of the school. There were many references to boys being sent from Kingswood or arriving in Canada but nothing that can be used to positively identify individuals.

In 1887 the Canadian authorities decided not to allow any further immigration of children who had been convicted of a crime. Charles Tupper, Minister of Finance, wrote to the Colonial Office, "I believe the Canadian Government has no desire to encourage the emigration of these children whether they are under discharge or under the license scheme".

The emigration of children from a reformatory was strongly defended; the Philanthropic Society pointed out that no difficulty had been experienced finding places for them and none had re-offended while in Canada. After much discussion the Canadian Government withdrew its objections and boys and girls continued to be sent from reformatories in Britain, including Bristol.

Problems were being experienced in England; when children were sent to Canada they were released on licence but once they reached Canada, some of the more enterprising young boys realised that they were now free of the rules that kept them in school. Many had saved enough to return and had been found living freely back in England, sometimes returning to their "old lives".

In 1891 a report was published with details of the reformatory children who arrived in 1890. Listed were nine boys who were brought out by Mark Whitwill through the Bristol Emigration Society. Two boys left in 1902, one went to Pittsburgh, U.S.A. to take a job in an iron foundry and one went to Montreal to work on a farm. In 1907 one boy left to go to Manitoba and eventually joined the Canadian Expeditionary Force during the First World War. Several boys left in the years 1902, 1906, 1907 but there is no information about their lives. There were only five boys names with additional information about their journey and where they were working. Marge Kohl, in her book, *The Golden Bridge* wrote that in 1862 there were 131 children who emigrated from reformatories in Britain whereas by 1914 there were only 39. Legislation in 1891 now asked for the consent of the parent, the child and the Secretary of State before a child from one of these institutions could be emigrated.

EMIGRATION FROM THE WORKHOUSE

THE 1834 POOR Law Act clearly stated that children were not to be sent away to another country without friends or family and although there is some evidence that boards of guardians ignored this ruling, no children were sent away by Bristol or Barton Regis Guardians at that time. As out relief was firmly discouraged, the poor had no choice but to seek shelter in the newly formed workhouses which were full very quickly. Concern was felt in government circles because one third of the paupers living in these workhouses were children under 16; a matter of concern for many people but costly for the rate payers. In 1850 the Government passed the Poor Law Amendment Act which now gave boards of guardians the opportunity to send their child inmates to another country without friends or family, if they wished, but certain procedures needed to be followed:

1) The guardians must get approval from the Poor Law Commissioners every time they wished to send a child away.
2) Parents and family must be informed and permission sought in writing.
3) The child must go before the Justices of the city in order to show that they understood what was going to happen to them.

The Bristol Board of Guardians did not send children to Canada at this time; trade was good and fathers of young families were able to find work. It wasn't until the end of the 1860s that the guardians began to seriously consider sending groups of children away. A letter from the Bristol Incorporation of the Poor, dated June 30, 1870, set out a list of children who were chargeable on the common fund of the Incorporation at £9.2.0. per year, seeking consent from the Poor Law Board for emigration. Four of the youngest children did not have settlements within the city and the Justices refused consent. In arguing for emigration the letter stated that, "the guardians are satisfied that it would be very much to the advantage of these little creatures to be sent to Canada where they would be adopted, and in all probability, be better provided for than many of the older children".

The guardians also added that they would be glad if the Poor Law Board could see a way for these children to be taken to Canada by Miss Rye. It appeared that the guardians were asking the board to proceed as if the Justices had already approved the emigration. Some of the children were young. Two were four-years-old, one was five, one was six, and the rest of the children in the group were slightly older - 10, 11, or 12-years-old. The guardians didn't appear concerned about asking the board to break the rules.

Newspaper reports on the work of the board of guardians recorded that Maria Rye attended one of its meetings and explained that she wished to take their orphaned and deserted children to Canada where good Christian families were waiting to receive them. Using a fairly forthright manner, she told the guardians that as she had chosen the homes for the children, she could promise they would have good food and be able to go to school. The guardians were impressed by her promises and allowed her to take a group of about 100 children.

MARIA RYE

Maria Susan Rye was born in 1829 and came from a superior background - being born into a well-educated, professional family and, unusually for a woman at that time, had received a good education. In her early years she became interested in women's rights and the position of women in society. Described as a strong and forceful woman, she was actually difficult to work with because she was so certain that taking the children to Canada was the right action to take. At 40 years of age, and influenced by the plight of the children on the streets, she became totally convinced of the need to save them. She saw it as her duty to take them away from their disreputable families and send them to Canada. It has been claimed that she thought only of the child's soul; as it was their souls she wished to save and didn't seem to see them as

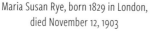

Maria Susan Rye, born 1829 in London,
died November 12, 1903

Annie Macpherson, born 1883 in Scotland,
died November 27, 1907

children with their own special and individual needs. In 1869 she took her first group of street children, including some from the Bristol Workhouse, to the town of Niagara-on-the-Lake. Her friends and supporters had refurbished an old jail and courthouse. She called it "Our Western Home", and it became the receiving and distribution home for all the children taken out to Canada by Maria Rye.

ANNIE MACPHERSON

Annie Macpherson was another woman influenced by the plight of the street children and felt the call to do something about saving them. Born in Glasgow in 1833, she was well educated and came from a family of teachers. She herself trained as a teacher. As seemed to happen to many people involved in working with street children, she experienced a profound religious experience which left her wanting to work for her God. A devout and evangelical woman she moved to London in 1862. She began to teach in the East End and it was here she found a level of poverty she had not met before - children living on the streets and surviving in any way they could. Annie was moved to set up and organise Sunday Schools for the street children. She told them stories from the Bible but also taught them the skills of reading and writing.

On one occasion, when exploring a house, she reached the attic and came

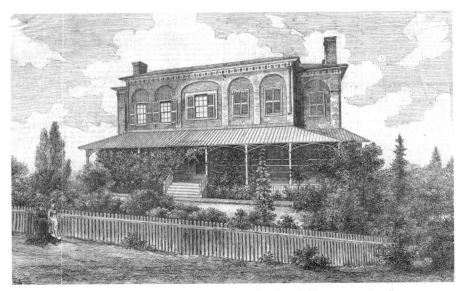

Maria Susan Rye used this home at Niagara-on-the-Lake called "Our Western Home"

upon a group of young girls, some as young as four, who were making match boxes. The conditions under which these young girls were working so appalled her that she likened it to slavery; this experience fired her determination to find an alternative way of life for these children. Taking them away from the dirt and grime of the city streets and finding them good homes in the fresh air of Canada became her life's work. Annie planned to collect children from the big cities and bring them to a home she had set up in Spitalfields, London; there they could rest and get to know each other before sailing to Canada. She also set up a receiving home in Belleville, Ontario. The house was called Marchmont and all the children she brought to Canada would live there until she had found places for all of them.

MARCHMONT

Annie Macpherson and Maria Rye worked with boards of guardians all over England and it is somewhat difficult to know exactly how it worked. Did the guardians contact the women when they had a party of children ready to leave? Or did these women inform the guardians when they were organising another passage on a ship? What we do know, because the newspaper reports of the time tell us, is that these two women were tireless in their search for those

Annie Macpherson used a home in Belleville, Ontario called Marchmont

children who needed to be saved from a life on the streets of the cities. Both women were devout practising Christians who wished, very sincerely, to do God's work and believed they were doing this by saving the children. Taking them from the streets where, the women thought, all that was waiting for them was degradation and despair and, at the same time, remove them from their unworthy families and take them to Canada where they would be adopted. They really did believe, as did many people at this time, that these children would get a better start to their lives by going to Canada. The word adoption was used quite liberally by these two women but as Canada did not have any adoption procedures at that time, it took one 16-year-old girl to explain the meaning of the word adoption to a visiting inspector. "Adoption sir is when folks make you work without wages." And she was right. In the early days it appears that quite young children, some still in their pushchairs, were taken out to Canada, and that these children were successfully adopted.

Although Annie was to take children from different parts of the country, she became very involved with the emigration of children from Bristol. In 1869 she contacted Bristol Board of Guardians and offered to take a group of children out to Canada and find them homes. It was agreed she would take a group of 70 children and, as they did with Maria Rye, the guardians recorded their approval. This first group of Bristol children sailed on the ship *Peruvian*; they were joined by children who had been collected from different parts of the country, and were accompanied by Annie and her friend Ellen Bilbrough. Born in Leeds in 1841, Ellen had also worked in the slums in the East End of London and supported the belief that emigration for these children was their only chance of a better life. It was Ellen who recognised the necessity of having a receiving home for the children, a place where they could rest after their journey and stay until homes were found for them. When Marchmont was made ready for the children, Ellen happily agreed to run it and thereafter she received many groups of children brought to Canada through the organisation run by Annie Macpherson. In 1887 Ellen married the Rev Wallace; they ran Marchmont together until Ellen died in 1901. Rev Wallace married again and eventually retired from Marchmont in 1913. The home closed in 1925.

When the first large group of children was taken out to Canada in 1870 by Maria Rye, it cost the Bristol Board of Guardians the sum of £12 for each child, a sum which had to be approved by the Poor Law Board. This appears to be a large sum of money but the guardians worked out that, as they would be saving the yearly costs of these children over a number of years, then it represented a saving.

Over the next few years, several groups of children were taken out by these two women from the Bristol Incorporation of the Poor until 1875. Then a letter from the Local Government Board, (previously known as the Poor Law Board), received in March 1875, stated that they had not received any applications from the guardians of the Bristol Incorporation looking for sanction for the emigration of children from that Board.

The groups of children taken out to Canada by Maria Rye were taken straight to her receiving home at Niagara-on-the-Lake, called Our Western Home, where the children were able to rest after their long journey. Maria often notified people in the area that she would be bringing out a new group of children and would invite them to apply for a child. Children were allocated to a farm or homestead without, it appears, any inspection by herself or any appointed agent. When questioned about this she always explained that she had asked the local minster if the receiving family were good Christian people. She accepted the answer and thought that this was enough. In the Archives of

New Brunswick there's a document which shows that farmers wishing to have a child appeared to be passing money to Maria Rye. The manuscript shows a list of applicants for servant girls, still to be brought out by Maria Rye, but subject to the payment of 30 dollars to be paid on arrival. It seems that Maria was making money from her philanthropic work.

Maria Rye preferred to bring girls although there were boys in the groups she brought to Canada. As it was believed important to take the children away from their unworthy families, it was also believed important to split brothers and sisters in case of contamination. Ellen, along with her two sisters, left Bristol and arrived at the home in Niagara-on-the-Lake in 1871. The three girls were sent to different families and not told where each was sent. Ellen wrote to Maria Rye, from her home in Queenstown, County Lincoln, asking if she would tell her where her sisters were. Ellen mentioned that her master and mistress were very kind and that they had a very pretty baby. This letter was included in The Rye Report which was written in 1878 - we don't know if Ellen ever received a reply. The irony is that, today, the whereabouts of Ellen's sisters has been traced in the census for that time.

MARIA STACEY

There is a letter in the archives written by a woman called Maria Stacey from Horfield Gaol in Bristol giving permission for Maria Rye to take her two children, Louisa and Emily, to Canada because she was in jail and could no

---

letter dated July 10th 1872

Bristol Goal

July 10th 1872

I shall feel obliged if the Governors of the Goal will inform the authorities of St. Peters Hospital that I should wish my children Louisa and Emily to go to Canada next month under Miss Rye's care as it is impossible for me to maintain them. I shall be discharged from this place on 17th of this month and will call to see them.

Maria Stacey

Witness
    Harriett Parrott   Warder

---

longer support them. The letter was witnessed by Harriott Parrott, one of the warders. Maria Stacey was in prison for stealing a joint of meat from a meat safe in a back kitchen. When you realise she had three children then you can understand why she might have stolen the meat. Louisa, aged 10, and Emily aged 12, went out to Our Western Home at Niagara-on-the-Lake in 1872. Ada, aged seven, followed them a year later.

Annie Macpherson preferred to bring boys and was not happy to bring girls over the age of 10. She was concerned about the moral issues of bringing the older girls and events were to support her concerns.

Both Annie Macpherson and Maria Rye used a form of indenture (below) formally presented on paper and the farmer was asked to sign that he agreed to lodge, feed and clothe the child.

FORM OF AGREEMENT TO BE SIGNED BY A RECEIVING FARMER

I agree to board, lodge and clothe .... during the time he or she is in my Home, if under the age of 12 years, to see that he or she attends school until he or she attains that age, and, after attaining the age of fifteen years to give him or her adequate wages, and, if at any time .... should leave my home to inform the government agent at St John of his or her whereabouts.

They were to give them wages at age 15 and send them to school in the winter. This was not unusual since most Canadian children only went to school in the winter as they were expected to work on the farm during the summer. Some farmers clothed and fed the children reasonably well whereas others did not. Deductions were often made from their wages for clothing and broken tools but some children did not receive any wages at all. A lucky few might leave the farm at the age of 16 or older with a cow as their wage and a very few were lucky enough to get a piece of land. A boy called Norman, who was sent out from Park Row in 1870, wrote back to the school in 1874 claiming he was now the owner of a large farm. They were proud but questions might have been

THE STORY OF WILLIAM

William was just nine when he was orphaned. In 1872, when he was 11, he was sent by the Bristol Board of Guardians to Canada with a party of children being taken out to Marchmont by Annie Macpherson. After resting for a couple of weeks, he was taken with 11 other boys to a barn about 13 miles outside of Belleville. Farmers from the area gathered hoping to choose a boy from this group. William was the only boy chosen, possibly because he looked the strongest, and he went to live with the man on his farm. He worked for this farmer for 10 years. When he was 19, William left the farm. He had attended a Revivalist meeting in the area which persuaded him to train for work in the church. Much later he wrote an account of his time on the farm and his comments are worth recording.

He said that he was never beaten but nobody cared about him. Shoes which he had been given in Bristol were taken away and he worked all the time in bare feet. This made him feel humiliated. William learned all the jobs on the farm until he was running it but he still had money deducted from his wages for breakages and for clothes. He would have liked to move but as the farmer was the most powerful man in the area, no one else would take him on. In his journal William said that no one from the home in Belleville ever came to see him to make sure that he was alright. This simple statement underlines the lack of supervision practised by these people.

Depictions of 19th century farming at Kings Landing heritage centre in New Brunswick, Canada

raised about that claim.

The next clause was of huge significance to the people who sent the children. They must be put into homes of the same faith of their family, living back in England. Unfortunately Protestant children were put into Catholic homes and Catholic children were put into Protestant homes which became a matter of great concern to the sending agencies and the Roman Catholic Church.

For a boy or girl who was being badly treated, that child could decide to run away and even if or when the farmer informed the agent, there was little that could be done to locate this young person unless neighbours had taken them in. Many of the children disappeared in this way and made their way across the land, perhaps taking on odd work as they went. It is thought that some joined the lumber companies working with the logging gangs in the North. Some had little choice but to stay and hope that someone would come to check on them and change their place. In 1882 a group of 12 Bristol boys were sent across the land from St John to Annapolis. By the time they had arrived in the town only seven remained. Five had disappeared!

Farmers would be given a girl or boy who might prove to be suitable for their requirements but more often than not the child would be sent back to the agent at the end of the year, with the farmer asking for a stronger child. Children living on the streets and scrounging for any food they could find were, quite simply, not fit and strong enough to do farm work.

Annie Macpherson eventually set up three homes in Canada; Marchmont in Belleville, Ontario; then in 1871 a home called Blair Atholl at Galt, Ontario. This was a farm of 100 acres which was run by her sister, Louisa Birt, and used to train the children in good farming practices. Her third home, Knowlton in Quebec County, opened in 1872, and was run by Rachel Merry, another of Annie's sisters.

REPORTS FROM BRISTOL BOARD OF GUARDIANS

Bristol Board of Guardians held weekly meetings at St Peter's Workhouse, a beautiful old building situated in the centre of Bristol, once used as a sugar house and before that a mint. Unfortunately, most of the official records for the guardians were destroyed in a bombing raid in 1940. However, as the meetings were attended by reporters from the local papers, the reports in the Western Daily Press and the Bristol Mercury are a valuable source of information on the proceedings as summarised below.

- On April 26, 1873, a Charles Wintle questioned the sending of pauper children to Canada and stated he had long opposed the practice. He didn't agree with the way the list was made out, with children just being asked if they were willing to go and then a list was made of the willing! They needed the consent of the children and must be careful not to influence them. If the consent was a nonsense, then the law was a nonsense. As a lawyer he was the last person to find fault with the practice; kindest thing that could happen to some of them. He argued that magistrates took the common sense view but he thought they should be better informed about where the children were going.
- He made the point that here were people in England willing to take children as servants. During the last three years, there were 56 applicants for servants, 51 accepted, and five declined for the best of reasons. There were 39 applications for apprentices, 18 sent out and 21 declined.
- He pointed out that if children had not been sent to Canada, there would be no places for people willing to take them into their homes; it was said they are so bad no one would have them. This was not true. He advised the Board to support two women; to reduce pauperism; to train all the children, and to make them more useful as servants and apprentices. He didn't understand adoption.

The comments of Charles Wintle are a little confusing on how he felt about emigration as compared with finding work placements for the children in this country. Many other people would no doubt have shared his thoughts.

Until 1874, the guardians seemed to agree with the philosophy surrounding the emigration of children who had been put in their care. The system seemed, to them, to be working well and many children had been sent to Canada from the workhouse. Some guardians became concerned that there were children who had only been in the care of the guardians for a short time and began to suggest that a stay of one year in the workhouse should be normal before

This building became known as St Peter's Hospital, as so many of the paupers were old and ill. In around 1870, the wards used by the paupers were taken over for the treatment of mentally ill patients.

emigration was considered. It was argued by some that a stay of only a few short months before sending orphaned and deserted children to Canada turned the workhouse into an emigration office. During the debate that followed, a small group of guardians who proposed alternatives to emigration, argued for more effort into placing out children in this country using the boarding out system. A resolution for action put to the meeting following this debate was defeated by 16 votes to nine, followed by loud applause! Belief in the value of emigration was restored but one Guardian remarked that the subject had become very embittered and had been so for some time.

VISIT TO BRISTOL BY MARIA RYE

At this point the guardians were asked if they would allow Maria Rye to speak to the meeting as she had travelled from Bath and was waiting outside. A show of hands was taken and it was decided, by a majority of one, they would like to hear what she had to say. She pointed out that she didn't want to give a speech but was prepared to answer questions. In her answers she explained that she didn't work through committees as she didn't believe in them, but persons of a *good social standing*, living close to the children, were used to report to her on their welfare. She sent every child out with an indenture and if they were not comfortable in their home or were not well treated then they were recovered. The danger arose that they might be too well treated and over indulged, rather than treated unkindly.

She also made the point that she never placed out a child without making strict enquiries into the home. People were so anxious to have a child that they had needed to reject 300 applications just recently. When the guardians asked as to the motives of the people wishing to take a child she replied that people in Canada married much earlier than in England. They had been left childless at the early age of 40 and were anxious for a child to bring up as their own. She did acknowledge that some were only looking for a child for the work they could do but even so she felt that children had a far better chance in Canada than in England. She explained that she was thinking of leaving in May with another group of children. The guardians then thanked her for her courtesy and she left the meeting.

Several letters had been received from children who had been sent out by the guardians that gave glowing accounts of their new homes and their new lives in Canada and these were acknowledged by the guardians.

In March 1879 the board of guardians received a letter from an Amy Simmons of 10 Captain Cary Lane, Old Market Street in Bristol. She wrote-:

"I hope you will pardon this liberty taken in troubling you with this writing this note to ask you if you will be so kind to put me in the way so I can find out about my daughter Sarah Jane Simmonds she was sent out to Saint John at 7 years of age by the guardians of St Peters. By the name of Rev Shrives of St John and cannot find any answer to the letter. The Rev George Rogers told me if I wrote to you about my child you will kindly look into it for me and find out about her for sure. I should be only so glad if you will be so kind and find her for me. A broken hearted mother."

Written across the letter in red ink are the words, "Name not on the list of emigrants sent out by the Colonial Office." We don't know if Mrs Simmonds ever found out where her daughter had been sent...

EXPERIENCE OF A BRISTOL HOME CHILD

Western Daily Press, April 7, 1871. Letter from Mary Coakley to a Miss Cogle.

Mary travelled on the *Peruvian* to Quebec on very stormy seas and we learn that she was very sea sick; from Portland they continued their journey in cars, coaches on a train, for a night and a day until they reached St Johns in New Brunswick. Sixty of the children then went on to Niagara and Mary and the children in her group stayed in the St John's Orphan Asylum. Some children moved on to their new homes the next day but Mary stayed there for a week and went to her new home on November 19, 1871. Mary wrote about Mr and Mrs Hayward and a small boy of 10 years and of Mrs Hayward's sister who was also living in the house. Her sister was not with her and was still in the Asylum but she said she saw her often.

It was Christmas time and there were parties and presents and she had been enjoying all the excitement of that time. Mary had lessons every day and attended Sunday school. She explained that her sister had lessons in the Asylum and could read very well, thus giving us some indication that the sister was learning more than Mary. Smallpox was a problem in St John's and the doctor visited houses to ensure that everyone, including Mary, was properly vaccinated. Mary seemed to be enjoying herself and sent her love to the teachers she knew in Bristol. Two pieces of information appear to be missing - comments about her master and mistress and, considering that Mary was now 16, what work was she doing in the house?

It was a very well written letter, full of information; clearly Mary was homesick and missed everyone she knew in England but there was an impression that we haven't been told about her real feelings. This letter seems to fit in with the letters written to the board of guardians which Mr Pethick, a Bristol magistrate, called "bogus letters" as he felt they were written under supervision.

CONCERN ABOUT LACK OF PARENTAL AGREEMENT FOR EMIGRATION

The board of guardians sent a boy called John Walcott to Canada in a group of 13 other children from Bristol Workhouse. They left Bristol on March 30, 1874, to embark on the ship *Prussian* from Liverpool under the care of Annie Macpherson. His mother had not given her permission; in fact, most of the

EMIGRATION FROM THE WORKHOUSE

accounts clearly stated that she did not wish for him to be sent away. A Mr Charles Wintle, the guardian responsible for St Stephens Ward where the family lived, wrote letters in support of Mrs Walcott and outlined his concerns about the emigration of young children. William Pethick, magistrate for the same ward, also pointed out that although the guardians claimed that John had been deserted, they still did not have his mother's permission.

Charles Wintle, now very concerned and clearly wanting a serious debate on the subject, wrote to the board of guardians and to the Bristol Times and Mirror, "We are told that the Bristol Board of Guardians are a very ancient and important body, but their views are not followed by other Boards".

There were 650 boards of guardians in England. In the Government Poor Law Board report for 1871 to 1872 it was reported that, out of all the 650 boards, the percentage of children emigrated by the Bristol Board was slightly more than one ninth of all the children sent. The authorised expenditure by the Bristol Board was £1,464 out of £7,451, about one fifth of the authorised expenditure for all England. Wintle went on, "I think this shows that the Bristol Board are carrying out the system to excess". He had also learned that questions about control and inspection of child emigration would be debated in the House of Commons and he drew their attention to the Local Government Chronicle of May 9, 1874. Other people were asking questions. Mr Secretary Fisk of the American Government pointed out that these children were sent out without accompaniment of anyone who knew them or was close to them. Returning to the case of John Walcott, Charles Wintle was concerned that the family was Roman Catholic and that he had read that Miss Macpherson refused to place children with Catholic families. When children leave for Canada the Bristol Board of Guardians lose all supervision over these children; they are placed out, given away, and as we have heard from Miss Rye herself, there is an utter lack of supervision and responsibility from that time. Only a few weeks previously the Board had heard of one "little waif" who had been transferred to four different families in as many as four months. He then writes of the letters received from some of the children calling them "bogus" letters written under supervision from the master or mistress of the house.

This was followed by a letter from a Mr Naish who answered all of these questions claiming that Mr Wintle had not proved any of his statements; his objections were groundless and were based as they were on newspaper stories and are not proved. His point about "bogus" letters is totally incorrect because how can he know that this is happening. He then takes up the stance for emigration asking who are the "we" that Mr Wintle talks about; "no doubt the little knot of objectors, the domineering minority who have cavilled at everything connected with emigration and have so charged and so objected, as well as made a great many other objections equally groundless and unfounded."

It appears that in 1874 the Bristol Board of Guardians was split into two distinct camps on the subject of emigration - with the far larger group strongly in favour. Perhaps at this point it might be wise to point out that the weekly meetings of the Board did indeed get very lively.

1874 appears to have been a year of confusion and upheaval for the Bristol Board of Guardians. Perhaps this is why the books containing the correspondence to the board of guardians exist for every year except 1874. Charles Wintle wrote a letter to the Bristol Times and Mirror on June 2, 1874, in which he expressed his concern that John Walcott had been sent for emigration by the Bristol Board of Guardians without his mother's permission. He was worried that the guardians were tending to send children without due care and when these children arrived in Canada all responsibility for them passed to an unknown family.

A MOTHERS ATTEMPT TO BRING HER SON BACK TO BRISTOL

The Walcott family lived in the Ward that Charles Wintle represented. Mrs Walcott, a widow, had been taken ill and a relieving officer had called suggesting that she give permission for John to be sent to Canada which she refused. She had been taken into hospital and her boy went to live in the care of the guardians but when she came out of hospital she did not collect John and the guardians assumed she had abandoned him.

The relieving officer called on her again for permission to send him to Canada and again she refused. It was said that the boy went to stay with his mother but ran away and came back to the guardians asking them to send him to Canada which they did. Now his mother asked for his return. The local magistrate attended the meeting of the guardians much to their annoyance, and asked them to organise John's return. They were not inclined to do this and so Mrs Walcott appealed to the Local Government Board. This then became a serious matter for the guardians and there was a lengthy discussion about limiting the damage this might cause them; they would ask an inspector to investigate and advise them as to where they might be making any mistakes. The report from the inspector agreed that the guardians had acted unlawfully but didn't seem to take any action.

Several weeks later Mrs Walcott set up a court action to get her boy back. She asked for a 'Writ of Habeas Corpus' to be presented to the person who had taken her boy John so that he might be brought back. But the Board of Guardians had given him to Annie Macpherson, who had in turn given him to a Mr Mckay, a respectable farmer who lived in Canada, and there were difficulties about serving a writ on someone who lived in another country. John Walcott was not returned to his mother. John Walcott was, quite clearly, sent out without permission from his parents and apart from the Local Government Board's stance, the lapse wasn't taken too seriously.

ANDREW DOYLE SENT OUT TO INSPECT THE WORK

Bristol Board of Guardians had allowed Annie Macpherson and Maria Rye to take large groups of children from the workhouses in Bristol to Canada without, seemingly, placing any constraints on them. The guardians became concerned when expected reports about the children had not been received. Questions concerning the placement and welfare of these children were raised with members of the Local Government Board. Similar concerns had been voiced from other Boards of Guardians and, in 1875, an Andrew Doyle was charged with visiting Canada to investigate and evaluate the emigration of British children.

It took him six months before he felt ready to return to England and write his report. Doyle was to visit the children who were living on the farms, often in isolated places, away from the rail and road networks. It could take him all day to visit one farm to report on the care of one child and many stories were told about his journey. People living in a community would be aware of how the British children were being treated but were often unable to intervene because they were also part of the community. He met a woman as he was nearing a township and asked for directions using the name of the boy. The woman told him that the boy was being beaten and asked that he would not tell them her name, because she does their washing and she didn't want to lose her job. It also became clear that the children couldn't be honest about their life as the master or mistress was often present when he asked them questions about the way they were being treated.

After returning home Doyle worked on his report for most of the winter and then on February 8, 1875, it was made public. Kenneth Bagnell in his book, "*The Little Immigrants*", writes that "in both England and Canada it hit like thunder". Doyle was very critical of the way child emigration was being organised; supervision was poor, children had been lost, some had been abused and others over-worked. He asked for stricter controls on both sides of the Atlantic; he emphasised that reports must be sent back to the sending agencies and asked for all children to be medically examined before leaving Britain. He praised the volunteers who worked in both countries and was inspired by the dedication of Annie Macpherson and Maria Rye. He understood they had accomplished much and realised the hardships they faced.

He then condemned everything about the work, from the way the children were collected to the way they were given to Canadian families, including the subsequent lack of supervision. His report directly concerned the two women because they took a mixture of children, some from the workhouse and some from the vagrant children who had been gathered up from the streets of the cities. Doyle thought this mixing of waifs and strays or the 'Street Arabs', as they became known, with the children from the workhouses was disgraceful. Doyle condemned the practice of mixing the workhouse children who had had the benefit of two years schooling, with the 'Street Arabs', who were considered of the lowest class with possible criminal tendencies. The workhouses, he said, were shelters of despair but they were not schools of vice; the streets, however, were another matter. There was one aspect of the work where he found a clear success rate; children under the age of five years who had been taken out but not expected to work, had been found homes where they were adopted. He visited many of these homes and, in all cases, found the results most satisfactory. Again and again he stressed the need for an adequate system of supervision.

Annie Macpherson recognised that there were faults in her system and worked to remedy the situation. She set up a system of supervision, but, as she explained to the Emigration Committee, all her helpers were volunteers and each supervised 200 children. The committee questioned her about the financial records and, upon inspection, discovered that the money was barely adequate for what she was trying to do.

Maria Rye, however, did not recognise that her system failed the children, and expressed her views very strongly. She had chosen the receiving families herself after ensuring that they were all God fearing people, devout Christians; she did not need to organise any follow up visits. Her friends who lived in the townships were of the highest class of people; they visited their neighbours and would report any problems immediately. She totally failed to recognise that if the foster parents realised that they were not going to be overlooked, then it was possible they would take advantage of these young people.

After the Doyle report was published Annie decided to take only younger children. The girls must be under 12, and from the homes but not from the workhouses. To Annie her work had a missionary character; she was saving these children from a life of hard labour and finding warm and loving homes for them. She really failed to understand that she was promoting emigration to provide cheap labour for the Canadian farmers.

Doyle also commented on the arrangements made by both women when the children arrived in Canada. He pointed out that they talked and wrote about the children calling it an adoption, but he called it simply, an apprenticeship where the children served the farmer without wages. Both women asked the farmers who took a child to sign a piece of paper agreeing how they would treat the child, but this piece of paper had no legal validity. It seems that the farmers did not view it as binding; wages were often withheld to pay for broken tools and clothes, and many children were kept at home working during school time. When the British children were sent to school they had a very hard time; their clothes were wrong, they spoke in a funny way and if there was any trouble it was always the British children who were blamed. Many children were put into homes of a different religious persuasion from that of their families back home because neither Annie Macpherson nor Maria Rye took enough time to match the children.

Ellen Bilborough was praised for the way she managed Marchmont. She ran the home with three important principles in mind, efficient training in the home in the old land, this training to be continued in the Canadian home. After the children are placed out, this influence and care must continue. Most children sent from the Canadian Emigration Home for Girls in Bristol were sent to the Marchmont Receiving Home in Belleville.

The Doyle report was sent to the Canadian Government. The committee responsible for Immigration and Colonisation in Canada was asked to give it their immediate attention. There is a Copy of Order dated September 25, 1875, on the report of Mr Andrew Doyle and the children brought to Canada by Miss Rye and Miss Macpherson. The select committee of Immigration and Colonisation recommended to the Government, that Doyle's inspection, being based on a partial inspection, should be set to rest. Children in the most part have been settled in Ontario and comparatively few in New Brunswick, Nova Scotia and Quebec. They recommended that any inspection would be best carried out by a person having a special acquaintance with the condition of immigrants to Canada, who must also be authorised to organise a detailed inspection of the condition of the children by competent persons.

The committee questioned both ladies and studied other pieces of evidence and had been in correspondence with a variety of persons, some of whom had given the children employment. All these reports correlated the evidence taken from Rye and Macpherson. Overall there was a favourable response to the ladies' work although they agreed that there were some failures but these were few in number. Doyle had suggested that Canadian workhouses might receive the children. The committee rejected this idea as they considered the sooner the children were placed out the better. The committee agreed about the lack of supervision but the ladies had already set up procedures for change and suggested that maybe they should settle the question by having a fuller inspection.

From 1869, Maria Rye had brought 1,000 young children to Canada. Annie Macpherson began her work in 1870 and by 1876 she had brought out 2,000 children of which 800 were girls and 1,200 were boys. 350 were from various workhouses and 1,650 were from distressed and orphaned families or waifs gathered from the streets of the larger cities.

It appears there was little support in Canada for the findings of Andrew Doyle and it was doubtful that any recommendations made by him were implemented. The farmers still needed young men to help on the farms!

BACK IN LONDON

An article in the Western Daily Press of March 6, 1875, discussed Doyle's report which had been included amongst the Parliamentary Papers on that Monday.

A letter published in The Times newspaper on May 17, 1875, written by the Chairman of the Liverpool Shelter Home, run by the Macpherson family, commented on the Doyle report. He had read the report written by Mr Doyle but had no doubt as to the value of the benevolent work in which they were engaged. Perhaps he might offer some changes to the system. The emigration of children under the age of nine years had been a complete success. He did not accept that of the 6,000 children already taken out, a certain number who were older on emigration, had not turned out satisfactorily. He underlined that Mr Doyle only visited 400 children and that of all the insinuations he made, Doyle did not produce one child who had been cruelly treated. Then he wrote of cruel step mothers and drunken fathers and gave details on the ill treatment and hardship that children had suffered in this country.

Although Doyle's report was shelved some changes did occur. Children had to be medically examined before they sailed and their medical papers must accompany them to Canada. Many children were not strong, they suffered infections of the chest, eyes, ears and skin. Some had deafness and eyesight problems and there was also a problem with bed wetting. The Bristol Board of Guardians did seem to take these changes seriously and now the children were examined by a doctor in the homes before leaving. However, the declaration at the top of a piece of paper giving a list of maybe eight children, simply that stated that these children were free from any disease and were a suitable case for emigration. This was not the more detailed or individual statements the Canadians might have expected to receive for each child. There is a photograph which appears to show boys of about eight years lining up by a warehouse door at a port; standing in front of them is a doctor who is clearly giving them a quick "look over". There is a feeling that he just says something like, oh yes you look alright, off you go!

Some institutions issued an individual form to certify that the named child was in good health. Others listed groups of children. The Cumberland Boys

Home in Bristol reports stated they are free from all disease and mentally and physically fit for emigration. In all of these papers there is a form of wording that declares that the child is, in all respects, a suitable subject for emigration. You get the feeling that a tick box system is used; if all the boxes are ticked then he or she must be suitable and can be emigrated. Later, medical forms also included information to say that the children had been vaccinated.

Maria Rye was deeply shocked by the criticism in the Doyle report and used her contacts to campaign against it, with the result that most of the recommendations were shelved and weren't put into practice for another 20 years. On August 18, 1877, a copy of a letter sent to the Local Government Board by Maria Rye was published in the Western Daily Press. In the letter she justified the work she did with the children, and quoted acknowledgments received from Kirkdale, St Georges in Hanover Square and the Bristol School Committee. They tell of the work she had done in saving the rates by £2,000 to £3,000 per year. She had written to 1,000 families with whom she had placed children and with the replies had come 500 photos of the children placed with them; they were just not recognisable from the waifs she had placed with the families, there was such an improvement!

It was two years before Maria Rye sent any more children. By then she was only taking children from the East End of London. Between 1869 and 1896, when her home was taken over by the Anglican Church, Maria Rye took to Canada almost 5,000 children. The Canadian Government had undertaken to carry out inspection visits but they certainly were not rigorous. As for Maria Rye, to the end she refused to carry out any type of inspection and even criticised those who believed in it. When she retired in 1896 her home and work was taken over by the Church of England Waifs and Strays Society, which operated it until 1913.

The Local Government Board took serious notice of Andrew Doyle's report and stated that if Britain was to continue sending children then there must be more systematic control over emigration and subsequent inspections. Annie Macpherson decided not to work with the Local Government Board anymore and did not take children from the workhouse again.

THE CANADIAN EMIGRATION HOME FOR LITTLE GIRLS

I
N 1881 Annie Macpherson opened a Canadian Emigration Home for Little Girls at 9 Bishop Street, St Paul's, to receive and shelter little girls (under the age of 13) whose surroundings were bad or where they had been neglected by their parents. These children were to be trained for a few months in order to make them ready to be sent out to new homes in Canada. The home was under the management of a committee of ladies, all of whom appeared to live in Clifton and were daughters or wives of professional men. They worked with a manager, Mrs Lilian Birt, who was the sister of Annie Macpherson. There doesn't seem to be any guiding principle which would support any decisions taken about the girls; certainly none that was written down, when, two years after the home was opened, a report was published on Tuesday March 20, 1883.

Mrs Birt reported that 11 little girls had been sent out to Canada in the company of Mrs Merry, another sister of Annie, but first they were to spend a few weeks in the Macpherson home in London, so they could get to know the other children. This company of children arrived at the Macpherson home at Galt, Ontario, in early July 1883. A second company left Liverpool on July 27, reaching Galt on August 8. The committee report said, "that every child sent, if left, in all probability will become a criminal or a member of the pauper class in England, in Canada they will become a happy and useful member of Society".

Reports about the business of the home appeared annually in the local newspapers and the committee always sought to increase the numbers of

The first house used was at 9 Bishop Street. It was a home for little girls

little girls sent to Canada. The Bristol Mercury of December 9, 1885, reported that during the year, 13 children were sent to Canada through the Macpherson homes; four had gone to America with the support of Mark Whitwill; one to the Cripples' Home in Clifton; one to Barnardos and six were returned to relatives. Supporters were informed that an experiment had been tried taking in young brothers of some of the girls. This was to be continued and boys under eight became a part of the regular intake. Overall, 85 children had been received, sent out to Canada and good accounts had been received. The meeting was told that an indenture had to be signed binding adoptive parents to treat the little ones kindly, to send them to day school and Sunday school and to keep them well clothed. Official visitors had inspected the homes and reports were sent to Mrs Wallace of the Marchmont home, who forwarded them on to Bristol.

On March 14, 1885, a meeting was held at the Victoria Rooms where Annie Macpherson was invited to give an address describing her work on settling children in Canadian homes. She defended the work pointing out that she now had two homes, Marchmont at Belleville, Ontario, run by Mrs Ellen Wallace, and Knowlton, which was run by her sister, Lilian Burt. She stressed it was important to know that it was the law in Canada for every child to attend school for four months each year until they reached the age of 12. Mark Whitwill presided over the meeting and expressed his interest in the subject. In the past 15 and 16 years many Bristol boys had been sent to homes in Canada and the United States. Every year Park Row Industrial School sent boys to New Brunswick and he had much to do with sending a considerable number of girls from a local industrial school. He had visited on three occasions to see the young people in their new homes and he was delighted to see the happy circumstances in which they were living; their homes were merry and bright and the children had a good chance of getting on in life. An appeal was made for the Canadian Emigration Home for Little Girls which, it was said, was not as well-known as it should be. Hymns were sung by the girls from the homes.

Unfortunately any records which might have been kept by the committee running the Bishop Street home have not survived. It seems that from about 1894 the home was examined on a regular basis and reports appeared in the correspondence to the board of guardians for Barton Regis and later for the Bristol guardians. Combining these reports with the articles from the newspapers at the time, it is possible to understand how the home was run.

On December 9, 1887, the Bristol guardians received a letter from the Bishop Street committee asking for outfits to be supplied for a family of four illegitimate children whose mother was a problem. If the money could be found the children would be sent in to Canada the following Spring.

Whatever doubts were expressed at the public meeting in March 1885, the home seemed to go from strength to strength. In November 1888 the home was moved to Parkfield House, Leigh Road South, Redland, enabling the committee to offer a larger number of places. A rather sharp comment was included in the annual report: "Three dear children, after all the training, had been removed by mistaken friends; sometimes it happens that a family is disappointed and takes the child back". There is a report on Leigh Road South about taking in illegitimate children and a discussion about the cost of supplying outfits at £25 for putting them into the Canadian home

A photograph of five children in the book, "*Children of the Empire*", by Gillian Wagner, shows five young boys dressed in their sailor suits, ready to

The Home was moved to Parkfield House in Leigh Road South in 1888

go to Marchmont in 1892. One is called Dickie, aged just four years. There are six boys on the database who sailed in 1891 - Edward Bashford, Luigi or Herbert Taylor, Herbert Edwards, Albert King, Harry Mitchener and Kenneth Shepherd. They might well be the boys in the photograph but like much to do with the Bristol children, we cannot be sure.

The people supporting and running the home were so convinced that they were doing the right thing for the children that the annual meeting in 1893 emphasised the following: "Canadians liked the little girls, whom they adopted, to forget their old friends so that the bonds of affection might not be weakened by regrets on the part of the child at leaving their English homes". The current President, Miss Pease, said that it was highly desirable that old associations should not be remembered. If left in this country these children would probably grow up to be a curse on society. Clear evidence then that children were encouraged to forget home and family when they arrived in Canada.

A report from the Barton Regis Board of Guardians in 1894 on the

A group of boys from the Bristol Emigration Home who were sent to the Marchmont home in 1892

Canadian Emigration Home for Girls currently established in Parkfield House mentioned that the matron was a Miss Bergendale. She reported that they currently had eight girls and two infants in-house and that 22 girls had been emigrated since the last visit in April 1893. The house was not considered big enough so, in November 1894, it moved once again, this time to Aberdeen Terrace in Redland, where it requested a change in certification as it wished to take in little boys from two years to eight years, with no boy being kept after the age of eight.

In 1895 the committee proposed that, in the future, the rules for taking in the children should work for motherless or otherwise destitute and neglected little girls; so keeping up a steady rate of emigration. Rules were to be relaxed which made it compulsory that consent for emigration must be given before a child was admitted. This left the committee free to keep a child longer in the house, if necessary, and this was more desirable. Costs of emigration had now risen to £20 per child.

Mark Whitwill had a lot to say about people who objected to emigration

The home moved to Aberdeen Terrace in Redland

of children; he thought it was purely from a theoretical idea and the practical workings may not be known and understood.

On February 10, 1896, the report from Aberdeen Terrace asked for certification for 25 to 30 children; girls from the age of two to 13 and boys from two until eight years; the costs to keep each child in the home being £5 per week. Emigration would take place in April. There was an application for a certificate to designate the home as an orphanage, so that it could then use the Barnardo facilities. This was denied because the house was in such a dreadful state and to make it safe for children would involve considerable cost and they didn't have the money. By May 1896 the guardians did issue a certificate for Aberdeen Terrace and authorised payment to be received for two girls who were training to go to Canada. A letter was sent to the guardians that set out the regulations of the home and justified the work they were doing. A Catherine Woollam, who was on the Barton Regis Board of Guardians, became involved in the home at this point.

In 1897, 14 children went to Canada with Miss Woollam and she agreed to

A much larger house at 25 Richmond Terrace, Clifton, was taken over in 1901

tell the board of guardians about the placement of the children after they had arrived. The guardians sent a letter certifying the institution for 1897 and after their inspection, stated that not more than 30 children are to be maintained in the home.

On June 28, 1899, the home was inspected by the board of guardians inspector, Dr Wethered. He referred to it as a training school for service and emigration. At this time there were four boys and 20 girls who all attended the local elementary school at Anglesea Board School, Redland. Miss Mollett was the matron of the home and she was helped by two girls, aged 15 and 17. The inspector questioned whether the house was big enough.

The 1900 inspection listed the children presently in the home. Most were from Bristol but one was from Bangor in Wales, one from Ross-on-Wye and one from Dursley. Again he questioned the size of the house and noted the committee was looking for a larger place.

In 1901 the home moved to larger premises at 35 Richmond Terrace. The committee asked for an inspection. It was now called The Children's Home and supported wholly or partially by voluntary subscriptions. It received destitute and deserted children for the purposes of training them with a view to emigration (if possible), for employment in England, or transference to another institution for further training. We also learn that the committee claimed to consider each case and could not bind itself to receive or refuse any special kind of case. Before being inspected the children needed to undergo a careful medical examination. The children attended Clifton National School twice daily and attended church on Sundays and Bible classes in the afternoon run by the ladies. The older girls were taught housework. Bristol Board of Guardians, now being responsible for the old Barton Regis area, allowed five shillings each week for every pauper child admitted. For other children payment was expected from relatives, parents or friends. Only very urgent cases were admitted free. Payment was made once a year for reasonable expenses involved in the maintenance and education of the pauper children.

The committee appeared to have the power to make quite major decisions on behalf of the children. All eight members were women and all were classed as 'ladies'- five were listed as wives of gentlemen; two as daughters of gentlemen and one as the daughter of a physician. The secretary was a woman and the president was an unmarried woman who had been involved in this kind of work for some time.

The house at Richmond Terrace was much larger, with three floors and it seemed as though this institution can now settle down. The managers, however, decided that all the children they accept must be of the Church of England religion. The board of guardians was not happy as it would seem the managers were matching religion to the children. Since they took children sent by the union, as well as parents, the guardians asked the committee to add an amendment stating that their policy was nondenominational but they would accept children of the Protestant persuasion. The certification was cancelled by the guardians until there could be agreement.

In the early days all the children sent from the Bristol Home for Little Girls seem to have been sent to the Macpherson home at Marchmont. The children would be identified, garments found and they were taken to Annie's home in Peckham, where they would stay and meet the other children who would be travelling with them. When all gathered together they would proceed to

Liverpool to board a ship for Canada. In later years some of the children arrived in St John, New Brunswick, and found their way to homes through the services of the agent who worked for the Bristol Emigration Society.

LOCAL DIRECTORIES GIVE CERTAIN INFORMATION

- 1885 Directory. Stated that there was an Emigration Home for girls at 9 Bishop Street in St Pauls which was established in 1881 and was in the care of Miss Annie Macpherson.
- 1890 Directory. The Canadian Home was at Parkfield House, Redland, established in 1881 for the purpose of collecting and training neglected girls under 13 years of age for emigrating purposes to Canada. A few young boys were received if their expenses are paid.
- 1901 Directory. The home was described as a children's home at 35 Richmond Terrace, Clifton, which was established for the purpose of finding a home for neglected, destitute and orphan girls under the age of 15 years with a view to emigration in suitable cases. A few boys from four years to eight years were accepted. For several years, 20 or 30 children were sent out annually but the number had now reduced.

The language used in the advertisements for the home changed over the years; the earliest entry was a simple and rather curt statement whereas over 16 years there was an attempt to be very clear about its purpose.

It has been possible to identify the names of the 78 children sent from the Canadian Emigration Home for Little Girls. There are others, names still unknown, who were taken out by women who supported this cause - Eliza Luce, Ellen Dicks and Catherine Woollam to name those most involved.

THE BRISTOL EMIGRATION SOCIETY

B RISTOL EMIGRATION SOCIETY was set up in 1884 and ran for around 30 years. It was set up by Agnes Beddoe, wife of Dr. John Beddoe who had established a medical practice in Clifton. Agnes had worked with Mary Carpenter, helping her when she set up her ragged school in St James Back, and was very aware of the difficulties experienced by the poor of Bristol, particularly the women and girls.

She formed a committee from interested citizens and the Bishop of Bristol was invited to become president of the society, a task which he accepted. Information explaining the purpose of the society was placed in the local newspapers and the Directories of Bristol gave a clear description of the procedures to be followed.

> *Bristol Emigration Society*, 27, Queen square. For the purpose of supplying information to intending emigrants, and giving advice as to the selection of a field for their labour, and in some cases assistance with clothes and money. An Agent investigates the cases before they are considered by the Committee. When assistance of money is given the emigrants are requested to write a promise to repay the advance made on their account so soon as they are able, so that the committee may again assist others. President, Bishop Marsden; Vice Presidents, Rev. John Percival, D.D. and Mrs Beddoe, Lt.-Genl. R. Luard, C.B., Rev. U. R. Thomas; Treasurer, Miss S. K. Tyndall, the Fort, Bristol; Hon. Secretary, H. C. Barstow, esq., Fern house, Clifton down; Agent, Mrs. M. E. Forster, 27 Queen square, Bristol.

Every year a notice was placed in the Bristol Directory

TRANSPORTING CHILDREN TO CANADA

The Bristol Emigration Society became responsible for sending children from the orphanages, reformatories, industrial schools and workhouses to Canada from around 1886. Most of the children were sent to the port of St John in New Brunswick and passed into the care of an agent who found homes or placements for them. They did not maintain a receiving or distribution home for the children in St John. Their agent often made a claim that they used the Sailors home in St John and, when under pressure, they named the home of a Mr Wallace in New Glasgow. On some voyages the children were taken to St Georges home in Montreal before travelling further and occasionally to the Marchmont home in Belleville, Ontario.

The committee appointed an agent to handle the business side of the emigration; in 1886 it was Charles Birt but after two years he appears to have handed it to his wife Louisa, a sister of Annie Macpherson. In 1889 a new agent was appointed; Margaret Forster. She stayed in post until the society closed down sometime between 1914 and 1915. Aged 50 at that time, Margaret Forster was a married woman with nine children. She lived at 27 Queens Square which was also the offices of the Bristol Emigration Society. Her husband didn't appear to have any involvement.

Supporting emigrants proved to be an expensive business and raising money became an important activity for the committee. A fancy dress ball was held once a year at the Victoria Rooms, to which the great and the good of the city of Bristol were invited. Newspaper accounts of the grand occasion of the Diamond Jubilee Ball held on Wednesday, May 19, 1897, described walls draped in silk and of a mass of flowers; the music being supplied by the band of the Grenadier Guards. This was to be a grand occasion which would advertise all the good work they do supporting would-be emigrants of this city. It was, of course, designed to raise as much money as possible.

Reports of the annual meetings of the society were published in the newspapers and give some understanding of the work it did. On March 5, 1888 the report from 27 Queens Square, set out details of the organisation. The committee met every Monday at 47 Royal York Crescent and Fridays in Queens Square when required. Meetings were always advertised in the Western Daily Press and headed by the title, "The Bristol Emigrants Friend", followed by

Montreal – A Scene at the Immigration Sheds, *artist unknown. A newly arrived batch of Miss Macpherson's boys at dinner. Taken from* Canadian Illustrated New *May 17, 1873.*

A group of children brought out by Annie Mcpherson sitting on the dockside waiting to be told about where they might go.

examples of the help given to families and then reports from Canada.

The agent was expected to report on her work and on June 28, 1899, the Bristol public was presented with a clear account of the difficulties of travelling with a party of children from Avonmouth to Canada. Her report on the 25 children who left on the ship, *Montrose*, on June 25, 1899, described the details: "The weather was cold and wet, seas were rough, everyone was sick and the boys in particular became very weak". It must have been very unpleasant but apparently the food was excellent as was the sleeping accommodation. Unfortunately the party arrived at Montreal too late to catch the train to St John and they used the St Georges home until the next train. The party set off again at 3.30 pm on July 11, and arrived at St John for 2.30 pm on July 12, 1899. They were met by Samuel Gardner, agent for the Canadian Government, at the Port of St John in New Brunswick, who straightaway sent the boys and girls to placements already arranged for them. There was one exception; one small boy was left without a place to go. Mr Gardner said he had no place for a boy who was so small and had made that clear to the society before the party had left England. The agent went on to say that as she had been instructed to visit as many Bristol children as time would permit in the locality of Belle Isle Point and St John, she would take the boy with her, but she failed to say if she found him a place.

For this group of children, on leaving the one place that was familiar to them, they had to endure a long and difficult journey and, upon landing in a strange place were sent, without rest, to a placement such as a farm or house and were often put to work on arrival.

The Canadian Government expected the Bristol Emigration Society to set up a reception and distribution home for the Bristol children. Most other societies taking out large groups of children did provide such a house but the committee, in the person of Margaret Forster, gave assurances that they were able to use different homes in New Brunswick. These answers were later proved to be untrue. It was said that a home in New Glasgow was used; this was owned by a farmer called Edward Walters, an ex-Park Row boy, who had done well and now had his own farm. When challenged, the society later claimed it used a home for sailors in St John but there is no evidence to support this claim. It was simply a delaying tactic to keep the Canadian Government happy. The society did not have the money to set up a home for the children and although they were told quite clearly that if they didn't provide this home they must cease their emigration activities, the children were still sent. The truth was quite simple; these children were needed to work on the farms; there were children in Bristol, ready to come out to Canada, to supply the needs of the farmers. Somehow the Canadian authorities never quite banned the work of the Bristol Emigration Society.

The annual report of Wednesday June 10, 1891, reported in detail the work covered by the society confirming that its sphere of operations was confined to Gloucestershire and Somerset. They seem anxious to be clear that the work is not sectarian but is about rescuing the young of both sexes from degraded homes, re-uniting wives with husbands and assisting men of families to join relations in a new home. The treasurer reported that the subscription list had declined from the previous year by 25% but donations had increased.

Some of the money had come from intending emigrants paying in towards their travelling expenses and some were repayments from settled emigrants. The committee thought that this indicated that the society was now dealing with a superior class of person and this entitled them to more support from the general public. In the last year they had sent 192 emigrants, 101 males, 91 females, among whom were 19 families with two to seven children between them; 111 of them had gone to Canada, 43 to Australasia, 30 to the Americas and eight elsewhere; in total 192 emigrants. They had assisted 100 children to emigrate but don't give details.

Mrs Beddoe, vice president, reported that the 1891 fancy dress ball in the Victoria Rooms had raised £150 and that the sum would relieve the society of its debts but left little over for the work. She said that the colonies used to take people out for nothing but that now they had withdrawn that boon. Most clients were too poor to pay much but they were good working people and would do well in the colonies with boundless land available for use.

The agent, Margaret Forster, had the responsibility to collect payment for the children being sent to Canada and to gather together all the papers, medical certificates and legal documents needed for the voyage. Part of her responsibility was to provide a suitable escort for the children while travelling on board ship. At best it can be said that she was careless and at worst she was plainly inefficient. A number of parties of Bristol children travelled across the Atlantic without adult supervision and without the necessary papers. It seems that the committee, in the writing of their public reports to those who supported them, publicised the affairs of the society as more organised than was apparent in practise.

Samuel Gardner, the Immigration Officer of the Port of St John in New Brunswick, was also the Emigration Officer for the Bristol Emigration Society. His role was to find places for the children being sent out; he was to meet them and ensure they arrived at their destination placement or new home. His stature in St John was assured as he came from an influential family already established in the business of men's clothing; they introduced readymade suits to the residents of St John in 1900 which ensured good trading for the next century. His family was known, his credentials were established and farmers were happy to make and maintain contact with him. Samuel Gardner filled the position of immigration officer for the Port of St John for 20 years until he was officially retired. He appears to have entered into an agreement with the representative of St John in the Federal Parliament, a Judge Mcleod, that he might continue his duties as Immigration Officer for the port. In order that he might receive his full pay it was agreed he would receive two cheques; one with his superannuation and one to make up the difference between that and

BRISTOL'S PAUPER CHILDREN

his full pay of office. In 1900, Samuel Gardner was aged 90, and still in office. Pressure from officers in the Federal Government forced him to resign from the post of immigration officer and as agent for the Bristol Emigration Society.

This did not suit the society and on August 1, 1896, Mark Whitwill, a committee member and a man who had personally been involved in the emigration of children from Bristol, wrote to the Ministry of the Interior in Canada. He argued that Samuel Gardner should be retained in spite of his advanced years because he was so good at his job and he, Mark Whitwill, could provide letters from seven boys who had been at Park Row Industrial School in Bristol to support this.

Whitwill's efforts went unrewarded however, as a John Lantalum was appointed by the Canadian Government as Immigration Officer for the Port of St John. Lantalum was also expected to take on the job as agent for the Bristol Emigration Society. He was very unhappy at being expected to take on this dual role, seemingly concerned that one person taking on two roles would lead to tension and conflict. John Lantalum was outspoken over his concerns about the Bristol Emigration Society. He said that they didn't insist on a written agreement and they didn't have a receiving home for the children. He was also concerned about there being no clear organisation for easy communication.

However much he protested, it does seem that he was expected to take on both roles and eventually appeared to agree and settled into the work. However, other concerns raised took a different direction when it was discovered that John Lantalum was of the Roman Catholic faith. When this fact came to the attention of Mark Whitwill he wrote a letter to the Canadian Government asking about Protestant children whom, he said, were put into Catholic homes. He argued that, as John Lantalum was of the Roman Catholic faith, he would favour the homes of people of the same faith and will put English Protestant children into those homes.

Whitwill now gave notice that no more children would be sent by the Bristol Emigration Society because of their concerns regarding the settlement of children into Homes not of their family faith. Samuel Gardner, now the ex-agent for the society, anxious to get his job back, responded quickly by writing to Frank Pedley in the Immigration Department of the Canadian Government. He claimed that now John Lantalum was in post, no Protestant children will be sent and he writes that, "This is a pity because we need 50 children annually". He claimed that there were 14 girls ready to come out to Canada but the Bristol Emigration Society had kept them back. Mark Whitwill, who Samuel calls 'the ruling spirit', had written to the secretary because he could not risk the possibility of them being placed under the influence of Roman Catholic priests.

However, it also appears that Margaret Forster had written directly to Samuel Gardner asking him to meet and care for the Bristol Protestant children; Frank Pedley was informed of this by letter from Bogue Smart, Chief Inspector of British Immigrated Children and Receiving Homes for Canada. This was fast becoming a problem for the Canadian Immigration Department and in trying to calm things down, Pedley suggested in his reply that Lantalum might like to find someone to look after the Protestant children. In his reply John Lantalum declared that Mrs Forster might establish a home in Fairview for the Bristol children and work from there but he still doesn't think it a good idea to work for two organisations. Forster also responded that she didn't think it a good idea that the immigration agent should be a member of the Roman Catholic Church as most of the children were Protestants.

Gardner wrote to other institutions informing them that John Lantalum could not find Protestant homes for the children because he was a Roman Catholic. At no time had he, Gardner, ever refused to find Protestant homes for Protestant children. Clearly feeling under pressure he explained that he was not opposed to finding situations for non-Catholic children: in fact, he had already placed some Bristol children with Protestant families. Bogue Smart then wrote to these institutions saying that, as Samuel Gardner was nearly 90-years-old, they must not give too much importance to his communications.

Mr Keyes, a representative of the Federal Government, wrote to all interested parties and declared that Samuel Gardner was no longer an emigration agent and that John Lantalum was now in place, and that Lantalum was willing to look after the children in the same manner as Gardner and would work with the same degree of interest in their welfare. On January 30, 1901, a letter was sent to Margaret Forster telling her of the arrangements and that no special agent would be appointed for the Bristol children.

It does seem strange now that so much concern was placed on something that might happen rather than something that had happened. The people involved in organising the emigration of the Bristol children really did expect that children be placed in homes following the same religious views as that of their families back in Britain. Information that this did not always happen filtered back to Bristol and had caused considerable concern. Children sent from other parts of Britain had been placed out in Protestant homes although they were of the Catholic faith.

Thomas Barnardo was very active sending children from his homes out to Canada. He so believed in the merits of child emigration that he often ignored the Government ruling on parental permission. A large number of children had been taken out to Canada through his organisation without that important document and the parents of these children had turned to the courts for help in getting their children returned to them. More than 60 parents took the Barnardo organisation to court and, in all cases, the judge ordered that the children be returned. The organisation who paid for these court cases was the Roman Catholic Church - very concerned that Catholic children had been put into Protestant homes.

The first two parents who went to court were from Bristol. Even today we would not see them as good parents. Harry had been sold by his mother to an organ grinder who had abandoned him. He had been found wandering the streets of Folkstone, hungry and alone, by a clergyman who had taken him to a Barnardo refuge. Martha had been so cruelly treated by her mother and step father that she had taken herself off to the doors of Mullers Orphanage in Ashley Down, Bristol. Since Martha was illegitimate, Mullers would not take her in and instead sent her to a Barnardo refuge. Both mothers were informed about the whereabouts of their children but neither signed the Canada clause giving permission for the Barnardo organisation to send the children to Canada, but that is exactly what happened. A gentleman wanted to adopt a boy of 10 or 11 and he liked the look of Harry. Barnardo seemed happy to agree that Harry should go with this man and not leave any address! Martha is supposed to have been taken by a woman living in the south of France and although her mother had written to Barnardo asking that Martha be sent home, she was sent away to a secret address in the country. It is believed that she was probably sent to Canada although this news was kept from her parents.

Neither of these children were returned even though the courts had ordered it. These stories not only show just how easy it was for parents to lose track of their children but also how devious the "child savers" could be in their zeal to save the children.

The Bristol Emigration Society believed that it was working to achieve a better life for all of their emigrants by giving them the chance to go to Canada. It was reported that this same desire to improve the life of the children, who were taken to Canada by the efforts of the society, was lauded and welcomed by many people in the city. The report about the work of the society published on April 1, 1887, printed the words of the Bishop of Huron from Canada, who wholly supported the work: "it was of immense importance to remove the children from unhappy circumstances and the control of so-called friends who allowed them to grow up in evil habits".

Writing in "*The Globe*", a St John newspaper on March 23, 1912, James Gilchrist, Provincial Immigration Officer in New Brunswick, described how newcomers were received at the port. The churches and the Salvation Army were involved in the reception of the children. They believed the moral attributes of these children needed attention and, due to the good work undertaken by volunteers, the addresses of these children were followed up. From this paper we understand that a home for girls destined for domestic work had opened in St John.

It appears that farmers, who were wishing for extra help on their farm or farmers' wives needing help in the house or in caring for their children, sent their requirements to the agent for the Bristol Emigration Society in St John. James Gilchrist's job was to meet the parties of children, find food for them and, while they were resting on the dockside or in one of the immigration sheds, give out their train tickets.

The children, being told their destination, were then placed onto the train, given their ticket and the name of their station and told to get off there and wait for the farmer to collect them. Children tell of their need to find the toilet but were too frightened to move in case they missed the station. Then, there was often a long wait for the children; farmers were often unable to collect the child from the station until their days work was over. Girls who were taken into the town of St John destined to become servants may be collected in

Advert from 1882 showing Mark Whitwill's involvement in the shipping trade and particularly between Bristol and Canada

horse drawn carriages and taken on to their new homes. Rarely were boys or girls allowed to rest after their long and often exhausting journey and were often put straight to work on their arrival. It was all very casual and although no written explanation exists, there is no doubt that if a child placed with a farmer was not able to carry out the farm work demanded by that farmer, he was taken back to the agent at the end of the year, with a request for a stronger child. It is not surprising that many, when reaching adulthood, did not see themselves as worthy citizens.

An article appeared in the Bristol Guardian newspaper of Saturday, November 9, 1902, entitled, "Illogical Bristol Guardians", following their meeting where two reports were presented. The Bristol Emigration Society had asked the guardians for a subscription towards their work. They pointed out that they had given the guardians much assistance taking both boys and girls to Canada and quoted the numbers as set out below. It was thought a subscription of five guineas would be a suitable sum.

Numbers of children sent out in the following years:

1888 - Four boys and two girls
1889 - 11 boys and two girls
1900 - 11 boys and two girls
1901 - 17 boys and two girls
1902 - Nine boys.

The second report, presented by the Schools and Boarding Out Committee, considered there was no difficulty placing girls in suitable service positions; a great demand existed for boys in workshops and factories with every chance of rising to a good position. The reporter raised questions for sensible citizens of Bristol, "Why send them to Canada or anywhere else when we are giving free admission to England of the scum of the continent, making room for them by sending out our lads?" This was in 1902 not 2017 - but there are similarities. He ended his article, "The ways of the Board of Guardians are past finding out".

However, the Bristol Emigration Society did continue to take children from the Poor Law Guardians into the next century. The Western Daily Press of November 24, 1904, printed a piece about the Bristol Board of Guardians who sent 121 children away over the last six years, through the hands of the Bristol Emigration Society. The papers continue to document their involvement as the Western Daily Press of April 7, 1906, carried a report from the Schools and Boarding Out Committee of Bristol Board of Guardians, enabling a Mr Sheppard to authorise the first steps towards the emigration of 23 children. He was expected to get consent from the parents, except for those who had been deserted or were under the control of the guardians, who had the authority to give consent. It was agreed that the Bristol Emigration Society would outfit the children as last year but the committee would not finally commit themselves unless it was assured that the children would receive adequate supervision. The clerk was authorised to interview the Local Government Board with a view to seeking that assurance. The discussions and concerns about adequate supervision was still an issue for investigation; perhaps the guardians should be commended because, at last, they were asking for guidance.

The last group of Bristol children was taken out to Canada in 1915 through the Liverpool Shelter Home and not through the Bristol Emigration Society. They were taken to 51 Avon Street, Stratford, under the guidance of William Merry, nephew of Annie Macpherson.

When did the society finally close down? It appears that the society played a major role in taking children from both boards of guardians from 1887 until 1912. There are 366 names of children taken out to Canada by the society, but the final number is not known as the records have not survived.

The name of the society had disappeared from the Directories by 1903.

EMIGRATION FROM INDUSTRIAL SCHOOLS

MANAGERS AND FRIENDS of the industrial schools in Bristol used emigration to ensure that some of their pupils would not return to friends or homes in the city when they left school. The general belief that a child would receive a better start in life if they went to Canada away from their home city was shared by managers and staff.

EMIGRATION FROM CLIFTON DAY INDUSTRIAL SCHOOL

In the 1869 annual report of Clifton Certified Industrial School the managers indicated that they were prepared to consider emigration to Canada for those boys for whom a strong influence would be exerted to draw them back to their families when they left the school. Writing that they believed "a well-considered scheme in connection with emigration" would be fruitful, they were prepared to examine their options. The report published the following year recorded that two boys were sent to America and five boys to Canada; the first mention of an actual emigration in the records of this school. In the 1871 report the committee announced that they had found a trustworthy agent who would ensure that the Clifton boys would be taken to Canada and found suitable employment.

This was Reverend Shipperley, a man well known to Bristolians; he lived in Abbotsford, Quebec, and would organise the ship's passage and find homes for their boys. It was one thing to decide that emigration was a good thing for the boys but it was another to find enough money. This became a key issue for the members but after a long and difficult discussion in a general committee meeting, agreement was eventually reached. It was decided to take the costs of emigration out of their general funds. This was regarded as a legitimate way of

The two men are standing on Hotwells Road. The large building on the left is the Clifton Industrial School for Boys. The large building on the hill is the Clifton National School.

handling the expense. During what was a difficult discussion, it was clear that some members possessed strong feelings about the boys who were orphans and even who those who had families.

They argued strongly that it would not be safe to allow the boys to go back to those families who were considered unworthy. Interestingly the committee minutes don't record any description of what might be considered "an unworthy family". Reverend Shipperley visited the school in the summer of 1871. He was travelling home on July 18 and would take some boys with him - an offer he called, "a special opportunity for the boys". He explained to the committee that they would take a ship to New York and continue by rail to Quebec. Once there, he would find places for the boys and would be able to oversee the boys for two to three years. The committee considered that five boys were fit to go and agreed the cost which would be £10 per head. Quebec was, and still is, a French-speaking county; it must have been hard for these boys, going to live in a new country, living with strangers who speak a language they didn't understand.

By August 1871 the committee had changed its organisation. Perhaps realising that emigration had become a viable option for placing out their boys, it set up a special fund to pay the costs of emigration. Six more boys were sent out at a much lower cost of £6.6.0 per boy, but these boys were to travel steerage on the ship, a much cheaper option. It was recorded in the minutes that "the boys appeared before the committee to receive a Bible each and some words of wholesome advice". When travelling steerage the boys needed to take their own bedding. Reverend Shipperley reported back to the school about the six boys sent in January 1873. He informed the committee that the boys had arrived, were in good health and had been placed out in a situation but their bedding had been stolen on the voyage. Enquiries were made by the school but no follow up reports were noted, and it is open to speculation that the boys had seen a way of making some money! By 1874 the Canadian Government was paying the equivalent of £2 towards the cost of each boy sent out to Canada, a very positive incentive to the committee to send more boys. Reverend Shipperley wrote to the managers to encourage them to send more boys and from the tone of the committee meeting it seems certain that this offer would be gratefully accepted. Reverend Shipperley remained involved with this school for a number of years, with the records showing that he also took the Clifton boys to St John in New Brunswick, and he used the services of Samuel Gardner, the agent for the Bristol Emigration Society.

EMIGRATION FROM PARK ROW INDUSTRIAL SCHOOL

The records of Park Row Industrial School show that boys were encouraged to emigrate and were sent out during the early years of the school. Mary Carpenter, the first superintendent, certainly believed that sending the children away to Canada would give them a better start in life and although there are no details of the actual emigration, she did report on their progress.

Early records date from 1859 and there are lists of boys sent out but they give little detail. Edward Walters was sent out from the school in 1870 on the ship *Strathblane*. At some point he arrived in New Glasgow, Nova Scotia, acquired a farm of his own and appeared to be doing well. The school often used him to act as a receiving agent and would occasionally send a boy directly to him. It is not known whether he took the boy to work on his farm or passed him on to another farmer. There was no doubt that the school was very proud of their boys who, like Edward Walters, appeared to do well and their achievements were recorded in their personal files.

A boy called Norman, after only two years, was running a large farm of his own, but boys were not sent to him. The committee minutes of June 1862 record that two boys were sent to Canada. Biggs and Jones were brought into a committee meeting, congratulated on their luck, and presented with a Bible. It is to be hoped that those wishes proved to be an accurate forecast. Their passage to Quebec and subsequent transfer to Marchmont in Belleville had been arranged by Mark Whitwill, a manager of the school. These boys travelled with Mr Barker, Superintendent of Kingswood Reformatory, and six boys from that institution, by train to Liverpool. An interesting comment was recorded in the minutes that, "once on the ship, they travelled the rest of the way on their own"; presumably Mr Barker came back to Bristol.

Sets of clothing were supplied to any boys who were sent to Canada, as this was an expensive item for those who sent them; it took up some debating time in the committee meetings. The cost of giving the boys warm coats to see them through the hard winters was very controversial. The following list was fairly standard throughout all the schools and all items were packed in a tin or box.

One suit of working corduroy
One suit - new
One suit of cloth given by friends
Two new shirts
Two old shirts
One new pair of strong boots
One pair of second hand boots
Four pairs of stockings
Two neck handkerchiefs
One box value three shillings
Tinware for mess etc.
Old knife and fork
Bible, hymn book and copy books
Prayer book given by Rev. Knight
Beds, coverlets given by Red Lodge

A box used by the boys of Park Row Industrial School to carry all their belongings to their new life in Canada.

The remainder of the outfit was purchased at the boys own expense.

Sometimes the boys were expected to buy their own box, which in 1870 cost three shillings. All of their belongings were packed inside and these boxes were to become the emotional tie linking them with their old lives. They were treasured and became an important part of their new lives.

While researching the stories of these children the author was contacted by the daughter of a woman who had been sent out from Bath. Describing the emotional trauma her mother had suffered when she was sent away to Canada, she explained that, still sitting in the corner of her living room, was the box her mother had taken out to Canada. The box would not be thrown away; her mother had returned, bringing back her box and it now symbolised all those emotional memories.

On March 30, 1863, the managers of Park Row Industrial School sent four boys from Bristol to Canada on the ship *Ottilia*. It was expected they would take the railway to Ottawa City and be received by the agent of the Reformatory and Refuge Union who were involving themselves in the emigration of these boys. They were offering grants of £5 to assist towards expenses so now the committee had only to find £4; money and support for these children came from different sources.

It appears, from the minutes of the committee meeting in October 1863, that Mary Carpenter seemed quite upset. She had heard that a boy called Nicholas, thought to be safely in Canada, had been seen on the streets of Bristol. She had been personally responsible for finding the money that enabled Nicholas and three other boys to emigrate and she searched the city looking for him. He was found working in a tailor's workshop and clearly she questioned him quite sharply. His explanation described what had happened to many of the children. They had worked for six months on a large farm and none had received any wages. Another boy was on his way home and two other boys from Kingwood Reformatory were also thinking of returning. All this was reported back to the committee. It would have been interesting to hear Mary Carpenter's personal comments, but unfortunately they were not recorded. Having read the committee minutes and knowing that the boy Nicholas was an excellent tailor, even winning prizes in school for his work, it does seem odd that he was sent away to work on a farm. The committee did decide to send a letter of complaint to the Refuge and Reformatory Union agent in Canada.

In 1864 the school received a visit from an American gentleman, the Rev Van Meter, who ran the Howard Mission Home for Little Wanderers at 37 New Bowery, New York. He told them that he had been running the home for 10 years and, in his words, saving the children who lived on the streets of New York. He claimed he could place 1,000 children, take them across the Atlantic, at a cost of 33 shillings and four pennies, and place them with respectable people. His total cost would be £8 per boy plus an outfit. This seemed costly but after some bargaining, four boys were sent out to New York although there were no guarantees that reports would be sent back to the school. Boys who were sent out this way would be found places on farms in the Western States. In 1879 Mark Whitwill, having business interests in New York, visited the Howard Mission and did not find it pleasing or of a satisfactory character. He explained he had requested a detailed report of all the boys sent out in the last three years but there was no information that had been received. However he had ensured the conditions of the establishment were reported to her Majesty's Inspector, Major Inglis. It seems astonishing that the Park Row managers, after just one visit from the Rev Van Meter, and no separate enquiries made, were happy to send boys out to the New York home. By 1878 it was reported that the Howard Mission was under new management but no more boys were sent.

In June 1865 a letter was received from the National Colonial Emigration Society. It wished to inform the schools that although it supported the emigration of destitute and other children between the ages of 12 to 15, they wouldn't take criminals, ie any child who had been found guilty of a crime by the courts in this country. It seemed that a number of organisations were now in the business of child emigration, and were ensuring that their activities in this field were known by the schools and homes.

REV GEORGE ROGERS OFFERS HIS HELP

It was Rev George Rogers, a Bristol man now living in Canada, who persuaded the managers of Park Row Industrial School to send boys to Springfield in County Karrs, New Brunswick. He was convinced of the value of such a move for these boys and promised to meet them, find a suitable place for them and report back on their progress. A number of boys were sent out and were found places on local farms in the area of Springfield. In 1873 Rev Rogers, now suffering from poor health, returned to Bristol where he met with the managers of the school and promised places for another 38 boys on farms in the area. In persuading them to send more boys, he promised that they would feel quite at home, as there was now a large colony of Park Row boys in the area.

Mr Robert Shives, the Canadian Government Emigration Officer based in St John, had undertaken to continue his work ensuring that the boys would be put with a farmer for one year and during that time would work for their board, lodging and clothes. At the end of the year fresh arrangements were to be made for each boy. Although he didn't go into detail about these arrangements, he did tell the managers that it was possible for boys to get a yoke of oxen by the end of three years. Most of the managers ran very commercial businesses in a big city. It is interesting to wonder how they might consider that news, perhaps speculating about the value of a yoke of oxen. The Rev Rogers also promised a visit from a Dr Clay, the Government Immigration Officer at Halifax, who would report on their progress. He explained that Dr Clay was regarded by the boys as their friend and protector; this was someone to whom they could appeal if they were in trouble.

Reports to the manager at their regular meetings might include news from boys who had emigrated and any letters from the boys were laid out on the table for reading. Comments taken from these letters were added to the boys' record but there were many gaps where, presumably, these boys did not write back to the school. For those who did, the recorded comments were often quite short.

- Stephen was advised to come home because of ill health and he intended to return as soon as he could. He was a fine looking young man.
- Harry returned because he was in trouble with the police. He joined the army and a newspaper report pointed to him as the tallest man in the army!
- Not all good news though. In July 1893, William Shephard dived into a river and broke his neck.
- James reported he was doing well and wanted to persuade his father to join him.
- Two boys returned to Bristol in a ragged condition and Rudge returned because he said he was not met. They reported that Powell went out on the first passage of the *Aragon*, courtesy of Mark Whitwill, and several boys travelled out on the ship, *Great Western*.
- William Bryce came back to visit his family and brought treats of eggs and cakes for the boys in the school. Sometimes boys returned to Bristol, as they could when they were 16-years-old, stayed a while, but often returned to Canada.

The 1850 Poor Law Act was very clear about the emigration of any child under 16. Permission had to be given by any parents still living and the child must also attend before the Justices of Bristol to explain that they understand what emigration meant and that they knew what was going to happen to them. After the Doyle report in 1875 there must be an examination by a doctor to certify

The steam ship *Aragon,* seen here moored at Narrow Quay, owned by Mark Whitwill's company, took Bristol children out to Canada

that the child was fit in mind and body and suitable for emigration. These were children put in an industrial school until they were 16; therefore permission must be obtained from the Secretary of State to send a child any younger. The Secretary of State also had to ensure that all documents were in order and that included the written permission from the parents, if they could be found.

Andrew Doyle had reported all children under 16 were expected to sail with three or four pieces of paper, most showing that the laws had been obeyed and permission had been obtained. The most controversial piece of paper, and the one that caused much concern, was the permission of parents. It must have been really hard for parents to sign that "Canada clause" which gave permission for the authorities to send their children away to another country but sometimes they had little choice. Equally the children found it difficult to accept that their parents had written that vital letter.

Sometimes a boy has sailed to Canada before the formal discharge came from the Secretary of State and there were times when children were held back until they were 16 as permission from the parents was not forthcoming. Staff at an industrial school made those decisions as the children who were sent to an industrial school were free to leave when they became 16-years-old.

Stanhope School in Somerset Street

EMIGRATION FROM CARLTON HOUSE AND STANHOPE SCHOOL

Two industrial schools for girls in Bristol were involved in the emigration of their pupils. Records for the Stanhope House School for Girls, founded in 1866, and sometimes called the Bristol Industrial School for Girls, have not survived. We do know from notes made in 1876, and reports from the Bristol newspapers, that since the school opened in 1869, 192 children had left, 25 had found situations abroad and most had done well. Three had gone to Africa, one to Queensland and some to America.

Carlton House Industrial School for Girls, in Southwell Street, was certified in 1874. From its start, the managers were interested in the idea of emigration for some of the girls. It seemed that decisions were often taken at very short notice. Although permission must be sought from the Secretary of State, this was rarely refused and girls would be removed to the dockside with very little warning. Parents were expected to give their permission and pressure to agree was often put upon the family, sometimes by the girl herself. If a parent refused permission for their child to be sent to Canada, and the committee really believed that it was in the best interests of the girl, they waited until she became 16 and then she was put on board a ship. Staff at the school made judgements about the parents and that influenced how they dealt with the child.

On April 21, 1887, two girls were to be sent to Canada; one was allowed to go home and say goodbye to her mother because her mother was thought to be a respectable woman, the other girl was not. Clearly her mother did not match up to the standards expected! There was a huge amount of pressure put on these children. One girl said that some people had come into the school to talk to them about Canada and made it sound so good that they all wanted to go. They thought it would be like going to the zoo for the day.

Mark Whitwill was a prominent figure in the life of this school; he was a great believer in the emigration of these girls and took a very active part in the process. Many of the girls travelled to the United States and Canada on board his ships, sailing from Bristol, Newport, Cardiff and other west country ports. With business interests in New York and the States he helped to find places for these girls both in this country and in Canada, and arranged for reports to be received about them. Some appeared to be carrying letters written by him, the assumption might be that they were letters of introduction.

Matron, who was a very powerful person within the school, was in favour of the girls being sent away from Bristol and often found placements for them before they left Bristol. Ex-pupils, already in Canada or the United States, would write with news of vacant situations and a girl would be dispatched to fill that vacancy. When these girls returned to England, sometimes to visit their families, many also came to visit the school. When Ada Holdsworth visited in 1882, bringing news of her successful life in New York, she was given a great welcome. However, when, in 1884, Elizabeth Nutt was persuaded by friends to reject the idea of going to America, staff did not approve of this decision and made their feelings known. Reading through the minutes it did seem that girls were anxious to go but it is hard to make judgements about this as it was the staff who wrote the records about the girls and the school.

Finding the necessary money to cover the costs of emigration, not only the fares but also enough money to fund suitable outfits and bedding for the girls, was a problem for the managers. In 1898 an outfit cost £5 and then £6-8-4 had to be found for the fare. Somehow they always seemed to find the money and were able to send a steady number of girls to Canada although the actual organisation of sending the girls on their way seems very casual.

In 1888 the matron took two girls to the station and just left them with an unknown family who were also travelling to Liverpool to board a ship. Girls were often taken to the docks at Newport or Cardiff in twos or threes, and then left with the crew, perhaps because there was a delay on sailing times. In 1891 two girls were sent off with a man, no name shown. We read he is from the Temperance League and would see them to the end of their journey. It was no surprise to find that Emily returned from America when the records show she was sent to Canada.

When concern was expressed about Ada and they decide she would never be fit for industrial work, they send her to her brothers in Canada as they were doing well. Ellen has kleptomania; the question is debated whether she should be sent to Canada or a reformatory. The decision was not recorded. It is tempting to think that emigration was also a tool used when considering how to place girls who had caused some concern to the staff at the school.

In March 1887 the records show that 42 girls had gone to Canada or America and that 38 were doing well. No concern is shown about the remaining four.

By 1903 there was no money for emigration. The committee could find money for the fare but no money for outfits. Much later, in 1913, the committee was asked if it would send Florence to Canada. Her mother was now living there and had asked for her daughter to be sent. It seemed that she was sent once but was rejected at the port. Passage to Canada was no longer a way to pass on a child who presented problems. There were concerns about Florence. She was underweight and not considered fit for domestic service. Florence stayed in this country and was eventually sent to Stoke Park Colony.

No more girls were sent from Carlton House and the school closed in 1924.

The costs of sending a child to Canada were found by many means; some schools opened a special account in order to save money for that purpose but most times the costs had to be taken from the funds used to run the establishment. It was seen as expensive and the fact that the necessary money was found is a testimony to how the staff of these schools considered emigration.

EMIGRATION FROM THE WORKHOUSE AFTER 1884

A FTER THE DOYLE report was published in 1875, Bristol Board of Guardians did not send any more children out to Canada. There was no doubt about their concerns; they did not know what had happened to the children previously sent out to Canada. The magistrate of St James Ward was reported in the Bristol Mercury of March 22, 1878, as saying that he regretted the decision of the Local Government Board in stopping the emigration of pauper children and hoped to get the decision reversed. Two opposing points of view being presented by concerned Bristol citizens; which one would decide the future of the Bristol children?

BARTON REGIS BOARD OF GUARDIANS BECOME INVOLVED IN THE EMIGRATION OF POOR LAW CHILDREN

It wasn't until 1884 that the Barton Regis Board of Guardians commenced sending groups of children to Canada, their decision being prompted by a letter from Mark Whitwill, a member of the Bristol School Board and a manager of two industrial schools. As owner of the Great Western Steamship Company, he took children from these schools to train as apprentices; his belief that boys longed for an adventurous life on the open sea prompted him to place them on board his ships. He felt strongly that boys and girls would have a better start to their lives if they were sent out to Canada and wrote a letter to the board of guardians seeking to persuade them to start sending children. In a letter addressed to the board he explained there were seven boys who wished to go, he would like the guardians to consider the matter and promised to undertake the responsibility of forwarding them to homes in New Brunswick, promising that he had already successfully placed lads (and lasses) in that province.

A Loxton drawing of Barton Regis Workhouse, located at 100 Fishponds Road

About the same time Whitwill also asked for an interview with the president of the Local Government Board; he wanted to satisfy him that Bristol children would be given good homes and he, personally, could promise that the guardians would receive reports. He proposed that the children would be sent straight to St John, New Brunswick, and enclosed letters from Samuel Gardner, the Immigration Agent of the Port of St John, who wrote that the children would be properly cared for and he could find good homes for all of them. The reply from the Barton Regis Board of Guardians was not positive; they did not believe that the boys would be properly cared for if they were emigrated in the manner proposed by Mark Whitwill, and appeared very unhappy about the proposal.

Whitwill had to explain why he had always taken an interest in the emigration of pauper children and he would ensure that whoever was entrusted with the care of the child was a fit and willing person. He proposed that if just seven or eight children were taken out at any one time he, personally, would check that the procedures were properly carried out. He even offered to take them in his own ships and fund part of the cost himself. This offer to bear some of the cost must have engaged the attention of the guardians immediately. The boys would be put in the charge of a steward when on board ship and this man would hand over the boys to Gardner at the port. He had done this in the past and it worked perfectly.

Mark Whitwill, manager of two industrial schools; member of the Board of Education; promoter of the Suspension Bridge; Director of the Bristol and West Building Society; first President of the Childrens Hospital; city councilor and owner of the Great Western Steamship Company

Pushing for a positive reply, Whitwill then promised to write down all of these conditions for the guardians otherwise it would be too late for the summer and there were boys waiting and wanting to go. The guardians became adamant that Whitwill must send word of where and with whom the boys are placed, plus information about their welfare. Agreement was eventually reached; the boys would go before the Justices and the guardians sanctioned the expenditure of £7. Mark Whitwill does then make a point that these boys must be of the Protestant faith and he will ensure they will go into Protestant homes. The boys sailed in July 1884 and by August the guardians had received reports from Whitwill giving only details of the boys' placements but no comments on their welfare.

From this time small groups of children were sent out through the arrangement with Whitwill and Gardner and the guardians appeared quite willing to allow the children to go, although they always argued about the costs. In 1888 they gave permission for some boys to go but refused to sanction any more expense than £10 per head. By March of the following year they agreed £11 per child but refused to go any higher. Then they set some conditions of

The ship *Somerset* owned by the Great Western Steamship Company, based in Bristol. She took many of the industrial school children out to Canada and America

their own; each child must be placed with a family of their own religion, they now required more than just placement details; they also required a welfare report. Lengthy discussions about money occurred every time it was proposed to send a group of children to Canada.

THE GUARDIANS CONSIDER BOARDING OUT FOR THEIR INMATES

Barton Regis Board of Guardians allowed Mark Whitwill and the Bristol Emigration Society to take small groups of children for new lives in Canada but they were also beginning to "board out" children with suitable families. Boarding out for the children who were unable to stay with their families or who needed to be separated from unsuitable family members was now being seriously considered. A boarding-out committee was formed to organise and set up a system whereby boys and girls were sent to homes in the rural villages of Gloucestershire and Somerset on the outskirts of the Bristol. It was seen as a very successful way to support the children and to keep them away from the unhealthy and evil influences of the city and a growing number of children were being boarded out in this way. One of the influential members of this

Washwell House in Painswick, Gloucestershire, run by Harriet Wemyss

committee, Harriet Wemyss, lived in the village of Painswick in Gloucestershire and ran Washwell House, a home for wayward girls.

She described her work as saving girls from a wasted life. She found they were slovenly, stubborn and had a temper but she worked with them and found them work as servants by advertising in the papers. In August 1887 she had 27 children in her house; they were of a fit age to emigrate and she felt it her duty to consider this. She became involved with the Bristol children, some of whom were boarded out in the very rural village of Sheepscombe near Painswick. Harriet Wemyss became responsible for sending quite large groups of very young boys and girls, ages ranging from five to seven years, to Canada.

WOMEN ELECTED TO BARTON REGIS BOARD OF GUARDIANS INVOLVED IN THE EMIGRATION OF CHILDREN

Mary Clifford, standing for the Westbury-on-Trym ward in April 1884, was elected on a majority verdict and became a member of Barton Regis Guardians. She was one of the first four women who were elected at that time to serve on the board of guardians and became very active working with the children.

She was responsible for setting up the "boarding out" system and she became personally involved in organising emigration of the children.

In 1884 she arranged for 11 little boys from the workhouse school to go to Canada and by June 5, 1884, we are told that these boys had been given a new outfit and Mark Whitwill had funded most of the cost. Mary had words of advice and hoped for their future welfare and before sailing, each party of children was invited to her house for a farewell tea in her garden. She kept correspondence with these children over many years, writing to them frequently, reporting that, "although they express a longing in their letters for knowledge of their family, she doesn't answer as she only wants to send them gladness not sorrow". These children asked about their families and had a need to know about their families. This was a good example of the people who called themselves, "The Child Savers", so focused on saving the child, they don't perceive the child as a person with needs of their own.

On her visit to New York, Mary Clifford sent every boy and girl in New Brunswick a printed letter of friendly advice. News that one girl called the card "nice and holy like" did travel back to Bristol. Mary's niece, travelling in a train at end of the First World War, shared the carriage with a demobilised soldier. She discovered that he was one of "Mary's boys" and recorded that he spoke happily of his life in Canada and recalled, thankfully, the temperance pledge he had taken under her influence.

Mary Clifford was able to influence policy making at a time when many women had difficulty just making their voices heard. Her views were uncompromising; she believed that offering help to families – an example might be giving a pension to older people – would undermine family life. She influenced the passing of the Act of 1889, "which denied idle and vicious parents restitution rights over their children at the most important period of their training". For those interested in child emigration, her denial, to those children she corresponded with, of information about their families seemed cruel and unnecessary. This constantly reminds us that parents were judged on such evidence as poverty and expediency rather than an understanding of their position. Mary Clifford died on January 15 1919.

In 1894 Miss Catherine Woollam, also a Guardian, became interested in taking groups of children out to Canada. A letter written on June 8, 1894, was received from the Secretary to the High Commissioner for Canada stating clearly that any person responsible for emigration from Bristol must observe the conditions set down by the Canadian Government. Greater supervision must be exercised, forms are to be properly completed and the agent must complete the statuary declaration at the port. They asked if the guardians were in a position to assure them that Miss Woollam or the Bristol Emigration Society, with whom she was connected, had a distribution home in Canada and asked for the full address of the home. They pointed out that they were aware that Samuel Gardner received the children at the Port of St John and assigned homes to them but felt that this arrangement did not satisfy the conditions laid down by the Canadian Government.

The guardians wanted to know about these conditions and agreed that if the Bristol Emigration Society did not satisfy them on enquiry, then the board would act accordingly. The board then wrote to the High Commissioner stating that they intended to take the greatest possible care of the children. In return, they were told they must abide by the rules. News of Samuel Gardner's appointment as agent to the Bristol Emigration Society was brought to the notice of the guardians. It was important to note that children were still being sent out to Canada even though a receiving home for the Bristol children in St John still had not been established!

It is interesting to note that in 1897 the board asked the Local Government Board for permission to send children to the Marchmont home which was run by Rev Wallace and his wife. However, after some pointed discussion between the guardians, who were now asking for more information about the children, and the Rev Wallace, who was only prepared to send his usual reports, he announced that he didn't have room. The next party of children was then sent to the Rev Renaud in Montreal who apparently promised, without any argument, to send full reports. The guardians did appear to be trying to follow the rules and it was the Bristol Emigration Society who promised to collect yearly reports, who now reneged on that agreement.

William, Henry and Alice were put into the care of the Barton Regis Board of Guardians when their mother died and the father deserted the family. The boys were sent to the Cumberland Road home and were sent to Canada in 1899 on the ship *Montrose,* arriving in July at St John. William, aged nine, went to a farmer in Tennants Cove, Kings County, New Brunswick, but his family related that his time with the farmer was not good. As soon as he became 16 he moved to Boston to learn the carpentry trade. He returned to St John where he married and worked as a carpenter. The report on his welfare is dated 1901, two years after his arrival. It reads that he had an excellent home, did housework, and got his board, clothing and pocket money. The next report in 1903 said that he was employed at light work around the house; that he was not a robust looking lad but he attended Baptist church and school and he was an obedient lad. Teacher said he liked it here and did not want to return home. We can only wonder what William might have added to that report.

By this time the inspectors should have been checking on these children once a year but sometimes relied on what the master or what neighbours said rather than personally talk to the child. On the written report it might state that this was a good placement for the child whereas the child was saying something quite different. William didn't know where either Henry or Alice had been sent but now it has been possible for the family of William to get in touch with Henry's family, but sadly, not with the descendants of Alice. There is a report of an Alice of the right age recorded as suffering from consumption but she cannot be traced!

The guardians were still sending orphaned and deserted children in small groups to Samuel Gardner in St John, but sometimes the children had living parents who were just unable to support them. It is hard to imagine how it must feel, as a parent, to sign that piece of paper which takes your precious children away to another country. The workhouse records show how Alice, aged seven, and Florence, aged 11, were being sent to Canada. The girls and their mother Elizabeth, aged 33, had been in the workhouse for two years; the whereabouts of the father was apparently unknown.

Florence and Alice sailed to Canada in March 1899 on the ship *Vancouver* to St John with the Bristol Emigration Society; one of the voyages where a group of children sailed across the sea without an adult. On arrival Alice was sent to an ordinary house in St John and Florence was sent to a large house, on the hill in the best area of St John, both to work as servants. Information received from the granddaughter of Alice revealed that the family who had taken in Florence later moved to the United States, and they had taken her with them

CITY AND COUNTY OF BRISTOL.

GUARDIANS OF THE POOR.

EMIGRATION OF CHILDREN TO CANADA.

NOTICE is hereby given, that the undermentioned Children, now chargeable to the Common Fund of the said City and County, having consented to Emigrate to Canada, an application is proposed to be made to the Justices sitting in Petty Sessions for the said City and County, in pursuance of 13 and 14 Vict., cap. 101, sec. 4, in order that the Children may be so Emigrated, unless objections by their Parents or Relatives are communicated to the undersigned, in writing, before SATURDAY, the 18th April, 1903:—

Small, Henry.	Jones, William.
Davis, John.	Gilbert, Stanley.
Hunter, Albert.	Chaffey, Gertrude.
Smith, Frederick.	Curley, Rose.
Hawker, Frederick.	

By order,   J. J. SIMPSON,
Clerk to the Guardians of the City
and County of Bristol.
St. Peter's Hospital, Bristol, 27th March, 1903.

This notice came from the Avonmouth Advertiser of 1903. All these children were eventually sent to Canada

and her whereabouts were unknown. Alice had married, and brought up her own family and had a good life, so her granddaughter reported. In later life she developed tuberculosis; an examination at that time showed that she must have suffered this illness as a child. Following the records back in Bristol, it seemed that Elizabeth, after signing away her rights to her children, was still living in the workhouse but on going forward another year it was recorded that she had been taken to the asylum. Somehow this does not seem to be a surprising conclusion.

The guardians appeared to be meticulous about ensuring the rules were followed; permission from known parents was sought and a number of such letters have survived among the records. If parents could not be found then the names of the children were printed on posters which were attached to lamp posts or, in later times, printed in the local newspapers. Friends or family were informed that unless objections were received by a certain date then these children would be sent to Canada. Since many people were still illiterate this was only helpful if family or friends could read; but the letter of the law had been upheld.

BRISTOL BOARD OF GUARDIANS RENEW THEIR INTEREST IN CHILD EMIGRATION

Bristol Board of Guardians show no more interest in sending children to Canada in the years following the report of Andrew Doyle in 1876. Nothing is recorded in the correspondence to the Board of Bristol Guardians until 1893 when there was a request from one of the guardians of Barton Regis Workhouse, a Miss Catherine Woollam, who wished to send four boys to Canada. The guardians do not appear to be very pro-emigration and nothing appeared to happen.

An application in 1895 to send a boy called Joseph, (who we are told had no relatives), is rejected as the guardians consider it is the wrong time of year. Then the minutes recorded some information about Annie. Her mother had died but she had a brother, now in Canada, who was sent out from Park Row Industrial School, and she was very anxious to join him. The farmer, who employed the brother David, lent his support to the request but the guardians delayed with a number of questions. Annie had an eyesight problem, but that can be corrected with glasses; then they claim there was some enlargement of her tonsils and anyway the cost of £15 is expensive. Were they just making sure that this would be good for Annie or were they genuinely unsure about the value of emigration? Eventually Annie travelled to Canada in May 1897 with a group of girls from the Emigration Home for Little Girls. The receiving farmer, William Grant, sent a letter giving a good report. Here is one boy who had found a good home with a farmer who was also happy to offer his sister a place. In spite of the concerns of the Bristol guardians, this seemed to be a rewarding placement for these two children.

Catherine Woollam, on Bristol Board of Guardians, had this strong belief that emigration was essential to the future welfare of the children and became very proactive in organising small groups of deserted or orphaned children. She gathered together groups of boys and girls between the ages of nine and 14, and sent them to St John in New Brunswick. As these children would be chargeable to the common fund of Bristol Union, it was essential that the requisite amount of money was in place before the children were allowed to go. The children would arrive at the port where they would be met by Samuel Gardner, Immigration Officer for the Port of St John. He would have places

This is the entrance to the Bristol Workhouse at Stapleton

arranged for them and, with no rest or a chance to acclimatise themselves, the children were sent off to their placements by train or horse and cart. From this time Bristol Board of Guardians sent fairly small groups of children to Canada and most were sent out to Samuel Gardner or, in 1900, to his replacement, James Lantalum. They appeared to have passed the organisation of the journey on to the Bristol Emigration Society who worked through their agent, Margaret Forster.

When the boundary lines of the city of Bristol were expanded in the 1890's the Bristol Board of Guardians was also working with the inmates of the Barton Regis Workhouse and from this point any emigration involved children in both workhouses.

On May 10, 1899, the Local Government Board wrote to the Bristol guardians, yet again, to remind them of the need to send copies of written consent from parents, any known address of parents, and copies of the medical reports. The Local Government Board also formally reminded the guardians that, as a general rule, girls should not be sent to Canada above the age of 10 years, and in no case, unless there are special circumstances, be sent over the age of 12. They asked the board to inform them of any special circumstances, as in the case of two girls being sent out by Miss Woollam. Apparently both were anxious to go. One had a brother who was sent some time ago and neither appeared to have any relatives to take an interest in them. Although it appeared that both Edith and Lily were orphans, there was a note to say that sometimes when parents were traced they raised objections to their children being sent away. This is a comment that does not cause any surprise in the 21st century.

Some pressure to send children did come from the Canadian Government. In 1902 a letter from the Canadian Government outlined the many opportunities available for the children and included a plea for the numbers of emigrants to be increased. In a report released on March 13, 1903, the Committee of Emigration reported that "at no previous time in Canada have there been so many opportunities for absorbing, in so satisfactory a manner, young emigrants". Bristol Board of Guardians considered emigration as one of the best means of providing for orphans or deserted children under the care of the guardians. They underlined the reasonable cost of £15 and hoped the guardians would give the matter careful attention with a view to emigration for such children as are suitable for the purpose.

An interesting letter dated March 2, 1903, pointing out that if the written consent of the mother or the father has been refused then the parents can take action for their child to be returned to them. If the parents obtain a Magistrates Order under sub section 2 of Section 1 of the Poor Law Act of 1899 for the restoration of children or child to him or her, then the child can be brought back to them. I cannot find any examples where this has been successfully used but the law is now supporting those parents who have had their children taken away from them.

On Saturday, November 29, 1902, the Bristol Guardian and Avonmouth Advertiser carried an article on the front page entitled, "Illogical Bristol Guardians". The Bristol Board of Guardians presented two reports at their last meeting; in the first one the committee had considered the application of the Bristol Emigration Society for a donation and had agreed one of five guineas. The second report concluded that the committee found no difficulty placing out girls in suitable service and reported that there was a great demand for

The Bristol Children's Cottage Homes at Downend, Bristol. The homes were established in the early 1900's.

boys in Bristol, both in trades and factories. The writer posed the question that he presumed every sensible Bristol citizen would ask... "Why are we wasting the rate payers money sending our boys and girls to Canada when they could be well suited in the city?" Truly, he wrote, the ways of the Bristol guardians are past finding out.

From about 1883 Bristol guardians began to use boarding out for the children who were living in the workhouse. Arrangements were made for the children to live in private homes in villages away from the city streets; the receiving foster parents were expected to send them to the local school and treat them as family. In the late 1880's they also opened homes in such places as Montpelier and Staple Hill; 10 or 12 children lived in each home and were cared for by a step mother or step father, sometimes both. These children attended the local school. It was not unusual for these children to experience this kind of life for one or two years and then be sent to Canada.

Around 1900 the Bristol guardians decided to build a village near Downend, a country area just outside the city. Houses were built which would accommodate a group of ten or 12 children and, of course their step parents. Even though the Guardians now felt that they were addressing the needs of these children they continued to send small groups to Canada and used the services of the Bristol Emigration Society until 1906. When the society became short of funds they turned to the services offered by the Macpherson family. Louisa Birt, sister to Annie, was now running the Liverpool Emigration

Liverpool Sheltering Home, Myrtle Street, Liverpool

Louisa Birt was the sister and colleague of children's emigration promoter Annie Macpherson. From 1873 to 1915 she was the Superintendent of the Liverpool Sheltering Home.

Home and taking the children to one of their homes in Knowlton. This home was originally an old tavern situated in a remote country village 70 miles south of Montreal. There was no running water, just oil lamps and box fires. By all accounts it was a lonely place. Louisa and Annie converted the tavern into a home for the children themselves, calling it, "their Eastern Townships Home". In 1910 Lilian Birt, daughter of Louisa, took charge of the Liverpool home and Knowlton when her mother retired. Bristol children were sent to Knowlton through the Liverpool home for the next nine years, the last group being sent in 1915.

At last the need and desire for emigration had passed; Bristol communities were now looking out for and caring for these children; the age of the social worker had arrived.

CHILDREN SENT OUT BY THE BOARDS OF GUARDIANS FROM BRISTOL AND BARTON REGIS

Date	Boys	Girls
1888	4	2
1889	11	2
1900	11	2
1901	17	2
1902	9	
1903	11	1
1904	3	1
1905	40	32
1906	3	2
1907	10	1
1908	23	3
1909	16	5
1910	17	4
1911	16	2
1912	1	1
1913	12	2
1914	8	4
1915	9	3

ALFRED BATER

Alfred Bater, pictured below, was sent to Canada on the ship *Texas* on April 21, 1887, having been in the Cumberland Road Home for Boys run by the Bristol guardians. He was one of five children. In May 1879 their mother Elizabeth had died of Cancer. Just one year later, their father John, an excavator who worked on the railway, died in an accident.

All the children were then transferred to Barton Regis Workhouse in Bristol and three – Alfred, Charles and Hannah – were eventually sent to Canada.

Charles settled in Framingham, Massachusetts; he married but had no children. Hannah arrived in St John, married Charlie Miller, who died while still a young man, and as a single mother, spent 40 years in the poor home in St John, New Brunswick. She died in 1942 and is buried in the local cemetery. The rest of the family appear to have stayed in England.

Alfred's great grandson, Jamie, says that Alfred never knew his parents' names and that he just wrote the initials M and F on documents such as his marriage certificate. Jamie says he knows more about Alfred's immediate family than Alfred did, which he finds very sad.

Sadly the three siblings sent to Canada never had any more contact with each other once they had left the workhouse in Bristol. It has now been possible to put the great, great granddaughter of Hannah Bater in touch with the great grandson of Alfred Bater – and they have met and exchanged information.

A family split up by illness at a time when there were no support systems in place.

LIFE IN CANADA
FOR THE CHILDREN

THE CITIZENS OF Victorian Bristol were very aware of the children who lived on the streets of the city in the 19th century; in fact it would have been difficult to ignore them. There was an expectation that the better off citizen would give to help the poor and one way of doing this was to subscribe annually to a good cause. Many of our Victorian ancestors did give support in this way and had the satisfaction of seeing their actions recorded in the annual reports of these institutions; a cynical 21st century person might consider that this was a way to keep the money coming. For the guardians running the workhouses, the superintendents in charge of the industrial schools and reformatories, for the many who were dealing with such large numbers of orphaned and deserted children, they found the answer in emigration.

Individuals took up this work; there was William Quarrier working in Scotland; James Fegan in Kent; John Middlemore with his Emigration Home in Birmingham and Thomas Barnardo, who ran a home in Stepney, London, but gathered in children from all over the country. Women too played their part; Maria Rye and Annie Macpherson bringing children from all over the country to their homes in London before sending them to Canada. All seemed to have undergone a profound religious experience which strengthened their belief in God and left them wanting to do his work.

The idea that they might save the children from the streets, where all that was open to them was starvation and corruption, appealed to these child savers and gave them the compelling need to organise these homes for gathering in the children to send them to Canada. Thomas Barnardo was responsible for sending more children to Canada than any other organisation and although he had a habitation in Bristol during the 1890s, he doesn't seem to have particularly targeted children from Bristol. Although emigration of the Bristol children ceased in 1915, other organisations and individuals continued to send children, the Barnardo organisation sending their last group of children in 1934.

Passages were arranged on ships sailing from various ports: Liverpool, London and Bristol, and children were shipped off to Canada, sometimes in very large numbers. In the early days ships were small, not fitted with stabilisers, and as the children travelled steerage at the very bottom of the ship, they suffered badly from sea sickness. One young lad painted a vivid picture of the journey when he announced, "We sicked all over each other". The Allan Line ships were frequently used and their captains, very aware of the children on board, encouraged the crew to organise games on deck when the weather was good. Many of the children looked back on their journeys as a pleasurable time which might be in contrast with the reception they received in their new homes. It is interesting to hear how the children reacted to their time on board as often the small things stayed in their minds; a girl who loved the food served on the ships, reported, "We had jam on our bread every day!"

The last group of children to be sent by the Bristol Board of Guardians sailed in 1915. Some had parents and, although names are given, information on the whereabouts of the parents is not given. One father had been in the army but did not receive a pension, other parental occupations were given as collier, market gardener and cab driver, but for half of the children, that space was either marked deserted or had been left blank. One set of parents had been imprisoned for neglect and two mothers were resident in the workhouse. These children travelled to the Liverpool receiving home where they joined other groups waiting to be sent to the receiving home in Knowlton in Quebec or Stratford in Ontario. Certainly no more children were sent from Bristol after this time.

LIFE IN CANADA FOR THESE CHILDREN

Most of the Bristol children sent out to Canada over this period of 45 to 50 years were given to farmers as extra labour and expected to work in the house or outside on the farm. The expectation of the people who sent them was

There was so much land. Farms were isolated, the young men of Canada wanted to work in the cities; the children of Great Britain were sent to work on the farms

that the children would become part of the family and be treated as such; the word adoption was used regularly but there were no procedures to ensure this. Most children were used as hired hands or in-house servants. Instead of living in with the family, as expected by the people who sent them, many of the children lived in attics, barns and outhouses. They ate apart from the family and enjoyed none of the comforts of family life. When one summer visitor asked if the girl was going to eat tea with them, the farmer's wife replied, "Oh no, she's only the hired hand!" which seems to sum up the attitude of many Canadians to these children.

Those who sent them expected that the children would go to school with the Canadian children but many were kept back to look after younger children or to finish the chores. Just recently a letter was discovered by a descendant of one British lad, the writer refusing him admittance to the local school because he was not born in Canada. Her comments show that she knew the farmer disagreed with this ruling and did press for the boy to go, but this was unusual. Schools in Canada were one classroom schools with all ages working in one room. The British children were seen as wearing strange clothes; they had

Children living in the countryside would have attended a single class school like this one

funny accents and so stood out as being different. For the British children who were kept at home to finish the chores or look after the younger children there was a lifelong resentment that they missed out on their education.

In those first years, through the early 1870s, the children were often sent out to the less populated areas of Canada and it would be accurate to describe the farmers as working in pioneering times. The land was being farmed for the first time, much of it was stony, covered with bush, and many children found themselves clearing and cleaning land; it would have been hard for a grown man but for these children it was work they couldn't manage. Many found themselves being returned to the agent with an accompanying comment saying "please send me a stronger one" and when passed on to another farmer, then the whole process would start over again. This might happen four or five times until possibly the child had reached the age of 16 and could move about for himself.

Treatment was often harsh and comments from letters received from concerned neighbours, include phrases such as "the man treats his dog better than he treats the boy". Communities were small and people relied on each other for jobs and support; when children were not being treated well or being beaten, the whole community knew and it would often take an important member, perhaps the doctor, who was able to step in to change the situation. There are recorded instances of cruelty which seemed relatively minor but were traumatic for the child; the boy who was given a Christmas stocking as were the rest of the children in the family only to find that his held a rotten potato. It is only as these children get to their 70s and 80s that they have been able to share this type of memory with their families and with other people.

Children died because of the way they were treated. A nine-year-old girl who was put to sleep in the attic froze to death when the temperature plummeted at the beginning of the winter. When asked why he hadn't given her a blanket the farmer seemed bemused and explained that he didn't give his dog a blanket!

There were children who died as a result of beatings and we know of two Bristol boys who committed suicide; Tucker was found hanging from a rope in a barn by his mistress and Ernest when he lost the money to buy a return ticket to take him back to England. Dorothy returned to her family in Bristol while still in her late teens. She was severely traumatised, couldn't settle and eventually committed suicide. Part of a letter survives in the archives; it was written by a spirited girl to her father back in Bristol. She had been put into a home where she was beaten if she didn't get her chores finished; "I was beaten until I was black and blue", she wrote, and complained that her letters sent home had been scrutinised and letters sent by her father were kept back. In another letter she wrote that she was now in a new place where they were treating her well and she was able to write to her father and tell him everything that happened to her because these people don't read her letters. She had written to Maria Rye to ask for a change in place but her letters had not been answered.

Most of the Bristol children found themselves working in farms and houses in the counties of New Brunswick and Nova Scotia with Canadian families descended from pioneer families who had left their homeland seeking a better life. They had made a life for themselves despite the climate and the unforgiving land; and this had made them tough and uncompromising people. They demanded hard work from these children who had survived living on

Farming life in Canada was tough and uncompromising

the streets or growing up with little food or medical care. The children were unable to keep up with the demands of the people who took them in. There is also no doubt that some of the farmers were unkind, hardhearted and thought they could beat what they saw as laziness, out of the children. It is important to point out that any kind of supervision was either spasmodic or didn't exist; the people responsible for placing the children were often unable to oversee the large numbers of children in their care and so assumed they were well treated. Others, such as Maria Rye, left this task to the prominent members of the community failing to understand they might experience divided loyalties.

Unfortunately Maria Rye had written a letter to The Times in the early days of emigration, and had written about the "street arabs" who had been gathered up from the streets of the cities and sent out to Canada, so giving the impression that these were the children Great Britain didn't want. It was also unfortunate that many of the first children who were sent out had not been medically examined and were suffering from many different infections; very few were strong and fit for farm work. Most were suffering from various infections and a large number wet the bed at night. All of this supported the belief that there must be something fundamentally wrong with these children, the suggestion being that they had a deep seated disease or illness which would show itself in time. It gave the wrong impression to many Canadians that these were the children Great Britain didn't want and certainly there were many who did not view them as normal children or children who just needed help and understanding.

If a farmer was lucky enough to have a good strong boy then neighbouring farmers were quite happy to persuade the boy to come to work with them and, of course, offer higher wages. Letters to agents often complained of these back-handed tactics. These were city children who knew little of country life and so imagine the feelings of the boy who had never seen a cow and was told that his job was to milk this cow every day. It took him a week but he learned!

These children had been separated from the families they knew and the places they called home; taken to the land called Canada and most, not all, had been put to work on the farms. It was a very difficult time; the word "uprooted" has been used to describe how it was for them and many lost the memories of their early life in the process. Canadians gave this loss a name, 'absent memories'. A grandson talked of his grandfather who could not form good relationships with his family. William explained that his grandfather had married three times and of all his grandchildren, William was the only one who could reach him. This man, as a young boy, had lost his parents and was sent to Mullers Orphanage in Bristol, but he couldn't stay dry at night so his grandmother, who lived in an almshouse, took him away to get him dry at night but when she returned him to Mullers he reverted to wet beds again. He was then sent to Bristol Workhouse and, in 1888, was put on the ship *Ontario* to go to Canada.

I remember talking with an older woman whose mother had been sent out but returned and took up life again in Britain. Her message was clear; her mother did not know how to be a mother because she had not experienced being mothered. This daughter felt that she also had lost something important because of her mother's enforced emigration.

OPINIONS OF THE BRITISH PEOPLE WERE DIVIDED

A letter sent to The Times newspaper in April 1910, by a Mr Dunlop from

London, explored how a section of the population felt about the poverty being experienced in this country. He saw the extreme poverty as caused entirely by dependent children whose parents cannot afford to, or will not, maintain them properly. The neglected children of this generation are the unemployed or unemployable of the next generation and potential parents of the unemployed of the following generation. He wrote that they put themselves into poverty by begetting more children; he didn't write down any suggestions as to how they might avoid this. Dunlop advocated a policy to seek out the neglected children, take them from their parents and send them to the colonies where they would become self-supporting. He saw the poor law system as supporting this and wrote that this was money well spent.

For many people of this time emigration seemed a sound economic measure; after all the costs of sending a child away compared favourably with the annual costs of keeping a child until the age of 14 or 16 years. They also argued that sending children to Canada would give them a better start in life than if they stayed in this country. This letter was written at a time when the Bristol Board of Guardians still favoured emigration although they were to cease their activities within the next five years.

Other people saw the emigration of children in the light of Britain dumping her unwanted population on Canada. This was detrimental to the interests of both Britain and Canada where there was and still is a strong relationship between the two countries; for Canadians the perception at that time was seeing Britain as the mother country. Sending the children away to another country without family or friends could not possibly support their needs and for some there was the difficulty of distinguishing between the children and slavery transportation.

A report in the Western Daily Press, written after the weekly meeting of the Bristol Poor Law Guardians, drew attention to the fact that the guardians were giving away £5.5.0. to the Bristol Emigration Society, which was experiencing financial difficulties. The guardians gave details of the children who have been taken to Canada by this society. The reporter was incensed by this act of generosity using money intended for work with the poor. He pointed out that plenty of situations can be found in Bristol for both boys and girls; there were situations in trades and factories where there was every opportunity for boys to get into good positions and for girls to be placed in suitable service. He questioned, why send them to Canada or anywhere else, and then draws attention to the poisoning of our race by the free admission of the scum of the continent taking the jobs when in Britain we appear to be making way for them by sending our Bristol lads away.

Children became angry because their parents had given permission for them to be sent to Canada and found it hard to understand that their mothers had little choice in the matter. In the early years letters sent to the children from those families considered unworthy were kept back and letters sent by the children were not delivered. The families thought the children had forgotten them and the children thought their families had deserted them and, of course, neither was true. The agencies who were physically involved in the process of emigration saw their role as removing the children from the undesirable influences of their home life and placing them at a distance from their unworthy relatives who are likely to drag the children down to their level. They are therefore removing them from a position of danger to a more hopeful environment.

SOMETIMES IT WAS JUST BAD LUCK

The story of this Bristol family does show the process of emigration in a more sensitive light. This family lived in Green Street in an area of Bristol called Hotwells; they attended church regularly, having all their children baptised in the local church. In the 1891 census there were eight children in the family followed by the births of Ernest, Walter, Nelson and then James. In 1900 their father, a general labourer, died leaving his wife with a large family of children to support. It was an impossible task, with no possible widow's pension she might try to find a job but even if successful her wages would be about a third of a man's wage and what was she to do about her still small children?

The family was split up through no fault of their own; this was not a bad family, it is just that the wage earner had died. The older children were able to stay with their mother, they could find work as it was usual for 14 year-old children to work at that time but all the younger children were taken into the care of the local Poor Law Guardians. Walter, his older brother Ernest, and younger brother Nelson went into Bristol Workhouse and were adopted by the guardians. After a stay in a children's home they were sent to the Cumberland Boys School, also run by the guardians. In 1904 Walter was sent to Canada, his brothers Nelson and Ernest were also sent. The brothers were split up when they arrived in Canada. All contact with Nelson was lost. He eventually returned to England, but Walter and Ernest kept in touch. Ernest saved hard to buy a return ticket to take him back to England but his money was stolen. He couldn't deal with this and committed suicide in December 1913.

Walter married in 1917 and fathered six children; his granddaughter, Liz, wrote that he was a kind and gentle man and "would give anyone the shirt off his back if asked". Walter did not have an easy time when he arrived; he was put with a man called Ryder who was a bully and a hard taskmaster. (The report received by the guardians read that he was in a good home and although he did not get any wages, he got lots of other things instead.) Walter told his daughter that he was beaten regularly, he slept in the barn and not in the house and there were many evenings when he ate from the pig trough. He ran away once but was caught and whipped when the farmer got him back. The second time he ran away he managed to make it to the next farm about five miles away; the farmer's wife, Annie, brought him into the house, hid him under her skirts and stood at the stove stirring a pot of soup when the farmer came looking for him. Annie said that Walter was holding on to her legs and was shaking so hard that she was surprised that the man Ryder didn't find him. Annie and her husband decided to look after Walter; he lived with them until he married the daughter of a local farmer.

There were children who, being accepted into a Canadian family, enjoyed a happier way of life but for many the change of country and adapting to farm life was very hard. Yet it is important to explain that there were children who adapted to their new life however hard it was for them.

AUTHOR'S NOTE

One of my contacts is Kelly, a very proud great granddaughter who told me the story of her grandfather, Charles Henry, sent out from Bristol in 1881. He had a really hard time at the beginning, being moved from farm to farm and not treated at all well. When he was 16 he decided to start delivering milk to some of the houses in the place where he lived. His initiative grew into a successful dairy business delivering milk products to the whole province. I was able to tell Kelly that Charles Henry had been sent to Park Row Industrial School because he had stolen some books and was therefore seen as a petty thief. He had been sent to Canada by the school, travelling on the ship *Bristol* from Avonmouth; the story he told his family was much more exciting; he had stowed away on a ship and had been discovered halfway across the ocean! Certainly he was a resourceful and interesting boy.

VOLUNTEERS TO FIGHT IN THE 1914-1918 WAR

At the start of the First World War there was an opportunity for Canadians to join the Canadian Expeditionary Force to fight for peace in Europe. Of the first contingent of men who signed up at Valcartier, Quebec, in 1914, two thirds of them were British born and all were volunteers. Many of the British Home Children, now young men, signed up and fought in France and many didn't return. Of the 40 men from Bristol who joined the army and have been identified as being a Home Child, six were killed in action. A memorial plaque was erected on each side of the doorway leading into the Liverpool Emigration Home for Children, situated at 7 Myrtle Street in Liverpool, to commemorate the deaths of the boys who had been sent to Canada from that home.

George Gliddon arrived in Canada on the ship *Corsican* in 1909. He enlisted in 1914 and served in 4th Battalion of the Canadian Expeditionary Force. He died of his wounds February 28, 1916, aged 20 years and was buried in the Bailleul Communal Cemetery in the north of Calais.

Albert Hapgood was enrolled in 87th Overseas Battalion of the Canadian Grenadier Guards and was killed in action May 3, 1917.

Two of those names were boys from Bristol sent to the Liverpool home for shipment to Canada and both worked as farm labourers until they volunteered

This plaque flanking the door of the Liverpool Emigration Home names the children, sent from this home, who were killed in the First World War. At least two of the children named in the plaque came from Bristol; Albert Hapgood and George Gliddon.

to fight and both died at the age of 20. When those still alive returned to Canada, the Government offered to give a piece of land to each man who had fought in the war. Many took up the offer but, as sometimes happens, many did not find out about their Government's generosity until they were older. Copies of letters survive where ex-soldiers write a number of years later to claim their benefits.

Present day Canadians tell of a time when this immigration of thousands of children was never talked about. It was if it was a taboo subject. Descendants of these children did not know about their family background because their Home Child did not talk about it. One grandparent described her feelings, "I felt as if it was my fault, as if I had done something wrong". For some they say they didn't know who they were; they didn't know who their mother and father were; some talk of home sickness and others tell how they cried themselves to sleep. Many children found it difficult to develop relationships and became lonely, rather isolated people; one woman said, "It was as if the Lord had planned it for you before you were born". Sometimes grandparents talked to

Left: The British Home Stamp, released September 1, 2010, by Canada Post to mark British Home Children Day. Right: A badge designed in 1994 by Lizzie Smith of St Jerome, Quebec, whose father was sent through the St George's home in Ottawa. You can see the lion representing the mother country, the industrial towns where they lived and the ship being guided by the star of good hope. Sheaves of corn promise the children will never go hungry again and at the bottom the motto which translates as, "Our hope is in Canada"

their grandchildren and sometimes a father or mother to their child; some wrote journals or wrote their experiences into diaries and when the families read these stories they began to understand what had happened. It was the children and the grandchildren of the British Home Children who became concerned about what had happened to their ancestors, and who published these stories in newspapers and used the television to tell other people. In spite of these efforts made by descendants to tell of the experiences of their ancestors, many Canadians still do not know about this period in the history of their country.

In the summer of 2015, I talked to a group of 30 Canadians in England on a friendship visit, only to find that not one person knew about this immigration of British children into their country.

REUNIONS FOR THE DESCENDANTS

In 1980 George Barrett, a British Home Child, set up reunion meetings for boys and girls who were sent out from the Middlemore homes in Birmingham - the idea being that they might exchange stories of their experiences. They met every year and encouraged more people to join them but they also encouraged the descendants of the Bristol children to come along to tell their stories. Now a reunion is held every year in Frederickton, New Brunswick, and in 2015, 100 people enjoyed a discussion about the British Home Children who signed up to join the Canadian Expeditionary Force in the First World War.

I was able to attend that meeting and met descendants of the children sent out from Bristol all that time ago. This was not my first visit to the reunion of the Middlemore Atlantic Society; my first visit was in 2005 when the general feeling about this emigration was focused on the individual. The feelings being expressed by the group at that time was a grateful thank you for the part that their ancestors had played in the life of the nation of Canada; the Home Children were thanked for their hard work and contribution to Canadian life.

MAKING QUILTS

From very early times Canadians have made quilts, firstly to protect them from the cold winters but latterly because they enjoy this craft and have become very skillful. Descendants of these children design and create squares to feature their ancestor; proudly showing what they have achieved in their lives. All the squares are sewn together to make a quilt which then becomes a powerful record of the lives of these home children.

There is a square in the quilt commemorating the life of William Thorne added by Jocelyn his great granddaughter-in-law. Two boys left Bristol on the ship *Montrose*. They arrived in Montreal on July 10, 1899, and both boys were sent to New Brunswick. Their mother had died and their father had deserted the family. William, aged ten, and Henry, 13, with their small sister, Alice, were put in the charge of the Poor Law Guardians. Jocelyn, writing from Canada, explained that William was her husband's grandfather and tells how he was put with a farmer in Tennants Cove. Jocelyn wanted to share her story about William; this sense of wanting to share is very typical of the descendants.

Looking back over the years, the way in which we relate to our children has changed, not in great leaps but quietly and subtlety. In the past children had been viewed as an economic addition to the family income; bird scarers on the fields, collectors of rats and other unwanted vermin and paid from the village rates. Young boys and girls were apprenticed from the ages of seven and eight and removed from family support and as both sexes reached the age of 14 they were expected to work towards supporting family income; all monies earned

The quilt was made by descendants of the British Home Children in remembrance of their ancestors

went back into family finances.

Traditional family life as enjoyed in the villages was broken up as families moved into the industrial cities looking for work. Families often experienced extreme poverty which led to family break up and children living on the streets. A loss of a parent could not be cushioned by a supporting village family and as the years progressed it must have seemed to some people that, as a country,

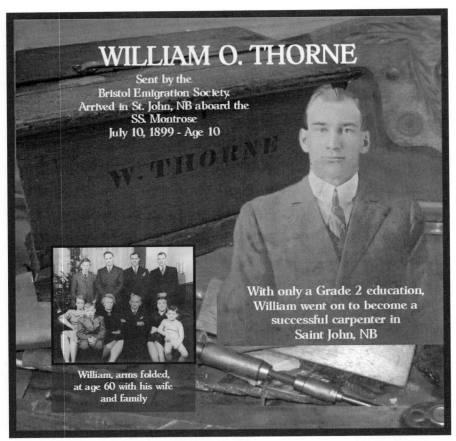

WILLIAM O. THORNE

Sent by the
Bristol Emigration Society.
Arrived in St. John, NB aboard the
SS. Montrose
July 10, 1899 - Age 10

With only a Grade 2 education,
William went on to become a
successful carpenter in
Saint John, NB

William, arms folded,
at age 60 with his wife
and family

One of the squares of the quilt, telling the story of William Thorne, a Bristol pauper child sent to a new life in Canada. The trunk he left Bristol with is shown in the background. It is now in the care of his descendants.

we were not tackling the problems, just patching things up best way we could. Calls for introducing an old age pension had been made for a number of years but wasn't implemented until 1908 and even then it was controversial. If only the Government had seen a way of paying a widows pension to the woman who had lost her man and had been left to support their children; then she might have been able to keep her family together. A man could not earn enough to feed his family because the hourly rate for a working man fluctuated when the economy of the country was suffering from a depression. Maybe an agreement to pay a minimum wage would have made a difference for families? All this was yet to come.

In the summer of 1940, at a time when the German armies had swept through France and there seemed to be a very real danger of invasion, the Children's Overseas Reception Board was organised to evacuate children of five to 16 years and take them to Canada. The children would live with a family until it was judged safe enough for them to return home. Initially 2,664 children were taken until, on September 17, 1940, the ship *Benares* was torpedoed by a German U Boat and 73 children died. No more children were sent after this although children were still sent to Australia, New Zealand and South Africa. This attempt to send children away was put in motion so quickly that little attempt was made to understand the emotional consequences, for the children, of such a long separation from their families. The foster parents came to know the children so well that when the children returned they experienced divided loyalties which, for some, was a gap that could not be bridged.

COMPARISONS WITH TODAY

In this year of 2017, if you walk the streets of the city of Bristol or any city in the United Kingdom, you will not expect to find children living there, bedding down in an alley with the beggars; nor would you expect to see children begging for food or dressed in rags. In the unlikely event that this might happen, then we expect help to be available; the child protected, parents sought and supporting mechanisms set up and hopefully help could be offered with the child's best interests in mind. It is to be hoped that now we understand that children have the right to know their father and mother, even if they cannot live with them. I would hope that we have given them a voice to tell us about what happens to them and, very importantly, we actually listen to them and take them seriously. In 2017 we should be able to offer to children an understanding and proffer solutions that match their needs.

Today it is estimated that 12% of present day Canadians are descended from the British Home Children and represent an important part of Canadian history that is only just recently beginning to be appreciated by fellow Canadians. In the province of Nova Scotia and Ontario, September 28 is being celebrated as British Home Child Day; it is hoped that this will spread throughout the country. This is a part of Canadian history that is slowly being understood as the efforts and achievements of these children are being recognised, their stories are being told and their voices, from down the years, are being heard. The children themselves faced huge challenges as they adapted to life in a new country, they were not always welcomed; some were treated harshly but, in spite of and sometimes because of this, they went on to lead successful lives. Many fought for Canada in the First World War and their families are now proud to call themselves Canadians.

Attempts in 2008 to get Federal support by individuals and groups of descendants of the British Home children failed. On December 7, 2009, a motion to designate September 28 in every year British Home Child Day, across the country of Canada, was passed. Canada Post issued a commemorative stamp marking the special occasion.

AN APOLOGY

On February 24, 2010, the then British Prime Minister, Gordon Brown, made a statement in the House of Commons, Westminster. He described how successive UK Governments had supported child migration schemes of children aged between three and 14, sending them to Australia, Canada, New Zealand, South Africa and Zimbabwe in the hope of giving them a better life. Many were sent without the consent of their parents, some were lied to and told that their parents were dead and were separated from their brothers and sisters. He went on to acknowledge that they were robbed of their childhood and instead of caring for them, our country turned its back and didn't heed their cries for help. This apology received full support from all parties in the House on that day. This followed a year after the Prime Minister of Australia, Kevin Rudd, had made an apology on behalf of the Australian Government for the way in which the British children had been received in their country.

In Canada the reaction to this apology offered by Gordon Brown was very mixed. There were people who celebrated this news, thought it was long overdue but voiced their opinion that they hoped he was apologising to all the children, not just those who were still alive. Others commented that they felt that their home child ancestors would not want this apology; they had come to love Canada and would not want to see themselves as victims. Many people just wanted to ensure that the story of the home children became known so that it could take its place in the history of the country. In 2005 I was invited to attend the annual reunion of the Middlemore children. At this time the general feeling of the people attending that meeting was very similar; they wanted this to be taught in the schools so that all Canadians might learn about the history of their own country. In the prayers at the end of that meeting the children were thanked for the contribution they had made to life in Canada.

In 2016 a strong call came from a huge number of the descendants of the home children for an apology to come from the Canadian Government. On February 16, 2017, a motion was passed unanimously by members of the House of Commons when Luc Theriault called on the house to "recognise the injustice, abuse and suffering endured by the British Home Children, as well as the efforts, participation and contributions of these children and their descendants within the Canadian communities". It is hoped that the Right Honorable Justin Trudeau, Prime Minister of Canada, will eventually put a voice to that apology.

NAMES OF BRISTOL CHILDREN SENT TO CANADA

(Derived from a database constructed by the author.
Unless otherwise stated, dates given are birth dates)

Abrahams, Henry, 15 Jun 1876

Ackland, Louisa, 4 March 1858

Ackland, (Walter) Frederick, 5 October 1859

Albany, Robert, Born abt 1891

Alford, Selina, 25 March 1884

Allen, William, Emigrated 19 May 1873

Allen, William, Born abt 1877

Allen als Burk, John als John Henry, Born abt 1860

Alsopp, Elizabeth, Emigrated 1890

Alsopp, Robert or Thomas , Born 1891 London

Alway, Lily, Born 1889 in London

Alway, Reginald, Born 1896/1897 Bristol

Anderson, Selina, Born abt 1867

Anderson or Henderson, Thomas, Born abt 1887

Andow or Andrew, Robert, Born 13 Jan 1880

Andrew, John, Possible emigration 1879

Andrews, Leslie, Born 25 May 1906 in Ross on Wye

Andrews, George, Emigration about 1870

Andrews, Ernest, Born abt 1886 in Sevenoaks

Andrews, Wm Stephen, Born abt 1861 Bristol

Andrews, Frederick, Born 10 Jan 1870 Bedminster, Bristol.

Andrews, George Edward, Born abt 1860 in Bristol

Aplin or Alpins, Albert, Born

abt 1854

Appleby, Mark, Born 24 June 1861 St James, Bristol

Ashman, Adelaide, Born abt 1877

Ashton, William, 12 Oct 1863

Atkinson, Bertie, 15 Sep 1879

Atwell, Elizabeth, Born 1876

Babb, Ruth, Born abt 1876

Babb, Charles, Born about 1870

Baber , William, 5 Aug 1878

Baggot, Fred, Aged12 years in 1889

Baggs, H, a male, Aged 14 in 1889, born abt 1875

Baggs or Biggs, James, Emigrated in 1862

Bailey, Henry A, Born 1899

Baker, Catherine or Kate, 16 Jun 1882

Baker, Victor Charles, Born 1898

Baker, Walter L, Born 1899

Baker or Baber, William, 5 Aug 1878

Bale, James, Born 31 May 1896

Ball, Mary, Born abt 1865

Ball, John, Born 1870

Ball , Elizabeth, Born abt 1858

Ballinger, James, Born abt 1856 Cheltenham

Ballsom, Ivy Lavinia, Born abt 1894

Balmont, James, Born 1884

Bamber, John, Born abt 1891 14 June 1890 in Bristol

Barclay, Sidney, 19 yrs born 1875

Barkley/Buckley, Emily, Born

abt 1864

Barman, Miriam, Born abt 1884 in Middlesex, London

Barrow, Joseph Henry, 11 Dec 1882

Barry, Ernest, Born 1862

Bartlett, Maud, Born 1894

Bartlett, Victor, Born 1894 in Bristol

Bartlett als Wilkey, Henry, Born abt 1859 in Bristol

Bashford, Albert Edward, Born abt 1885 Newport, Isle of Wight

Bashford, Charlotte, Born abt 1881 Newport, Isle of Wight

Bashford, Rose, Born abt 1888 Newport, Isle of Wight

Bassett, George, Born possibly 1861

Bastaple or Bastiple, Minnie, Born abt 1870 in Bristol

Bater, Charles Elias, Born 7 Green Street,18 Jan 1875

Bater, Alfred, Born Dec 20 1872 born 8 Morgan Court

Bater, Hannah or Annie, Born 1871 in Devon

Battle, Arthur, Born abt 1894

Baxter, John, Born abt 1862

Bayley, Emily, Born abt 1865 Redcliffe, Bristol

Bayley, Hannah, Born 1869 Redcliffe, Bristol

Bayley, Mary Ann, Born abt 1863 Redcliffe, Bristol

Beacham, John , Born 1895

Beachim, William, Born abt 1872

Beacon, A, No information

Beake, Charlie, Born about 1884

Beake or Beak, Annie, Born 24 May 1888 or 20 Jul 1887

Beake or Beak, Lucy, Born 27 July 1889 or 14 Mar 1890

Beal or Bool, Alfred, Born abt 1869

Beckington, Thomas, Born abt 1862

Bedford, Stuart H H V, Born 1899

Beechey, James, Born abt 1860

Beechey, Thomas, Born abt 1858

Beer, John C, Born 1896

Bell, James, Emigrated 1872

Bell, Mary, Talk of return in 1881

Bellringer, Elizabeth, Born 1895

Bellringer, Henry, Born 1895/1896

Belmont, Sarah, Born 1886

Belyea, Albert, No information

Bennett, Mary Ann, Born abt 1861

Bennett, Ellen, Born abt 1859

Bennett, Henry, Born abt 1861

Bennett, Clara, Born abt 1865

Bennett, Samuel, Born 15 March 1877

Bennett, Arthur, Born abt 1881

Bennett, William, Born 1897

Bennett, Fred or Freddie, Born 8/1/1899

Bernadine, William, Born abt 1889

Bernadine, William, 8 September 1892 Bristol

Bernardine, William, Born abt 1887

Berry, Frederick, Born 1906

Berry, William, Born 1907

Best, Frank Burman, Born about 1863 St James, Bristol

Best, William Alvin, Born abt 1860 St James, Bristol

Best als Stradling, John, Born abt 1865

Bevan, James, Born abt 1874

Bidgood, Ernest, Born 25

February 1869

Biggs or Baggs, James, Emigrated in 1862

Bird, George, Born abt 1860

Bird, William, Born 1899

Bird/Medlyn, John (Fred J), Born 1900

Birke or Birks, John, Born abt 1879

Blackman, Arthur, Born abt 1896

Blackmore, Walter, Emigrated 1895, d of b 27 Feb only

Blurton, Charles, Born abt 1868

Bobbett, Mary Ann, Born abt 1864

Bodley, Henry Francis/Thomas, Born abt 1861

Bond, Emma, No information

Bond, Wilfred, Born 1899

Bool or Beal, Alfred, Emigrated 1883 aged 14

Boon, Frederick, Emigrated 1869?

Bowden, Walter, Emigrated 1902

Bowditch, Henry or Harry, 18 Feb 1889

Bowditch, Henry or Harry, Emigrated 1897

Bowhey, Harriet, 11 Jul 1887

Bowhey, Elizabeth, Born abt 1864

Boyce, Mary, Born abt 1862

Boyce, Albert, Born 1899

Brace, Charles Henry, Born 1894

Brace, Henry, 15 Oct 1875

Bracey, William (George), Born June 1879

Brackett, Elizabeth, Born abt 1859

Bragg, Alfred, Born 1900

Brantz, Henry, Born 15 October 1875

Breen or Van Breen, Henry, Born abt 1862 Plymouth, Devon

Breen or Van Breen, Leslie May/Lena Helena, Born 10 August 1901

Breillat, Lena, Born 10 August 1901

Breillat, Louisa, Born abt 1857

Bretnell or Britnell, Phillip, Born abt 1859

Brewer, Alice, 3 Oct 1899

Brewer, Jessie, Born 6 April 1894

Brick, Esther, Born 1892

Bridges, Eliza, Born abt 1870

Brierley, James, Born abt 1874 in Bristol

Brighton, Sarah, Emigration 1870

Brinkworth, Alan or Alexander, 6 November 1870

Britnell or Bretnell, William, Possible emigration in 1880

Brittan, Alice, 3 Oct 1899

Britton, Mary Ann, Born 1890

Britton, Alice, Born 1894

Britton, Edward, Born abt 1885 Gloucester

Britton, James, Born abt 1888 Sevenoaks

Britton or Britten, William, Born abt 1892

Brock, Alfred (Leslie), Born 16 August 1893 Sevenoaks

Bromfield, Henry, Born abt 1889

Brook or Brooks, Arthur, Born 1896/1897

Brooke, William, Born 29th Sep 1883 Scarborough

Brooks, James, Born abt 1858

Brooks, J male, Born abt 1868

Brooks, Edwin, Born abt 1869

Brooks, Fred J, Born 8 November 1902

Broom, Fred J, Born 8 November 1902

Broome, George Bowden, 8 June 1891

Brown, William, Born abt 1874

Brown, Joseph, Born abt 1880

Brown, Alfred, Born abt 1884

Brown, Thomas, Aged 14 at emigration possibly 1897

Brown, Elizabeth, Born 1858

Brown, George, Born abt 1858

Brown, Daniel, Born 30 May

1870 8 Vickerys Building

Brunnel, Henry J, 16 June 1877

Bryant, Charles, Born abt 1874

Bryant, William, Born abt 1881

Bryant, John Henry, Born abt 1860

Bryant , Rose, Born abt 1870 in Bristol

Buck, William H , Born abt 1875

Buck , William Frank, Born 26 Sep 1887 Marylebone London

Buckingham, Frank, Born abt 1870

Bull/Buckingham, Eliza, No information

Bull, Albert, Born 17 May 1903

Bullock, Albert, Born 17 May 1903

Bullock, Isabella, Born abt 1882

Bullock, George Alfred, Born 3rd quarter 1882

Bullock, William, Born abt 1885

Bullock, Elijah, Born abt 1880

Bunell, Joseph, Born 15 August 1885 or 1883 Bristol

Bunnell or Burnell, Bertie, Born 1898

Bunock, Charles, Born 25 Aug 1873

Bunock, Elijah, Born abt 1881

Burbridge, George, 12 in 1894 Born abt 1882

Burge, Arthur, Born 10 Mar 1877

Burge, Alfred Ivor, Born in Bristol 1911

Burk als Allen, John William, Born 9 Nov 1882

Burke, John als John Henry, Born abt 1860

Burke, Mary, Born abt 1861

Burke, Jane, Born abt 1859

Burnell, John, Born abt 1893

Burnell or Bunnell, Alfred, Born 1900

Burnett, Charles, Born 25 Aug 1873

Burnett, Fred Charles/George, 10 Nov 1888 Bristol

Burns, W, Born abt 1887

Burns, Mary, Born abt 1860

Burns or Burrs or Burris, Sarah, Born abt 1862

Burroughs, Wm, Born abt 1882

Bush, Edward, Born abt 1862

Bush, Frank, Born abt 1866

Busker, Henry, Born 16 December 1864

Butland, Louis, Born abt 1875

Butler, Ellen R, Born 1901

Butler, Caroline, Born abt 1884 Bristol,

Butt, Luigi or Herbert K, Born abt 1886 Bristol

Butt, Lilian, Born abt 1879

Byford, Margaret, Born abt 1867

C, William, Born abt 1864

Caines, George, Born abt 1876

Callacot, William, Emigration took place 1875

Calthorpe, Sydney, Born abt 1889 Gillingham, Kent

Campbell, Francis, Born abt 1870

Cantello, Mary Ann, Born abt 1859

Cantello, William, Born 1896

Canton, William Henry, Born 1897

Canton, Frederick, Born abt 1885

Capp, William, Born abt 1879 St Philip and Jacob

Carloss, Henry, Born abt 1861

Carloss, Alfred, Born abt 1870

Carloss, Richard Insall, Born abt 1873 or 9 Sep 1875

Carpenter, Arthur Richard, Born abt 1871

Carpenter, George Alfred Isaac , Born abt 1858 Bristol

Carr, Morley, Born 28 May 1867

Carroll, William, Born 22 Jun 1878

Cautcher, George, Born 29 Apr 1880

Cavill, Clare, Born abt 1878

Cawley, Florence, Born abt 1890

Chadwick, William, Born 1872 or 1873

Chaffey, Frederick, Born abt 1870

Chaffey, Gertrude Florence, Born 1892

Chapman, William, Born 1898

Chapman, Florence, Born abt 1899

Chapman, Louisa or Louise Lilian, Born abt 1896

Chapman, Winifred, Born abt 1894

Chapman, Edward, Born abt 1870

Chapman or Williams, Frederick, Born 11 Jan 1879

Chappell, Fred/Mitchell/Moore, Born 19 April 1881

Chapple, William, Born abt 1870

Chew, Joseph, Emigrated in 1870

Chick, Daniel, Born abt 1870

Chilcott, Philip, Born 29 July 1877

Chillcott, William Thomas, Born 1896

Chivers, William T, Born 1896

Chivers, Edith Maud, Born abt 1893 in Bristol

Chivers, Lily A , Born 15/6/1897

Chudleigh, Samuel, Born 1896

Clancy, Albert, Born abt 1859

Clanfield, John, Born abt 1869

Claridge, E, Emigrated in 1883

Claridge, Adeline, Born 1896

Clark, Adeline, Born 1896/1897

Clark, Jessie, Born abt 1880

Clark , Ernest, Born 1864

Clarke, Arthur, Emigrated 1899

Clawson als Parker, Hector, Born abt 1889

Cleale, Alfred, Born abt 1875

Clements, John, Born 4 October 1878

Cleveland, William, Born 9 Aug 1870 Bristol

Clevely, Charles, Emigration 1871

Clifford, James, Born 16 Oct 1869 Bedminster

Coakley, Samuel, Emigration 1880

Coakley, Mary, Born abt 1858

Cobb, Sarah, Born abt 1858

Cockin, Charles, Born on 22 October 1870

Cockram, Thomas, Born abt 1869

Cockran, Emily, Born abt 1872

Cogan, Frank, Born abt 1859

Cole, William Charles/Walter, Born abt 1891

Coleborne, Elizabeth Annie, Born abt 1869 London Middlesex

Coleborne, Dorothy, Born 2 August 1895

Coleman, Lucy M, Born 6 December 1892

Coles, Frederick W, Born about 1870

Coles, Herbert, Born 1890 Bristol

Coles, Charles, Born abt 1892

Coles, James, Born abt 1859 Taunton, Somerset

Coles, Thomas, Born 26 February 1902

Collingbourne, George Edwin, Born 8 March 1897

Collins, Frederick, Born 22 Feb 1880

Collins , Sidney, Born 8 Feb 1870 Bristol

Comley, Henry C, Born abt 1868

Connor, John, Born abt 1877

Connor, Ellen, Born abt 1855

Coode, Frederick, Born abt 1882

Cook, Edwin, Emigration 1870

Cook, Mary Ann, Born abt 1855

Cooper, William George, Born 1 Jan 1870 Bedminster, Bristol

Cooper, Marion, Emigration 1892

Cooper, William George, Born abt 1869

Cooper, Frederick, Born 27 Aug 1887

Corbett, Percival R D, Born 1898

Cornish, Frank, Born abt 1867

Cornock, Edith, Born abt 1879

Cornock, Herbert, Born abt 1891

Coster, William, Born abt 1887

Cotten, Nathan, Born 20 Nov 1862

Cottle, Frank, Born abt 1887

Cotton, Frederick, Born abt 1860 Bristol

Cotton, John, Born 19 or 29 January 1883

Cottrell, Rhoda, Born 10 December 1884

Cottrell, Susan, Born abt 1854

Coward, Bessie, Born abt 1858

Cox, G M, Aged 18? in 1891

Cox, George S, Born abt 1863

Cox, Edwin, Emigration in 1874

Cox, Edward, Born abt 1859

Craddock, Herbert, Born 1896

Craddock, Bertha, Born abt 1874

Crane, Caroline or Carrie, Born abt 1876

Crane, Robert, Born abt 1873

Crees, Annie, Born abt 1876

Criddle, Edward, Born 7 July 1870

Critchley, Richard, Born abt 1890

Critchley, James, Born abt 1885

Croker, Sam, Born abt 1896

Crook, John, Born abt July 1871

Crutcher, Lucy, Born abt 1884?

Crutcher, Thomas, Born abt 1879

Curley, Clara, Born abt 1878

Curley, Frank (Francis), Born 1895 (7 June 1892) Bristol

Curley, William, Born 1 Jan 1889 (June 1889)

Curley, John, Born 16 Dec 1887

Curtis, Rose, Born abt 1890 Bristol

Curtis, Frederick, Born 03 Jul 1887

Cuzner, Joseph, Born abt 1865

Cuzzins, Alfred, Emigration took place 1875

Dale, Mary, Aged 8 years by 15 December 1893

Dale, John George, Born abt 1852

Dale, James, Born 1878

Davidson, William, Born 1880

Davies, John George, Born 9 Nov 1876

Davies, Henry J, Born abt 1892

Davies, William, Born abt 1893

Davies, Margaret, Born abt 1870

Davies, Emily, Born abt 1890 Bristol

Davies, James, Born abt 1899

Davies, James, Born abt 1883

Davis, William Peter, Born 1901

Davis, Ann, Born abt 1857

Davis, Albert, Born abt 1858

Davis, Frederick William, Born abt 1861

Davis, John, 1871 year of emigration

Davis, Charles, Year of emigration 1872

Davis, William, Born 8 July 1883 Weston super Mare

Davis, Annie, Born abt 1886

Davis, Issac, Born abt 1859 Liverpool

Davis, Charles, Born abt 1862 Bristol

Davis, George, Born abt 10 July 1873

Davis, George, Born abt 1894 Ross, Hereford

Davis or Davies, Henry John, Born abt 1892

Day, James, Born abt 1888

Day, John Henry, Born abt 1892 (20 June 1895 Bristol

Deacon, Arthur, Aged 11 in September 1882

Deacon, Albert, Emigration 1877

Dellmer or Zellmer, Absalom, Aged 20 years in 1902

Denman, Frederick, Born about 1862

Dennis, Thomas, Born abt 1858 Bridgewater

Dennis, George Thorne/Tom, 10 Jan 1880

Derrick, Thomas, Born abt 1876

Derrick, Ernest, Born abt 1880

Derrick, Richard, Born abt 1878

Derrick, Thomas, Born abt 1876

Derrick , R, Born 1878

Derrick , Charles James, Born abt 1883 (15 Dec 1889) Bristol

Derritt, Edmund John / Edward, Born abt 1886 (21 Dec 1891) Bristol

Derritt, George, Born 21 September 1886 Bristol

Derrousier, Emily Sarah, Born 25 September 1882 Bristol

Devine, J, Year of emigration 1880

Dew possibly Dean , Louis, Born abt 1887

Dick, Rosina, Born abt 1863

Dolman, Philip, Born 29 Jul 1877

Donelan, William, Born abt 1861 Walsall, Stafford

Dowling, Patrick, Born abt 1894

Dowsell, Samuel, Born 14 Jul 1863

Drinkwater, Henry, Born 2 April 1875

Drinkwater, Minnie, Born abt 1881

Drinkwater , H male, Born abt 1880

Driscoll, E male, Born abt 1875

Duddridge, James, Born abt 1861

Duddridge, Gertrude, Born abt 1887

Duddridge, Thomas, Born abt 1885

Duddridge, Alice, Emigration took place 1892

Dwyer, Lily, Emigration took place 1892

Dyer, Annie, Born 1883

Dyer, George, Emigration took place 1871

Dyer, Annie, Born abt 1882

Eager, George, Born 23 Dec 1884

Eaghton, Alice, Aged 9 or 12 years at emigration 1894

Eagleston, G, Emigration took place 1892

Eaves, Ruby V, Born abt 1885 in London, Middlesex

Edgeland, Kathleen, Born 1901

Edwards, Annie, Born abt 1893

Edwards, James Brown, Born abt 1883

Edwards, George B, Born abt 1888

Edwards, Herbert, Born abt 1887 Fulton, Somerset

Edwards, Emily, Born 1879

Edwards, Ellen, Born 1876

Edwards, Alice, Born 1882

Edwards, Annie, Born 1869

Edwards, Emily, Born 1884

Edwins, Mabel, Born 1885

Eldridge, G, Born abt 1874

Embro, Herbert, Born abt 1886

Emery, Eliza, Emigration took place 1873

Emery, Thos, Born abt 1882

Emery, William, Born abt 1883

English, Eliza, Born 1879

Enwright or Enright, John, Born abt 1873

Essex, Thomas, Born 3 Jul 1885

Evans, William, Possible emigration 1871 or 1866/7

Evans, Matilda Elizabeth, Born abt 1900

Evans, Thomas, Emigration took place 1873

Evans , Albert, Born abt 1859 Dursley, Gloucestershire

Evans , James John, Born abt 1859

Evis, John or James, Born abt 1859

Fackrell, Alfred, Born abt 1860 St Paul, Exeter

Faussett, Edward, Born 1 Sep 1884

Fear or Owen or Hitchins, Edward, Born 9 Nov 1868

Fedkin, Lily, Born abt 1896

Feltham, Emily, Born abt 1876

Feltham, Henry Reginald / Harry, Born abt 1892

Feltham, Ellen Amelia , Born abt 1891

Feltham, Alfred, Born 1895

Few, Alfred, Born 1892

Fisher, James, Born abt 1864

Fisher, Anne, Born abt 1864

Fisher, Alice, Born abt 1861

Fletcher, Martha, Born abt 1859

Fletcher, Hannah Maud or Maud, Born abt 1895

Flower, Agnes Gertrude , Born abt 1894

Flowerday, William, 17 years

Flowers, Minnie Florence, Born 1894 Bristol

Flowers, Dorcas, Born February 1877

Flynn, William Charles, Born abt 1870

Forrester, William, Born abt 1889

Fortune, Emily, Born January 1866

Fowler, Lionel, Born 20 Mar 1881

Fowler, Elsie May, Born abt 1892

Fowler, William Bert, Born abt 1895 (9 July 1895) London

Fowler, John, Born abt 1861

Fowler, William, Born abt 1859 Bristol

Foxon alias Kenzie, William, Born 1894/1895

Francis, Mark, Born abt 1879

Francombe, Harry or Henry, Born 14/11/1894

Francombe, George, Born Feb 1871 St Jude, Bristol

Francombe, Joseph, Born 7 March 1877

Francombe, Henry, Born March 1873

Frodsham, William, Born abt 1877

Frodsham, John, Born abt 1861 Scotland

Fry, Thomas, Born 1 Aug 1865 St Pauls, Bristol

Fry, Benjamin, Possible age 18
at emigration in 1886
Fry, Benjamin, Born abt 1869
Gage, Daisy, Born abt 1887
Gage, Leon, Born abt 1873
Gage, George William, Born
1896
Gale, Charlotte E, Born 1899
Galley, Robert, Born abt 1858
Galliford, Kate Rebecca, Born
abt 1886
Gally/Gully, Charles, Born 30
June 1862 Cardiff
Galvin, Kate, Born abt 1888
Garbutt, John, Born abt 1864
Garland, Martha, Born 9 Dec
1885
Garland, Georgina, Born abt
1862
Garland, Susan, Born abt 1857
Garrod/Garred, William, Born
abt 1860
Gazzard, Percy Philip, Born 11
Nov 1893
Geake, Henry, Born abt 1892
Gee , William, Born 31 Aug
1879
George, Daisy, Born 6 May
1890
Gibb or Gibbs, William, Born
19 May 1873
Gibbons, Jesse, Born abt 1888
Gibbons, Amy, Born abt 1880
Gibbons, Edith, Born abt 1877?
Gibbs, Seward, Born abt 1882
Gibbs , Major, Emigrated at 16
years, no date
Gibson, Jessie, Emigrated 1901
Gilbert, John, Emigrated 1872
Gilbert, Grantley, Born abt
1895
Gilbert also Gilbertson,
George, Born abt 1861
Gilbert also Gilbertson,
Stanley Alfred, Born abt 1892
(20 Dec 1893) Bristol
Gillard, Lilly, Born abt 1890
Gillard, Thomas Henry, Born
abt 1888 (19 Sep 1892)
Bristol
Gillard, Florence G, Born 1897
Gillard, John William, Born

1895
Gilvear, Thomas Edward, Born
1900
Gilvear, Elizabeth, Born abt
1894 Bristol
Gingell, George (William),
Born 5 Feb 1890 St Philips/
St George
Gingell, Emma, Born abt 1868
Glascock, George, Emigration
took place 1885
Gliddon, Sarah A, Born abt
1865
Gliddon, Frederick G, Born
1896
Gliddon, Ernest, Born 1894
Godwin, Sidney J, Born 1898
Good , Alfred, Born abt 1865
Good or Goode, Alice, Possibly
born 1878
Goodyear, William, Born abt
1871
Gough, Francis, Emigration
1875
Gould , John, Born abt 1862
Goulstone, Florence, Born abt
1880
Graham, Arthur, Emigration
1885
Grant, Ernest, Born 15
September 1874 Portsmouth
Grant, Richard or William,
Born 14 June 1876
Grant, Sidney, Born 1901
Granville, Sidney, Born 1901
Greathead, J J, Emigration
took place 1872
Green, Emma, Born abt 1863
Green, Florie, Emigration took
place in 1892
Green, Maria, Born abt 1859
Green, Alfred, Born abt 1864
Green, Walter, Born abt 1864
Green, , Born abt 1861
Green, David, Born abt 1863
Green, Joseph, Born 16 Feb
1869 St Philips, Bristol
Greenaway, Thomas Richard
, Born 27 September 1876
Greenland, Louisa, Born abt
1896
Grenville, Maria, Born abt 1867

Grenville, George, 1871 year of
emigration
Grey, William, 1871 year of
emigration
Gribble/Gubble, Charles, Born
10 Dec 1867 St George, Glos
Griffiths, Robert, Born abt
1862
Griffiths, William, Born abt
1864
Griffiths, William, Born abt
1863
Guxton/Grexton, William, Born
23 May 1879
Hackitt, Robert, Born abt 1861
Hale, Mary Ann, 1889 year of
emigration
Hale, James, Born abt 1897
Hale, John William, Born 1
November 1865
Hale, Henry, 1885 year of
emigration
Hall, W or A, Year of
emigration 1892
Hall, Rosina, Born abt 1880
Hames, George Frederick,
Born 21 Jul 1878
Hammond, Ellen, Born abt
1882
Hammond, Albert, Born abt
1869
Hancock, James, Born abt
1868
Hands, Emily, 1892 year of
emigration
Handy, James, Born abt 1875
Handy, John, 1870 year of
emigration
Hapgood, Samuel, Born abt
1881
Harding, Albert, Born 1899
Harding, Annie, Born
September 1878
Harfon/Harpur, William Alfred,
Born 1901
Hargarve/Hargrave, S A, Year
of emigration 1889
Harman, Louisa, Born abt 1860
Harmon, Philip, Born abt 1869
Harper, Agnes, Born
December 1868
Harper, Sarah, Born May 1875

Harper, Alfred, Born 23 Jul 1867 Baptist Mills, Bristol

Harpur or Harfon, John, Born 4 Dec 1871

Harrington, S A, Year of emigration 1889

Harris, Thomas, Born abt 1864

Harris, Henry George, Born abt 1887

Harris, Francis, Born abt 1892

Harris, Eliza, Born April 1866

Harris, G, 1889 year of emigration

Harris, Frank, Admitted to school 1869

Harris als Kinnersley, (Frederick) Charles, Born 24 Oct 1880 (2 June 1882) Bristol

Harrison, Henry George, Born abt 1887

Hartley, George, Born abt 1865

Havill, Richard, Born Jan 1871 Scotland

Havill, Emily, Born 5 Oct 1883

Havill, Mabel, Born 12 May 1889

Hawker, Florence, Born 3 May 1887

Hawkins, Fred, Born abt 1890

Hawkins, William, Born abt 1877

Hayes, Henry Charles, 1897 year of emigration

Hayes, Annie, Born abt 1885

Hayes, Mary Jane, Born abt 1858

Hayle, Dennis, Born 1847 in Cork, Ireland

Haynes, Issac, Born abt 1880

Haynes, Mary Jane, Born abt 1858

Hayward, Joseph/ Fred?, Born abt 1867

Hazell, William, Born 1896

Hazle, James, Born 1901

Headford, William, Born abt 1856

Headford, Lydia, Born abt 1895

Heale als Williams, Eliza, Born 1900

Healey, John William, Born 1 Nov 1865

Hearley or Hurley, John, Born 25 Oct 1876

Helveit, William Sidney, Born 12/11/1898

Hembrow, Florence, 1889 year of emigration

Hemmings, Henry, Born 30 October 1882

Henbury, Alfred, Born in 1892 (22 Jul 1893) Bristol

Henderson or Anderson, Florence/Flori/Flossie, Born abt 1887 Bristol

Hendy, Thomas, Born abt 1887

Hendy, Charles, Born 15 Apr 1877

Hendy, Samuel, Born 6 Oct 1880

Hendy, Bertram, Born 15 November 1903

Hendy, Charles, Born 6 January 1905

Hendy, Bertram, Born 15 November 1903

Hendy, Charles, Born 6 January 1905

Hendy or Hardy, Reginald, Born 1901

Hendy or Hembury, Charles, Born 15 Apr 1877

Hennessy, Helen, Born abt 1884 Bristol

Herbert, Bryan, Born abt 1878

Herbert, Henry, Born 15 Aug 1872

Herbert, C or T, Born abt 1875

Herman, T, Born abt 1873

Hewett, Charles, Born abt 1859

Hewlett, Charles, Born January 1873 Peckham, London

Hibbert, John, Born abt 1871

Hickman, Henry or Hy, Born 15 August 1878

Hicks, Arthur Henry, Born 1897

Higgins, Francis Sidney, Born 28 Jul 1879

Hill or Hills, Susan, Born 1 Mar 1885

Hillier, George W., Born abt 1886

Hillman/Hellman, Charles, Born November 1872

Hillman/Hellman, Charles, Born abt 1856

Hillman/Hellman, Frederick, Born abt 1858

Hiscox, William, Born abt 1858

Hitchings, S, Year of emigration 1875

Hitchins or Owen or Fear, James, Born 7 January 1879 Bristol

Hobbs, Lily, Born abt 1896

Hobbs, Lizzie, Born abt 1867

Hobbs, Mary Ann, Born abt 1870

Hobday, William, Born 15 Jan 1871

Hocking, Claude, Born 1 July 1870 Paddington

Hockley, Mary, Born in January 1877

Hodges, Sidney George , Born 29 May 1878

Hodges, William Isaac, Born abt 1880

Hodgetts, Frederick or Henry, Born 3 May 1876

Hodgetts, Maye T, Born 1902

Hodgson, Joseph, Born 10/5/1900

Holbrook, Fred, Born abt 1873

Holbrook, Annie Angelina, Born abt 1869 Bristol

Holcombe, Thomas, Born abt 1870

Holcombe, Mary Ann, 1897 year of emigration

Holcombe, Leslie Harold, Born 9 February 1904

Holder, Leslie Harold, Born 9 February 1904

Holdsworth, Samuel, Born abt 1863

Holdsworth, Ada, Born April 1868

Hole or Hold, Henry, Born 11 Mar 1863

Holland, Ada Amelia, Year of emigration 1892

Holloway, George, Born Aug 1868 St Philips, Bristol

Holly, William, Year of
emigration 1894

Hollywood, Albert, 8 yrs old in
May 1872

Holmes, Benjamin James,
Born 7 Jan 1869 Ireland

Holtham , Jane, Year of
emigration 1891

Honeybone, Joseph Frank,
Born abt 1890

Hope, Ellen, Born abt 1881

Hope, Annie , Born 2 April
1900

Hope, Charles, Born 22 August
1903

Hope, Elsie, Born 9 December
1901

Hope, Charles, Born 22 August
1903

Hope, Elsie, Born 9 December
1901

Hopkins, Annie , Born 2 April
1900

Hopkins, Henry James, Born
24 Mar 1876

Horton, Robert, Born
December 1873

Horton, Herbert or Henry,
Born December 1880

Howill, Thomas, Born 14 Nov
1878

Howill , Mabel, Born 12 May
1889

Howlett, Florence, Born 3 May
1887

Howse, John, Bristol

Hudd, Alice, Born abt 1864

Hughes, Leslie C, Born 1897

Hughes, Bessie, Born abt 1885

Hughes, Olive, Born abt 1885

Humphreys, Margaret Jane,
Year of emigration 1890

Humphries, Ellen R, Born 1901

Humphries, Ada, Born abt
1878

Humphries, William, Born abt
1880

Humphries, George, Born abt
1884

Humphries, Frank or Francis,
Born abt 1861

Hunt, William, Born abt 1861

Hunter, Matilda, Born abt 1861

Hunter, Florence, Born about
1891

Hunter, Alfred, Born abt 1893
Bristol

Hunter , Edith, Born June 1896

Hurley/Hindley, Lily, Born abt
1895

Huxtable, James, Born abt
1856

Jacques, James, Year of
emigration 1888

James, Arthur, Born abt 1883

James, John, Born abt 1830

James, Betty, Born abt 1882

James, Lily, Born August 1881

Jefferies, John Thomas , Born
19 Mar 1884

Jefferies, William, Born abt
1861

Jeffreys, Edwin, Year of
emigration possibly 1877

Jenkins, Lily, Born abt 1883

Jenkins, Ivor, Born 1891 at
Bristol

Jenkins, Ernest (James), Born
7 Oct 1893 Bristol

Jenkins, Minnie Kate, Born abt
1895 Bristol

Jenkins, William, Born 1898

Jennings, William, Born 1898

Jocelyn, Laura, Born abt 1891
Bristol

Jocelyn, Jane, Born 17 May
1885

Johns, Albert George, Born 6
July 1890 or 1891

Johns als Waygood, Henry,
Born 18 Jun 1865

Johnson, William, Born 2 Feb
1871

Johnson, Jane, Date of
emigartion 1891

Johnson, Charles, Born 6 Jul
1866

Johnson, Alfred, Born 10
November 1878

Jones, Ernest, Born 15 Jul 1883

Jones, Robert, Born 28 July
1892

Jones, Percival, Born abt 1883
Bristol

Jones, Teresa, Born abt 1892

Jones, Albert Philip Arthur,
Born 16 February 1897 4
William Street

Jones, Mary Jane, Born abt
1889

Jones, George, Born abt 1892

Jones, Florence, Born June
1897

Jones, Frederick, Born abt
1892 Weston Super Mare

Jones, Joseph James, Born abt
1858 Cardiff, South Wales

Jones, William, Year of
emigration 1862

Jones, David, Year of
emigration 1869

Jones, Robert, Born abt 1887

Jones, Henry John, Born 12
March 1873

Jones, Robert, Born abt 1892

Jones, Ernest, Born abt 1874

Jones, Henry, Aged 12 years
when emigrated

Jones, William, Born 1904

Jones, Alec Hubert, Born 1902

Jones, John Watts, Born 1899

Jones, Henry, Born 1897

Jones, William, Born 1880

Jordan, Henry, Born 1878

Jukes, Joseph, Born abt 1870

Kathroe Kithroe, James, Year
of emigration 1878

Keating, Mary, Born 1860 (BHC
website)

Keating, John, Born 1893

Keating, Fanny, Born abt 1888
Bristol

Keating, Edward (Arthur),
Born 1895 Weston super
Mare

Keating, Emily, Born 1894

Keen, Nellie, Born 1891

Keen or Ware, George, Born
September 1961

Kegan, Herbert, Year of
emigration 1891

Kegan or Keynes, Edith, Born
abt 1885

Keil, Josephine, Year of
emigration 1891

Keil, George, Born abt 1879

Kelly, William, Born abt 1882

Kempsford, Daisy, Born abt 1888 at St Gabriels Easton

Kempsford, Arthur, 16 years born 1870

Kennedy, Edward, 16 Feb 1867

Kenny, Peter, 16 Years no year of emigration

Kent, Albert Edward, 26 Jan 1892 Cork, Ireland

Kenzie als Foxon, Albert James, Born abt 1890 (15 May 1882?) Bristol

Kessel, Mark, Born abt 1879

Keynes or Kegan, John, Born abt 1882

Kilminster, Josephine, Year of emigration 1891

Kimford, Sidney, Born abt 1896

King, A, Born abt 1871

King, Lily, Born abt 1885

King, Walter, Born 1863 or 1859

King, Ernest, Born 28 Nov 1886

King, Albert, Born abt 1884 Bristol

King, Rose, Born abt 1868

King, Charles, 23 February 1872

King, William, Born abt 1872

King, Edgar Wm, Born abt 1891 Bristol

Kingdom, Lily , Born 1878

Kinnersley or Harris, Thomas Charles, Born 1899

Kithroe or Kathroe, Henry George, Born abt 1887

Knapp, Mary, Born 1860 (BHC website)

Knapp, Ada, Born abt 1877

Knapp, Florence, Born abt 1878

Knight, William, Born abt 1880

Lacey, E possibly Elizabeth, Born abt 1889

Lacey, Millicent Maud, Born 1 Aug 1892

Lampen/Lampion, Thomas, Born abt 1890

Lampin or Lampen, James, Born abt 1857 Cardiff

Landcastle, Charlotte, Born abt 1860

Lane, Joseph, Year of

emigration 1873

Lansdown, Francis Ball, Born 1857 (BHC website)

Lansdown , Lilian Gladys, Born 16 July 1891or 21 Nov 1891

Larcombe, Emily Rose, Born 10 March 1889 or 24 Jun 1890

Larcombe, Florence, Born March 1875

Laverton, James or John, Year of emigration 1869

Leachley/Gardiner, Edward, Born 10 Jun 1884 Melksham WH

Leachley/Gardiner, Mary, Born 1898

Leader, Albert, Born 1899

Leader, James, Year of emigration 1880

Leader, Alfred, Born 11 August 1873

Leader, Elizabeth, Born 1901

Leader , Susan, Born February 1899

Leavey, Thomas, Born 14 February 1875

Leaworthy or Seaworthy, Albert E, Year of emigration 1898

Lee, Albert, 6 Aug 81

Lee, Harold Bertie, Born abt 1894

Lees, Frank Robert, Born 7 Aug 1886

Leonard, Frank Robert, Born abt 1890

Leonard, Charles, Born abt 1867

Leonard, Albert or Alfred, Born abt 1858

Leonard, Samuel, Born 1864 or 1862

Leverin, Lucy, Born abt 1890

Lewis, Joseph Brieiting, Emigrated 1894

Lewis, James, Born abt 1884

Lewis, Samuel, Born abt 1875

Liberty, Hugh M, Born abt 1869

Lilse, Lizzie, No information

Llewellyn, Emily , Year of

emigration 1905

Lloyd, Frank/Frederick, Born abt 1860

Lockyer, Henry, Year of emigration 1895

Lockyer, James, Born 28 August 1896 Bristol

London or Leader, James, Born 1897

Long, Thomas, 14 Feb 75

Long, David, Year of emigration 1873

Lovell, George, Born abt 1870

Lovell, Lizzie, Year of emigration 1897

Lovell/Love, A E, Born abt 1874

Lovesay, Samuel George Allan, Born 26 Sep 1868 Bedminster, Bristol

Lovett, Arthur, Born abt 1875

Lovett, Bertie, Born abt 1885

Lowe, Eliza, Born abt 1882

Luceks, James, Born 5 July 1870

Lynch, Arthur, Born abt 1800

Lynch, Elizabeth, Born possibly 1863

Mable, Stephen, Born in 1848 in Liverpool

Maby, Sarah, Aged 10 years on 16 September 1886

Madley, Jesse, Born 15 Mar 1882

Madshaw, William, Born 7 Oct 1866?

Mahoney, C, Born abt 1889

Mahoney, Richard, Born abt 1858

Mais or Willoughby, G? S?, Born abt 1874

Maney/Naney, Charles, Born abt 1862

Manning, Thomas, Born abt 1858 St Augustine Parish

Manning, Emily, Born abt 1865

Manning, William, Year of emigration 1875

Mapstone, George, Born abt 1858 Bristol

Mark , Edward Fred, Born 1901

Markey, Frank, Born abt 1859

Marks, Charles, 15 August 1873

Marks, Alfred, Born 1896

Marsh, Walter , Born 1898

Marshall, Edgar, Born abt 1878

Marshall, Martha or EJ, 4 September 1883

Marshall, Hodgson or Hudson , Born abt 1867

Marshall als Newlon , James, Born 15 Jun 1881

Martin, William, Born September 1862

Martin, Alice, Born May 1870

Martin, Francis, Year of emigration 1869

Mason, Arthur, Born 1885

Mason, Henry, Born abt 1869 Derby

Masterman, C, Born abt 1886

Masters, Charles & George, Cousins aged 9 and 10 years

Mathias, Edwin, Born February 1869

Maudley, Mary, Born abt 1867

May/e, , 1871 year of emigration

Maye, Minnie, Born abt 1879

McKitterick/McKellerick, John, 1907 year of emigration

McCardle, Robert, Born abt 1870

McCarthy, Walter Bryant / Byron, Born 23/4/1891

McCormack, Annie, 1885 year of emigration

McDonald, Elizabeth, Born abt 1862

McDonald, Mary, Born abt 1870

McMaster, Frank, Born abt 1870

McMaster, Frank, Born abt 1892 Frome, Somerset

McNulty, John (Archibald), Born 24 Jan 1894 Frome, Somerset

Mead, Mary, Born abt 1856

Medlyn/Bird, Walter, Born 27 Apr 1881

Meredith, Fred J, Born 1900

Merrick, George, Born 1884

Micbrook, Kate, Born abt 1883

Miller, John, Born abt 1864

Miller, Arthur , Born 11 Jun 1867 St Philip & St Paul

Millinder, Albert, Born abt 1889

Millinder, Mary, Born abt 1893

Millinder, Alice, Born 1893/4

Mills, Frank, Born 1898/99

Missen, George, Aged 12 years at emigration

Missen, William, Born abt 1876 possibly Pontypridd

Mitchell, James, Born abt 1875

Mitchener, Edward J, Born 1889

Monk, Harry, Born 21 March 1883 Southwick, Sussex.

Monk, Robert, Born abt 1871

Monks, Samuel, Born abt 1870

Mooney, Sidney, Born 1898

Moore, George, Born 1 July 1875

Moore, Mary, Born abt 1871

Moore, Charles, Born abt 1860

Moore, Sarah Jane, Born 8 June 1864

Moore, William, Possible year of emigration 1876

Moore, Elsie Annie, Born 1896

Moore, Frederick, Year of emigration 1896

Moore, Gertrude, Year of emigration 1896

Moore, Martha, Year of emigration 1896

Moore, Harry or George, Born 26 January 1874

Moore, Mary, Year of emigration 1905

Moray /Morey/ Morly, James, Born abt 1888

Morgan, Ernest, Born abt 1890

Morgan, James or George, Born abt 1877

Morgan, Harry or Henry, Born 25 December 1892

Morgan, James, Born 9 Mar 1884

Morris, Ada, Born abt 1878

Morris, William, Born abt 1857

Morris, Geo Victor, Born abt 1893

Morrisey, Albt Edwd, Born abt 1894

Morrissey, George, Born abt 1867

Morse, Kate, Born abt 1864

Mosely, Chares, Born 1895

Mountjoy, William, Born abt 1860

Mudge, Edwin Possibly Emma, Born abt 1880

Mullins, Augustus, 1896 year of emigration

Mullins, Charles, Born 12 Aug 1864

Munday, George, Born 20 Dec 1881 (25 December 1883)

Murphy, C, Born abt 1874

Naish, Henry, Born abt 1866

Nash, Prince Albert, Born abt 1859 Bristol, Somerset

Neal, Thomas, Year of emigration 1873

Neale, Sarah Emily, Born abt 1866 Cardiff, Glamorgan

Neillie, Charles, Born 26 Dec 1878

Neillie, Frank, Born abt 1888

Nelmes, Albert, Born about 1888

Nelson, William Alfred, Born abt 1882

Nelson, Ellen, Year of emigration 1885

Nettle, Rebecca, Born 20 April 1872 Bristol

Neville, Jane, Born abt 1864

Neville or Walsh, Patrick, Born abt 1887

Newbury, Frank or Patrick, Born abt 1887

Newbury, Walter, Born abt 1887

Newbury, Thomas, Born abt 1889 (25 Dec 1889) Bristol

Newcombe, Fred, Born abt 1890

Newman, James, Born abt 1858

Newman, Charles, Born abt 1889 Bristol

Newport, James , Born abt 1881?

Newton alias Marshall, Ernest,

Born 1895

Nicholas, William, Born abt 10 Jun 1860

Nicholls, David, Born 1848 in Thornbury

Nicholls, Ernest, Born abt 1875

Nicholls, Florence, Born abt 1858

Nicholls, Jane, Born abt 1861

Nicholls, Henry, Born abt 1858

Nicholls, Samuel, Born abt 1862

Nicholls, Joseph, Born 23 Apr 1875

Nokes, Joseph, Year of emigration 1895

Norman, James, Born 1872

Norman, Bessie, Born abt 1882

Norman, , Emigrated 1866

Norris, Joseph , Born abt 1859 Cardiff, South Wales

North, William, Emigration 1895 b Bradford on Avon

Norton/maybe Newton, William, Born 1848 St James, Bath

Nutt, James, Born abt 1858

Nutt, Henry, Born about 1880

Nutt, Lizzie, Born 1868

Nutt, Elizabeth Jane, Born in June 1868 Bristol

Nutt, Edward, 30 November 1877

O Connor, Charles, Born 29 Dec 1881

O'Donnell, Alice Sabina, Born abt 1895

O'Hennessey, William, Born 18 February 1874

Oaten, G, Born abt 1874

Offer, Albert, 18 Jan 1883

Oldfield, William (George), Born 17 May 1884 Bristol

Oliver, Thomas, Born 1896

Oliver, Frederick, Born abt 1861 Phillack, Cornwall

Oliver, Walter, Born abt 1858 Phillack, Cornwall

Organ, Charles, Born abt 1858 Phillack, Cornwall

Osborne, Charles Henry or Harry, 21 Dec 1868 Newport,

Monmouth

Osborne, William (George), Born 5 March 1904

Ovens, William (George), Born 5 March 1904

Owen, Francis, Born abt 1758

Owen, Lewis, Born February 1862

Owen or Fear or Hitchins, Richard, Born 11 Jun 1881 (25 Dec 1884) Bristol

Owen/Fears/Hitchings, Lily, Born abt 1896

Owens /Hutching/Payne, Mary Ann, Born 1898

Oxley, James, Born 7 January 1899 (Jan 1897) Bristol

Oxley, Robert, Born 1877 St George, Bristol

Padfield, William, Born 1875 Redland Bristol

Paisley, Arthur William, Born June 1861

Palmer, Albert, Born abt 1859

Palmer, Annie, Year of emigration 1895

Palmer, Emily, Born abt 1861

Palmer, Alice, Born abt 1881 Bristol

Palmer, Minnie, Born abt 1886 Bristol

Parker, Nathaniel Arthur, Born 4 Feb 1891 Bristol

Parker, Rose, Born 2 Aug 1885

Parker, Thomas, Born abt 1892

Parker, S.A., Emigration took place in 1880's

Parker, William Frederick, Born 15 January 1903

Parker, William Frederick, Born 15 January 1903

Parker alias Clawson, George, Born 1901

Parker or Robbins, Alfred, Born abt 1875 or 1878

Parkes, Frank, Born 19 December 1883 (13 Nov 1883)

Parson, Frank, Born 9 Sep 1883

Parsons, Edwin, Born abt 1870

Parsons, Robert, Year of emigration 1872

Parsons, William, Born 13 Nov 1865

Paul, Thomas, Born 6 Nov 1865 Redcliffe,Bristol

Payment, William, Born abt 1874

Payne, Rose, Born abt 1892

Payne, Julia, Born abt 1859

Payne, Ellen, Born abt 1858

Payne, Robert Charles, Born 8 Feb 1894

Payne, George, Born abt 1882 Lewes, Essex

Peacock, James, Only placement details

Peacock, Henry, Born abt 1889 Bristol

Pearce, George, Born 28 Jun 1864

Pearce, Frederick (Charles), Born abt 1891 (24 Jan 1891) Bristol

Pearce, Alfred, Born 27 Nov 1875

Peart, George, Born on 15 Dec 1880 /23 Dec 1883

Peat, Charles Michael Victor , Born 6 Feb 1880 St George, Bristol

Peglar, A, Year of emigration 1884

Penfold, Wm, Born 10 Oct 1891 Herefordshire

Pennell, Noah, Born abt 1869 Port Talbot, South Wales

Penny, Henry, Born abt 1878

Penny, Aurora   or Laura, Born abt 1883 Fulton, Somerset

Penny, Amelia, Born 1878

Penny, Elizabeth, Born 1880

Penwarden, Maud, Born 1884

Peters, John, Born abt 1859

Peters, Kenneth William, Born 26 August 1876 Westbury Bristol

Pethick, Elizabeth, Born 17 March 1884

Phelps, William, Born abt 1874

Philips, Henry , Born 5 Feb 1889 South Wales

Philips, Henry Joseph, Born 18 June 1872 Bath, Somerset

Philips, Christina or Christine, Born abt 1881 Bristol, Glos

Phillips, Eliza, Born 1876

Phillips, Frederick , Born abt 1886

Phillips, Rose, Born abt 1888

Phillips, Wm, Born abt 1868

Phillips, William, Born 24 Jul 1880

Phillips, Albert Henry, Born 6 February 1877

Pick, H, Born abt 1876

Pill or Pitt, Edwin, Born abt 1870

Pinnegar, Edwin, Born abt 1894

Pitman, Margaretta, Born abt 1899

Plucknett, Rose, Born abt october 1865

Plucknett, Ivy Victoria, Born 15 October 1903

Pole, Ivy Victoria, Born 15 october 1903

Pollitt, Wilfred Hugh, Born abt March 1885

Pomroy, Ernest (Arthur) or James Ernest, Born 25 May 1891 (24 June 1889) Birmingham

Poole, Joseph, Born 25 Dec 1881

Poole, Amelia, Born abt 1866 Brislington, Somerset

Pope, Thomas, Born abt 1880

Pople, Edward, Year of emigration in 1894

Potter, Elizabeth, Born 1876

Potter, John Shadrach, Born 30 December 1902

Pound, John Shadrach, Born 30 December 1902

Pounds, Dorcas, Born abt 1864

Pow, Henry, Born 21 Jul 1862

Powell, Henry, Born 8 March 1889

Powell, Alfred, Born 5 Oct 1868 Bristol

Power alias Reece , James, Born 29 Apr 1879

Prater, George, Born abt 1869

Preece, George, Born abt 1858

Price, Hy, Born abt 1874

Price, Charles, Possible birth 1881

Proule, Frederick, Born abt 1860 Bristol

Prowse, Hetty Sophia, Born abt 1892

Puddy, John, Born abt 1874

Puddy, Frederick, Born 13 August 1870

Pugh, Thomas, Born 3 March 1877

Pugh, Sidney, Born 16 December 1900

Pugh, Sidney, Born 16 December 1900

Purnell, Henry, Born 1900

Purnell or Pennell, Louisa, Born abt 1876 Wrington, Somerset

Pyle, Henry, Born abt 1877

Pyne, Thomas, Born abt1880

Quick, William, Born abt 1859

Radford, Ellen, Only placement details

Ralph, Catherine, Born abt 1868

Rawle, George, Born 3 Dec 1884 Bristol

Rawle, Mary, Born 1897

Rawles, Beatrice, Born 1894/1895

Reddard, Harold B, Born abt 1887

Reece, Francis, Born abt 1894

Reeves, John, Born 22 Dec 1865 Bristol

Reeves, Kate, Born 26 Jul 1885

Rendle, John, Born 25 July 1882

Rendle, Henry, Born abt 1894 (22Aug 1896)

Rendle, Maud Beatrice, Born abt 1891

Rice, William, Born abt 1894

Richards, John, Born abt 1882

Richards, Walter, Born abt 1859

Richards, Fanny, Born abt 1868

Richards, Fanny, Born abt 1869 London, Middlesex

Richards, Ellen, Born abt 1867

Richards, Henry , Born 1896

Richardson, Randolph, Born 1894

Richardson, Priscilla, Born 11 January 1897 Swindon

Richardson, Harry or Henry, Born abt 1894

Riddiford, James, Year of emigration 1867

Riddiford, Charles Henry, Born 10 March 1897`

Roach, Eveline Grace, Born abt 1905

Robbins, Albert D, Born 19/1/1895

Robbins, David , Born 13 Nov 1881

Robbins or Parker, Annie, Born 26 Aug 1884

Roberts, Frank, Born 19 December 1883

Roberts, Emily, Born 22 July 1894

Rodd, Bessie, Born abt 1890

Roe, Henry, Born abt 1860

Roe, Albert Henry, Born 5 September 1876

Roper, Edward, Born 10 June 1878

Rose, George, Year of emigration 1875

Rossiter, Frederick, Born in 1862 or 1866 Quenington

Rossiter, John, Born abt 1863

Rourke, James, Born 1 Oct 1862

Rowe, Ro, Born abt 1883

Rowe, Arthur, Born 6 Jul 1886

Rowley, Alf, Year of emigration 1866

Rowley, Emily, Born 1904

Rudge, Samuel, Born 1892

Rush, Herbert George, Born abt 1868

Ryan, Mary E, Born abt 1863

Ryan , Katie, Born abt 1876

Sage, Alfred, Born 2 Jun 1880

Sage, George William, Born abt 1862

Sage, Albert, Born abt 1887

Sage, Bertha, Born abt 1891

Salsage or Salvage, Elizabeth, Born 1896

Salsage or Salvage, Laura, Born abt 1887

Sansom, Rose, Born abt 1892

Saunders, William, Year of emigration 1867

Saunders, Daisy, Born abt 1896

Saunders, George, Born 16 March 1879

Savary or Savery, William, Born 31 August 1884

Sayers, Joseph H or John Henry, Born abt 1875

Saygood, James, Born 26 Apr 1874 Bristol

Saysell, William, Year of emigration 1877

Scammell, Charles, Born 22 Oct 1889 Bristol

Scammell, Jane, Born abt 1892

Scarret, Alice, Born abt 1895

Scarry, Jonathan, Born abt 1860 Cirencester

Scotfield, Michael Thomas, Born abt 1866

Scourer or Needle, Elizabeth also Charles , Born abt 1884

Seal, Charles or Alfred, Born 24 December 1863

Seaworthy, Alfred, Born 25 Dec 1863

Seaworthy or Leaworthy, Albert, Born 6 Aug 1881

Sedgebear, Albert, Born 6 August 1881

Sedgebeer, Charles, Born abt 1886

Seymour alias Smaile , Frederick, Born abt 1888

Shaughnessy, William, Born abt 1859 Great Torrington, Devon

Shaw, George C, Born 12 May 1876

Shephard, Silvanus?, Born abt 1887

Shepherd, Kenneth, Born abt 1887

Sheppard, Louisa, Born 2nd November 1883

Sheppard, Caroline, Born abt 1870 Bristol

Sheppard, Albert, Born 6 Apr 1865 Bedminster

Sheppard, Henry, Born 18 Oct 1880

Sheppard, George, Born abt 1874

Sherrin, James, Born abt 1874

Shipperly, Thomas, Born abt 1871

Shoebrook, John, Year of emigration 1871

Short, John, Born abt 1872

Shortman, Mary Ann, Born abt 1859

Shute, William, Born abt 1865

Silk, William, Born abt 1873

Silk, Ernest, Born abt 1888

Silk, Walter, Born 14 February 1893

Simmonds, Nelson, 1905

Simmonds, William Albert, Born 1864

Sims, Frank, Born 1860

Sims, Edward, Born abt 1862

Sims, Henry, Born abt 1863

Sinnott, Nettie, Born 1903

Skelton, Mary Jane, Born 1869 3rd quarter Bristol

Skinner, William, Born abt 1995

Skuse, Lucy, Born abt 1858

Skuse, Jessie, Born September 1886

Skuse, Sarah, Born September 1882

Slade, Margaret, Born abt 1871 London, Middlesex

Smaile als Seymour, Henry, Born 1890

Small, William, Born abt 1859 Great Torrington Devon

Small, Hy Philip, Born abt 1889

Smallbone, Charles and a Henry, Born abt 1889

Smart, Thomas, Born 27 August 1885

Smith, Bessie Beatrice, Born abt 1871

Smith, Fredk, Born abt 1881

Smith, Maude, Emigration year 1892

Smith, Selina, Year of emigration 1892

Smith, Alice, Born abt 1892

Smith, Florence, Born abt 1887

Smith, Charles, Born abt 1856

Smith, Mary J, Born abt 1876 Bristol

Smith, Emily, Born September 1877

Smith, Sophia, Born abt 1871 Wotten under Edge

Smith, John, Born abt 1858

Smith, Fredk, Born 1892

Smith, Arthur William, Born abt 1891

Smith, Frederick, Born abt 1892 Weston Super Mare

Smith, Frederick Thomas, Born abt 1893 Weston Super Mare

Smith, Boreham, Year of emigration 1895

Smith, Richard, Born abt 1862 North or West Drayton, Middlesex

Smith, William, Born 4 Oct 1866 St Philips, Bristol

Smith, William Francis, Born 23 May 1882

Smith, Elsie, Born about 1888 Weston Super Mare

Smith, C Edwin, Born abt 1874

Smith, F, Born abt 1888

Smith, Jane, No date

Soloman, Thomas W, Born abt 1900 Liverpool

Sopp, John, Year of emigration 1895

Sopp, Ernest John, Born 1892 (1 Feb 1890 Bristol

Sopp, Frederick William, Born 1889 Bristol

Southcott, Albert (Edward), Born 24 January 1885

Spackman, Charles, Born 9 Mar 1880

Sparks, George, Born abt 1883

Sparks, Charles, Born abt 1897 (1 June 1895 Bristol

Sparks, Florence, Born abt 1895

Spear, Beatrice, Born 1910

Spear, Mary Ann, Born abt 1862

Spear, Dorothy Mabel, Born

1901

Speed, Reginald James, Born 1899

Speed, Rosina or Georgina, Born abt 1859

Speed, Harriet or Henrietta, Born abt 1864

Spencer, William, Born abt 1882

Spencer, George, Year of emigration 1869

Spicer, James, Born abt 1865

Spiers, Reginald Walter, Born abt 1893

Spiller, William, Born abt 1869

Spiller, Ernest James, Born 6 June 1887

Sprackett, Edith, Born abt 1889

Sproat, George, Born abt 1863

Stacey, Herbert, Born abt 1894 (13 Oct 1893 Bristol

Stacey, Louisa, Born abt 1862

Stacey, Emily, Born abt 1859

Staddon, Ada, Born abt 1866

Stallard, Alfred, Born abt 1879

Stanley, Charles, Born abt 1859 Cardiff, South Wales

Staples, William, Born 13 Nov 1879 Walsall, Stafford

Stauton or Stanton, Michael, Year of emigration early 1870's

Steer, Sydney, Born abt 1885

Stephens, Edward, Born abt 1878

Stephens, William, Born 28 Dec 1866 St Clements, Bristol

Stevens, Joseph Walter Tom , Born 17 Mar 1869 St Pauls, Bristol

Stewart, K, Born abt 1888

Still, Thomas, Born abt 1872

Stillwell, Henry William, Born abt 1856

Stillwell, Elizabeth also Mary, Born abt 1863

Stockman, Johanna, Born abt 1858

Stockton, Charles, Born abt 1894

Stockwell, Sidney George, Born on 29 May 1878

Stone, Charles, Born abt 1856

Stowell, Thomas John, Born 3 Sep 1881

Stower, Edgar, Born 1897

Stradling als Best, Thomas John, Born 3 Feb 1877

Strange, John, Born abt 1865

Strickland, Frederick, Born abt 1878 12 in 1890

Strickland, Thomas, Emigrated 1872

Strickland, Ethel, Born 1883

Stuckey, Gladys, Born 1884

Summerby, E, No year given

Summers, William, Born abt 1878

Summerville, William, Year of emigration 1889

Summerville, Alfred John, Aged 10 in 1871 census St Augustines

Surfr, Henry, Aged 14 in 1871 census St Augustines

Susten?, James, Bath, Somerset

Swash, E D, Year of emigration 1885

Sweeting, Henry, Born 3 October 1875

Symond, Robert, Born 1880

Tankins , S, Born 1881

Tarling, Eliza, Born April 1880

Taylor, Henry John George, Born 25 May 1879

Taylor, Wm, Born abt 1886

Taylor, Ada, Born 5 July 1885

Taylor, Augusta, Born abt 1866 in Bristol

Taylor, H, Year of emigration 1883

Taylor, William, Born abt 1872

Taylor, Matilda, Born abt 1888

Taylor, Albert, Born abt 1878

Taylor, Albert Ben George, Emigrated at 14 years

Taylor, William, Placement details

Thomas, A, Born 1875

Thomas, James, Born abt 1873

Thomas, Sarah, Born abt 1880

Bristol

Thomas, Frederick, Born abt 1862

Thomas, William, Born abt 1893 (5 Sep 1895 Bristol

Thomas, Frederick, Born about 1891

Thomas, Henry Pond, Born abt 1866

Thomas, Henry, Year of emigration 1895

Thomas, Emery, Born abt 1882

Thomas, George , Born 15 May 1877

Thomas, Herbert, Born abt 1866

Thompson, Wm, Born abt 1887

Thompson, Walter E, Born 1903

Thorne, Arthur Henry, Born 1898/99

Thorne, Querina, Aged 11 years when emigrated

Thorne, William, Born 17 Jun 1889 in St Philips

Thorne, Henry, Born 19 Jun 1885 Bedminster, Bristol

Thorne, Amelia, Born abt February 1897

Thorne, Alice, Born abt 1888 in Bedminster, Bristol

Thorne, Frederick, Aged 14 years in 1905

Thorne, Elizabeth, Year of emigration 1891

Thorne , Querina, Born 1879

Tilbury, Alice, Born abt 1885

Tiley, John (Raymond), Born 1898 (14 Jun 1897) Bristol

Timbrell, Fanny, Born abt 1869

Timmings, Elizabeth, Born 1 May 1886

Toogood, William, Born abt 1857

Tovey, Charles, Born 8 Aug 1879

Tovey, Emma, Born abt 1880

Tovey, Charles, Born 19 April 1888 Gloucester

Tovey, Ernest, Born 1899

Tozer, George, Born 1897

1885

Weston, Mary Ann, Born abt 1885

Wetheridge, Sarah, Placement Details

Weyman or Wayman, George, Born 20 Nov 1865

Whale, Richard, Born abt 1873

Whatley, Sabina, Born abt 1869 Bristol

Wheeler, Emily, Born abt 1873

Whitchurch, Henry, Born 13 Oct 1869

Whitchurch, Frederick, Born abt 1893

White, William, Born abt 1892

White, Arthur, Born abt 1882

White, Mary, Born abt 1875

White, Letitia, Born abt 1869 Cardiff, Wales

White, Male, Date of emigration 1867

White, William, Born 4 Mar 1871

White, William, Born 24 Jun 1875

White, Richard, Born 8 Aug 1878

White, Samuel, Born abt 1875

White, Thomas, Born 1900

Whitfield, Caroline, Born 1898

Whitnell, Ernest Edwin, Born 6 Sep 1890 Bristol from Exeter

Whitwell, William (Thomas), Born 21 Oct 1887 Bristol

Wicks, William, Year of emigration 1903

Wilcox, Grace, Born abt 1879

Wilcox, William Frederick, Born 10 June 1883

Wilcox, William, Born 8 Nov 1876

Wilkes, Sarah, Born abt 1884

Wilkes, Cecilia, Born abt 1867

Wilkey or Bartlett, Edith, Born abt 1894

Wilkins, Henry, Born abt 1859 in Bristol

Wilkins, David, Born abt 1882

Wilkins, Lily, Born 1 Aug 1886

William, John, Born 15 Jan 1872

William or Heale, Philip, Born abt 1882

Williams, John William, Born 1 Nov 1865

Williams, Annie, Born abt 1878

Williams, Mary Ann, Born abt 1856

Williams, George, Born abt 1883

Williams, George, Born abt 1858

Williams, James, Born abt 1858

Williams, Henry, Born abt 1855

Williams, John, Born abt 1859

Williams, William, Born abt 1863

Williams, Edith, Born 27 Aug 1887

Williams, Mabel or Isabel, Born abt 1880

Williams, Annie, Born abt 1867 Bristol

Williams, Annie, Born 11 January 1900

Williams, Herbert Cecil Frederick, Born 23 Mar 1881

Williams, Charles, Born 24 April 1873

Williams, Susan, Year of emigration 1895

Williams, Margaret, Year of emigration 1891

Williams, Ellen, Year of emigration 1888

Williams, Isabel, Emigration date 1891

Williams, John, Born abt 1872

Williams, Lizzie, Born abt 1876

Williams , Elizabeth, Born 1883

Williams als Heale, Edith, 12 yrs placement information

Williams or Chapman, John William, Born 1 Nov 1865

Wills, Frederick Mitchell Moore, Born abt 1880

Wilson, Frederick, Born 13 January 1874 Bristol

Wilson, William, Born 21 Aug 1863

Wilson, Annie, Year of emigration 1892

Wilson, Emily, Year of emigration 1892

Wilson , John, Born 1898/99

Wilton, Richard Patrick, Born abt 1871

Witchell, Beatrice, Born 1896

Witchell, Jessie(boy), Born abt 1893

Witchell, Thomas, Born about 1889

Witchell or Mitchell, Jessie, Born abt 1892

Witterage or Witteridge, James, Born 1895

Wollacot, George, Born abt 1866

Wood, Emily, Born 1875

Wood, Jane, Year of emigration 1870

Wooding, Ellen, Born abt 1871

Wooding, Arthur, Born abt 1871

Woodward, Walter, Born abt 1873

Woollacott or Wallacot, Henry, Born abt 1870

Wools, Charles, Born abt 1878 Bristol

Worgan, George, Born abt 1873

Worgan , Ada, Born abt 1878

Wren, Florence called Flossie , Born 4 Mar 1880 Bristol

Wright, Herbert, Born abt 1883 Bristol

Zebedee, Phillip, Born 1895/6

Zebedee, Henry, Emigrated 1871

Zellmer , Frederick, Born about 1862

PICTURE CREDITS

THE STREET CHILDREN OF BRISTOL
Page 16 Bristol Archives 17563-1-0449
Page 17 Bristol Archives 17563-1-0354
Page 19 George Morley Collection
Page 22 Bristol Archives PC-159-1
Page 25 Bristol Archives 17563-1-0864
Page 26 Bristol Libraries X1578
Page 28 Gustav Dore
Page 31 Victoria & Albert Museum

RAGGED SCHOOLS
Page 34 Bristol Archives 36867-5-5-9
Page 35 Bristol Libraries X1578
Page 36 Peter Higginbotham/Mary Evans
    Picture Library No.10424780
Page 37 Top - The Illustrated London
    News - April 21, 1894
Page 37 Bottom - George Morley
    Collection
Page 38 Left - Bristol Archives 33041-BMC-
    12-1-b-011
Page 38 Right - Bristol Archives
    33041-BMC-12-1-b-023
Page 42 Left and Right - The Illustrated
    London News - April 21, 1894
Page 51 Bristol Archives
    38087-CIS-A1-7-006

**DEVELOPMENT OF INDUSTRIAL
SCHOOLS IN BRISTOL**
Page 55 Bristol Museum BM 2307
Page 57 Bristol Archives 17563-1-0374
Page 60 Bristol Libraries - Loxton Drawing
    A54
Page 61 Bristol Libraries - Loxton Drawing
    A55
Page 62 Bristol Archives
    38087-CIS-A1-7-007
Page 64 Bristol Archives 38087-CIS-A1-021

Page 66 Thanks to Steve Saunders
Page 68 Peter Higginbotham/Mary Evans
    Picture Library No.11045779

LIFE IN AN INDUSTRIAL SCHOOL
Page 71 Thanks to John's family
Page 76 Top Bristol Archives
    38087-CIS-A1-7-004
Page 76 Bottom Bristol Archives
    38087-CIS-A1-7-014
Page 79 Top Bristol Archives
    38087-CIS-A1-7-007
Page 79 Bottom Bristol Archives
    38087-CIS-A1-7-0011
Page 81 Bristol Mercury, December 6, 1879
Page 82 Bristol Libraries - Loxton Drawing
    A53
Page 86 Bristol Archives
    38087-CIS-A1-7-015

THE FORMIDABLE
Page 94 Bristol Archives 38087-NS-X4-22
Page 99 Top Bristol Archives
    38087-NIS-A4-4
Page 99 Bottom Bristol Archives 17563-1-
    0282
Page 101 Bristol Archives 38087-NS-A4-4
Page 102 Bristol Archives 38087-NS-A4-4
Page 105 Bristol Archives 38087-NS-X4-1
Page 107 Bristol Archives 38087-NS-A4-4
Page 108 Bristol Archives 38087-NS-X4-22
Page 110 Author's Collection
Page 111 Bristol Archives 38087-NS-X4-6
Page 112 Bristol Archives 17563-1-0287
Page 113 Bristol Archives 17563-1-0011
Page 116 Bristol Archives 17563-1-0285
Page 117 Bristol Archives 17563-1-0291
Page 118 Bristol Archives 43207-9-1-029
Page 120 Author's Collection

ORGANISATION OF POOR LAW UNIONS IN BRISTOL

ORGANISATION OF POOR LAW UNIONS IN BRISTOL

The 1834 Act grouped together parishes into Poor Law Unions. The unions were set up between 1834 and 1838 by the Poor Law Commissioners.

The unions were managed by a Board of Guardians; these people were elected by the ratepayers of the parishes, the guardians taking on the duties normally carried out by the Overseers of the Poor before the 1834 changes.

Each parish was able to elect a number of guardians in proportion to the size of their population. Until 1894, a property qualification ensured that only relatively wealthy ratepayers might be elected to the Board.

Bristol

- St Peters Hospital was set up to house boys (old name meaning board and lodging)
- 1837 the old prison at Stapleton was converted into a new workhouse for the City of Bristol. St Peters became a hospital in the true sense of the word.
- By 1842 most Bristol paupers were sent to Stapleton.
- 1898 St Peters became the administrative centre for the Bristol Poor Law Union. All its contents were destroyed in the Blitz in 1940.
- 1898 The city boundary was extended and now included parts of Bedminster, Clifton, Barton Regis and Keynsham Unions. The Bristol Board of Guardians was now responsible for Barton Regis Workhouse at Eastville. Both workhouses were used to house paupers from this enlarged area.
- 1948 Bristol Workhouse became Stapleton Hospital.
- 1952 Renamed Manor Park Hospital
- 1992 Merged with Glenside Hospital - Blackberry Hill.

Barton Regis

- 1877 Clifton Union renamed Barton Regis Union
- 1847 Barton Regis Workhouse opened on Fishponds Road, known as Eastville Workhouse; also known locally as 100 Fishponds Road.
- 1898 Fishponds Workhouse now run by Bristol Board of Guardians; Barton Regis Guardians built a new workhouse in Southmead.
- 1902 Southmead Workhouse, including a large infirmary, now opened. These buildings eventually became Southmead hospital.

SOURCES OF INFORMATION/FURTHER RESEARCH

Records for all Bristol institutions can be found at the Archives and will be indexed by a code established for each organisation. The amount of information which can be found for any child will vary; it all depends on which records have survived and those which have been deposited. Those organisations that are still functioning may well hold their own records.

Bristol Industrial Schools

There are some good records for the industrial schools; the boys were sent to Park Row School, Clifton Day Industrial School and the ship *Formidable*. Girls went to Carlton House School and Stanhope School in the Kingsdown area; there was a small school in Hotwells. Some small schools were certificated to work as an industrial school for a short time only and were operating at Temple Back and Lewins Mead. The amount and type of records held for each school does vary.

Bristol Reformatory Schools

Records for Red Lodge Reformatory vary but there are some interesting accounts of how the school was organised. Kingswood records are closed.

Workhouse Records

Some records have survived; these include some Creed Registers for both Barton Regis and Bristol Workhouse. These can be accessed at the Archives along with some registers of births and deaths for Barton Regis, a school record for one year and a

few odd records relating to the guardians.

It is always worth consulting the Online Catalogue which can be found on their website.
Bristol Archives, "B" Bond Warehouse, Smeaton Road, Bristol BS1 6XN
www.bristol.gov.uk/archives

Bristol Library Service holds many different types of records; books, directories, newspapers and local images. Consult the Online Catalogue or the librarians.
Bristol Central Library, College Green, Bristol BS1 5TL
www.bristol.library.service@bristol.gov.uk

The museum service cares for many different types of documents, artefacts, images; it is worth making contact. Consult the Online Catalogue.
Bristol Museums, Galleries and Archives
www.bristolmuseums.org.uk

The books containing "Correspondence to the Board of Guardians" for both unions can be consulted at The National Archives, at Kew in Richmond, London. Copy books for 1900 and 1901 are also held at the Bristol Archives. Records relating to Child Emigration, Industrial Schools and Reformatories can be found in the Home Office Records.
The National Archives, Kew. Richmond, Surrey
www.nationalarchives.gov.uk

Newspaper reports can often back up these records sometimes filling gaps but also supplementing the information. Newspapers can also be found at local libraries.
www.britishnewspaperarchive.co.uk

Useful Web Sites for researching passenger lists
www.ancestry.co.uk
www.findmypast.co.uk
www.familysearch.org
ww.freebmd.org.uk

Web Sites for researching life in Victorian Times
www.victorianweb.org
www.workhouses.org.uk
www.hiddenlives.org.uk

Canadian Web Sites
Library and Archives of Canada
www.bac-lac.gc.ca/eng/Pages/home.aspx

British Home Children Advocacy & Research Association
C.E.O. Lori Oschefski
www.canadianbritishhomechildren.weebly.com

The British Isles Family History Society of Greater Ottawa
www.bifhsgo.ca

Tweetybird's Genealogy Page
www.freepages.genealogy.rotsweb.com/~tweetybirdgenealogy/hepasslist.html
Advise to put Tweetybird Genealogy into the search engine

New Brunswick Archives and Ships Lists relating to New Brunswick
www.archives.gnb.ca

Cyndi's List – Canadian Immigration, Emigration & Migration
www.cyndislist.com/canada/immigration/

There are a number of Facebook sites run by groups of descendants.

Other organisations which sent children sometimes this involved Bristol children
Barnardo's Homes
Catholic Organisations
Church Army
Church of England Waifs and Strays
Fegan Homes
Middlemore Homes
National Children's Homes and Orphanage
Salvation Army
Children's Friend society
Girls' Friendly Society

Author's own website and contact details
www.bristolhomechildren.co.uk
email: shirleyhod2@aol.com